AF661779

TOURISM: A WHOLE INDUSTRY IN ITS REALM

TOURISM: A WHOLE INDUSTRY IN ITS REALM

By

Nishant Arya

2008

CYBER TECH PUBLICATIONS
4264/3, Ansari Road, Daryaganj, New Delhi-110002 (India)
Ph.: 011-23244078. Fax: 011-23280028
E-Mail: cyberpublicationsdelhi@yahoo.com

TOURISM: A WHOLE INDUSTRY IN ITS REALM

Nishant Arya

© Reserved

First Edition 2008

All rights reserved. No part of this publication may be reproduced, stored in a retrieval system or transmitted, in any form or by any means, electronic, mechanical, photo copying, recording or otherwise, without the prior permission of the publisher.

Published by :

G.S. Rawat for **Cyber Tech Publications**
4264/3, Ansari Road, Daryaganj, New Delhi-110002 (India)
Ph.: 011-23244078. Fax: 011-23280028
E-Mail: cyberpublicationsdelhi@yahoo.com

Preface

The tourism industry, of which the hospitality industry is the core element, is one of the largest and the fastest growing industries worldwide. According to World Tourism Organization forecasts, the industry will continue to grow and employ more people in the twenty-first century. In parallel with the growth of the tourism and hospitality industry worldwide, consumer expectations and demands for quality are rising while consumer tastes are varying on the one hand, and competition among the firms, both nationally and internationally, is intensifying on the other.

In this business environment of heightened consumer expectations, distinct market segments that demand unique products and services, and stiff competition, tourism and hospitality organizations are looking for ways to excel in service quality, customer satisfaction, competition and performance. This book takes the view the most important resources or assets for tourism and hospitality organizations in their endeavor to provide excellent service, meet and exceed consumer expectations, achieve competitive advantage and exceptional organizational performance.

The purpose of this book is to emphasize the role of tourism and hospitality organizations and to examine the ways and means of managing their attitudes and behaviours for the mutual benefit of both government and the tourism industry.

—Author

Contents

1

INTRODUCTION

Tourism is travel for predominantly recreational or leisure purposes or the provision of services to support this leisure travel. The World Tourism Organization defines tourists as people who "travel to and stay in places outside their usual environment for not more than one consecutive year for leisure, business and other purposes not related to the exercise of an activity remunerated from within the place visited". Tourism has become a popular global leisure activity. In 2004, there were over 763 million international tourist arrivals.

Tourism is vital for many countries, due to the income generated by the consumption of goods and services by tourists, the taxes levied on businesses in the tourism industry, and the opportunity for employment in the service industries associated with tourism. These service industries include transportation services such as cruise ships and taxis, accommodation such as hotels, restaurants, bars, and entertainment venues, and other hospitality industry services such as spas and resorts.

DEFINITION

One of the earliest definitions of tourism was provided by the Austrian economist in 1910, who defined it as, "some total of operators, mainly of an economic nature, which directly relate to the entry, stay and movement of foreigners inside and outside a certain country, city or a region."

Hunziker and Krapf, in 1941, defined tourism as "the sum of the phenomena and relationships arising from the travel and stay of non-residents, insofar as they do not lead to permanent residence and are not connected with any earning activity." In 1976 Tourism Society of England defined it as "Tourism is the temporary, short-term movement of people to destination outside the places where they normally live and work and their activities during the stay at each destination. It includes movements for all purposes." In 1981 International Association of Scientific Experts in Tourism defined Tourism in terms of particular activities selected by choice and undertaken outside the home environment.

The United Nations classified three forms of tourism in 1994 in its Recommendations on Tourism Statistics: Domestic tourism, which involves residents of the given country travelling only within this country; Inbound tourism, involving non-residents traveling in the given country; and Outbound tourism, involving residents traveling in another country.

The UN also derived different categories of tourism by combining the 3 basic forms of tourism: Internal tourism, which comprises domestic tourism and inbound tourism; National tourism, which comprises domestic tourism and outbound tourism; and International tourism, which consists of inbound tourism and outbound tourism.

Intrabound tourism is a term coined by the Korea Tourism Organization and widely accepted in Korea.

Intrabound tourism differs from domestic tourism in that the former encompasses policy-making and implementation of national tourism policies.

Recently, the tourism industry has shifted from the promotion of inbound tourism to the promotion of intrabound tourism because many countries are experiencing tough competition for inbound tourists. Some national policy-makers have shifted their priority to the promotion of intrabound tourism to contribute to the local economy. Examples of such campaigns include "See America" in the United States, "Get Going Canada" in Canada, and "Guseok Guseok" (corner to corner) in South Korea.

Before people are able to experience tourism they usually need disposable income (i.e. money to spend on non-essentials); time off from work or other responsibilities; leisure time tourism infrastructure, such as transport and accommodation; and legal clearance to travel.

Individually, sufficient health is also a condition, and of course the inclination to travel. Furthermore, in some countries there are legal restrictions on travelling, especially abroad. Certain states with strong governmental control over the lives of citizens (notably established Communist states) may restrict foreign travel only to trustworthy citizens. The United States prohibits its citizens from traveling to some countries, for example Cuba.

HISTORY

Wealthy people have always travelled to distant parts of the world to see great buildings or other works of art, to learn new languages, to experience new cultures, or to taste new cuisine. As long ago as the time of the Roman Republic places such as Baiae were popular coastal resorts for the rich.

The terms tourist and tourism were first used as official terms in 1937 by the League of Nations. Tourism was defined as people travelling abroad for periods of over 24 hours.

Pilgrimage

The history of European tourism can perhaps be said to originate with the medieval pilgrimage. Although undertaken primarily for religious reasons, the pilgrims in the Canterbury Tales quite clearly saw the experience as a kind of holiday (the term itself being derived from the 'holy day' and its associated leisure activities). Pilgrimages created a variety of tourist aspects that still exist - bringing back souvenirs, obtaining credit with foreign banks (in medieval times utilising international networks established by Jews and Lombards), and making use of space available on existing forms of transport (such as the use of medieval English wine ships bound for Vigo by pilgrims to Santiago De Compostela). Pilgrimages are still important in modern tourism - such as to Lourdes or Knock in Ireland. But there are modern equivalents - Graceland and the grave of Jim Morrison in Père Lachaise Cemetery.

During the seventeenth century, it became fashionable in England to undertake a Grand Tour. The sons of the nobility and gentry were sent upon an extended tour of Europe as an educational experience. The eighteenth century was the golden age of the Grand Tour, and many of the fashionable visitors were painted at Rome by Pompeo Batoni. A modern equivalent of the Grand Tour is the phenomenon of the backpacker, although cultural holidays, such as those offered by Swann-Hellenic, are also important.

Health Tourism

Health tourism has always existed, but it was not until the eighteenth century that it became important. In England, it was associated with spas, places with supposedly health-giving mineral waters, treating diseases from gout to liver disorders and bronchitis. The most popular resorts were Bath, Cheltenham, Buxton, Harrogate, and Tunbridge Wells. Visits to take 'the waters' also allowed the visitors to attend balls and other entertainments. Continental Spas such as Carlsbad (Karlovy Vary) attracted many fashionable travellers by the nineteenth century.

It could be argued that Britain was the home of the seaside holiday. In travelling to the coast, the population was following in the steps of Royalty. King George III made regular visits to Weymouth when in poor health. At the time, a number of doctors argued the benefits of bathing in sea water, and sea bathing as a widespread practice was popularised by the Prince Regent (later George IV), who frequented Brighton for this purpose.

Leisure Travel

Leisure travel was associated with the industrialisation of United Kingdom - the first European country to promote leisure time to the increasing industrial population. Initially, this applied to the owners of the machinery of production, the economic oligarchy, the factory owners, and the traders. These comprised the new middle class. Cox & Kings were the first official travel company to be formed in 1758. Later, the working class could take advantage of leisure time.

The British origin of this new industry is reflected in many place names. At Nice, one of the first and best-established holiday resorts on the French Riviera, the long esplanade along the seafront is known to this day as the Promenade des Anglais; in many other historic resorts in continental Europe, old well-established palace hotels have names like the Hotel Bristol, the Hotel Carlton or the Hotel Majestic - reflecting the dominance of English customers.

Winter Tourism

Winter sports were largely invented by the British leisured classes, initially at the Swiss village of Zermatt (Valais), and St Moritz in 1864. The first packaged winter sports holidays took place in 1902 at Adelboden, Switzerland. Winter sports were a natural answer for a leisured class looking for amusement during the coldest season. Organized sport was well established in Britain before it reached other countries. The vocabulary of sport bears witness to this: rugby, football, and boxing all originated in Britain, and even tennis, originally a French sport, was formalized and codified by the British, who hosted the first national championship in the nineteenth century, at Wimbledon. The Fun Ski & Snow Festival, which has been organized annually by Korea tourism organization since 1998 and participated by about 10,000 tourists from Asia, is one of the most successful winter tourism products in Asia. The festival provides a variety of events such as ski and sled competitions, ski and snow board lessons, performances and recreational activities. Majority of the event participants are foreign visitors who come from countries with a warm climate that have no snow. The event offers them opportunities to enjoy winter and winter sports in Korea. In addition, southern South American countries making up the Patagonia region in Chile and Argentina attract thousands of tourists every year. Skiing is extremely popular in the mountainous areas.

Mass Tourism

Mass travel could only develop with improvements in technology allowed the transport of large numbers of people in a short space of time to places of leisure interest, and greater numbers of people began to enjoy the benefits of leisure time.

In the United States, the first great seaside resort, in the European style, was Atlantic City, New Jersey, and Long Island.

In Continental Europe, early resorts included Ostend (for the people of Brussels), and Boulogne-sur-Mer (Pas-de-Calais) and Deauville (Calvados) (for Parisians).

In Britain

The pioneer of modern mass tourism was Thomas Cook who, on 5 July 1841, organized the first package tour in history. He arranged for the rail company to charge one shilling per person for a group of 570 temperance campaigners from Leicester to a rally in Loughborough, eleven miles away. Cook was paid a share of the fares actually charged to the passengers, as the railway tickets, being legal contracts between company and passenger, could not have been issued at his own price. There had been railway excursions before, but this one included entrance to an entertainment held in private grounds, rail tickets and food for the train journey. Cook immediately saw the potential of a convenient 'off the peg' holiday product in which everything was included in one cost. He organised packages inclusive of accommodation for the Great Exhibition, and afterwards pioneered package holidays in both Britain (particularly in Scotland) and on the European continent (where Paris and the Alps were the most popular destinations).

He was soon followed by others (the Polytechnic Touring Association, Dean and Dawson etc.), with the result that the tourist industry developed rapidly in late Victorian Britain. Initially it was supported by the growing middle classes, who had time off from their work, and who could afford the luxury of travel and possibly even staying for periods of time in boarding houses.

The Bank Holidays Act 1871 introduced a statutory right for workers to take holidays, even if they were not paid at the time. By the last quarter of the nineteenth century, the tradition of the working class holiday had become firmly established in Britain. These were largely focused upon the seaside resorts.

The spread of the railway network in the nineteenth century resulted in the growth of Britain's seaside towns by bringing them within easy distance of Britain's urban centres. Blackpool was created by the construction of a line to Fleetwood, and some resorts were promoted by the railway companies themselves - Morecambe by the Midland Railway and Cleethorpes by the Great Central Railway. Other resorts included Scarborough in Yorkshire, servicing Leeds and Bradford; Weston-super-Mare in Somerset, catering for the inhabitants of Bristol; and Skegness, patronised by the residents of the industrial East Midlands. The cockneys of London flocked to Southend-on-Sea, mainly by Thames Steamer, and the South Coast resorts such as Broadstairs, Brighton, and Eastbourne were only a train ride away, with others further afield such as Bournemouth, Bognor Regis and Weymouth.

For a century, domestic tourism was the norm, with foreign travel being reserved for the rich or the culturally curious. A number of inland destinations, such as the English Lake District, and Snowdonia appealed to those who liked the countryside and fine scenery. The holiday camp began to appear in the 1930s, but this phenomenon really expanded in the post-war period. Butlins and Pontins set this trend, but their popularity waned with the rise of overseas package tours and the increasing comforts to which visitors became accustomed at home. Towards the end of the 20th century this market has been revived by the upmarket inland resorts of Dutch company Center Parcs.

Cox & Co, the forebear of Cox & Kings were in existence from 1758 largely entwined with the travel arrangements for the British Army serving around the Empire. While acting as 'agents' for various regiments, they organised the payment, provision, clothing and travel arrangements for members of the armed forces. In the 19th century their network of offices contained a banking and also travel department. The company became heavily involved with affairs in India and its Shipping Agency had offices in France and the Middle East.

Other phenomena that helped develop the travel industry were paid holidays:

- 1.5 million manual workers in Britain had paid holidays by 1925
- 11 million by 1939 (30% of the population in families with paid holidays)

NGOs and government agencies may sometimes promote a specific region as a tourist destination, and support the development of a tourism industry in that area. The contemporary phenomenon of mass tourism may sometimes result in overdevelopment; alternative forms of tourism such as ecotourism seek to avoid such outcomes by pursuing tourism in a sustainable way.

International

Increasing speed on railways meant that the tourist industry could develop internationally. To this may be added the development of sea travel. By 1901, the number of people crossing the English Channel from England to France or Belgium had passed 0.5 million per year. Shipping companies were anxious to fill cabin space that was under utilised.

For example, P&O found that the majority of their passengers for India and the Far East joined the ship at Marseilles. Consequently, they marketed holidays based upon sea trips from London to Lisbon and Gibraltar. Other companies diverted their older ships to operate cruises in the summer months.

However, the real age of international mass travel began with the growth of air travel after World War Two. In the immediate post-war period, there was a surplus of transport aircraft, such as the popular and reliable Douglas Dakota, and a number of ex military pilots ready to fly them. They were available for charter flights, and tour operators began to use them for European destinations, such as Paris and Ostend.

Vladimir Raitz pioneered modern package tourism when on 20 May 1950 his recently founded company, Horizon, provided arrangements for a two-week holiday in Corsica. For an all inclusive price of £32.10s.-, holiday makers could sleep under canvas, sample local wines and eat a meal containing meat twice a day - this was especially attractive due to the continuing austerity measures in post-war United Kingdom. Within ten years, his company had started mass tourism to Palma (1952), Lourdes (1953), Costa Brava (1954), Sardinia (1954), Minorca (1955), Porto (1956), Costa Blanca (1957) and Costa del Sol (1959).

These developments coincided with a significant increase in the standard of living in Britain. Further, the contribution of affordable air travel in combination with the package tour enabled international mass tourism to develop. The postwar introduction of an international system of airline regulation was another important factor. The bilateral agreements at the heart of the system fixed seat prices, and airlines could not fill blocks of empty seats on underused flights by discounting. But if they were purchased by a tour operator and hidden within the price of an inclusive holiday package, it would be difficult to prove that discounting had taken place - even though it was obvious that it had!

Another significant development also happened at the end of this decade. The devaluation of the Spanish peseta made Spain appear a particularly attractive destination. The cheapness of the cost of living attracted increasing numbers of visitors. Mass package tourism has at times been an exploitative process, in which tour operators in a country with a high standard of living make use of development opportunities and low operating costs in a country with a lower standard of living. However, as witness the development of many tourist areas in previously poor parts of the world, and the concomitant rise in standards of living, when there is equality of bargaining power, both parties can gain economic benefits from this arrangement.

Spain and the Balearic Islands became major tourist destinations, and development probably peaked in the 1980s. At the same time, British tour operators developed the Algarve in Portugal. The continuing search for new, cheaper, destinations spread mass tourism to the Greek Islands, Italy, Tunisia, Morocco, Turkey, and more recently Croatia.

For someone living in greater London, Venice today is almost as accessible as Brighton was 100 years ago. Consequently, the British seaside resort experienced a marked decline from the 1970s onwards. Some, such as New Brighton, Merseyside have disappeared. Others have reinvented themselves, and now cater to daytrippers, the weekend break market or business conferences.

RECENT DEVELOPMENTS

There has been an upmarket trend in tourism over the last few decades, especially in Europe where international travel for short breaks is common. Tourists have higher levels of disposable income and greater leisure time and they are also better-educated and have more sophisticated tastes. There is now a demand for a better quality products, which has resulted in a fragmenting of the mass market for beach vacations; people want more specialised versions, such as 'Club 18 -30', quieter resorts, family-oriented holidays, or niche market-targeted destination hotels. As well, people are taking second short break holidays. The developments in technology and transport infrastructure such as jumbo jets and low-budget airlines have made many types of tourism more affordable. There have also been changes in lifestyle, such as retiree-age people who living as a tourist all the year round. This is facilitated by internet purchasing of tourism products. Some sites have now started to offer dynamic packaging, in which an inclusive price is quoted for a tailor- made package requested by the customer upon impulse.

There have been a few setbacks in tourism, such as the September 11, 2001 attacks and terrorist threats to tourist destinations such as Bali and European cities. Some of the tourist destinations, including the beach resorts of Cancún have lost popularity due to shifting tastes. In this context, the excessive building and environmental destruction often associated with traditional "sun and beach" tourism may contribute to a destination's saturation and subsequent decline. Spain's Costa Brava, a popular 1960s and 1970s beach location is now facing a crisis in its tourist industry. On December 26, 2004 a tsunami, caused by the 2004 Indian Ocean earthquake hit Asian countries bordering the Indian Ocean, and also the Maldives. Tens of thousands of lives were lost, and many tourists died. This, together with the vast clean-up operation in place, has stopped or severely hampered tourism to the area. The terms tourism and travel are sometimes used interchangeably. In this context travel has a similar definition to tourism, but implies a more purposeful journey. The terms tourism and tourist are sometimes used pejoratively, to imply a shallow interest in the cultures or locations visited by tourists. Sustainable tourism is becoming more popular as people start to realize the devastating effects poorly planned tourism can have on communities. Receptive tourism is now growing at a very rapid rate in many developing countries, where it is often the most important economic activity in local GDP.

In recent years, second holidays or vacations have become more popular as people's discretionary income increases. Typical combinations are a package to the typical mass tourist resort, with a winter skiing holiday or weekend break to a city or national park.

Niche Tourism

Physical activity or sports-oriented niche tourism includes adventure tourism such as mountaineering and hiking (tramping); Backpacker Tourism; Sport travel to do skiing, golf and scuba diving or see a sports event (e.g., FIFA World Cup); and extreme tourism for people interested in risky activities. Learning-oriented niche tourism includes audio tourism and audio walking tours; bookstore tourism, in which travellers visit independent bookstores; creative tourism workshops; educational tourism for classes; ancestry tourism, to visit birth places; Hobby tourism (such as garden tours, amateur radio DX-peditions, or square dance cruises).

- The cultural sub-type of learning-oriented niche tourism focuses on cultural and arts activities, including cultural tourism, music tourism, and heritage tourism. The nature and environment-oriented sub-types include Coastal Tourism; Ecotourism (e.g. sustainable tourism in Rainforests or national parks); Garden tourism; and Rural Tourism such as Agritourism.

Lifestyle-oriented niche tourism types include Gay tourism; Gourmet tourism; Wine tourism; Health tourism; Medical tourism; Inclusive tourism (or Accessible Tourism) for people with disabilities; Mystical tourism (e.g., involving Meditation, yoga, and rituals).

Other miscellaneous types of niche tourism include:

- Dark tourism includes travel to sites associated with death and suffering, such as the scene of the Hindenburg airship disaster, or to the sites of disasters (Disaster tourism).
- Drug tourism, (e.g., to use drugs in Amsterdam)
- Sex tourism (e.g., to have sex with prostitutes).
- Free Independent Traveller: a sector of the market in which the tourists select their own accommodation and transport, rather than using the established tourism booking system.
- *Pop-culture tourism*: tourism by those that visit a particular location after reading about it or seeing it used as a location in a film (e.g., the Lord of the Rings film sets in New Zealand).

- *Perpetual tourism*: individuals always on vacation; some of them, for tax purposes, to avoid being resident in any country.
- *Pilgrimage Tourism*: pilgrimages to ancient holy places (Rome and Santiago de Compostela for Catholics, temples and stupas of Nepal for the Hindus and Buddhist, Mount Athos or Painted churches of northern Moldavia for the Orthodox), religious sites such as mosques and shrines.
- Sacred travel or metaphysical tourism is a form of New Age travel where believers travel to and perform rituals at religious sites
- Shopping tourism promoting shopping festivals such as the Dubai Shopping Festival.
- *Space tourism*: traveling in outer space or on spaceships.
- Vacilando is a special kind of wanderer for whom the process of traveling and discovery is more important than the destination.
- *Visiting Family and Relatives (VFR) Tourism*: traveling to visit persons related by close family ties and combining this with vacation-type activities; distinct from ancestry tourism, which involves genealogical research
- *Armchair tourism and virtual tourism*: not traveling physically, but exploring the world through internet, books, or TV.

Trends

The World Tourism Organization (UNWTO) forecasts that international tourism will continue growing at the average annual rate of 4 %. By 2020 Europe will remain the most popular destination, but its share will drop from 60 % in 1995 to 46 %. Long-haul will grow slightly faster than intraregional travel and by 2020 its share will increase from 18 % in 1995 to 24 %. With the advent of e-commerce, tourism products have become one of the most traded items on the internet. Tourism products and services have been made available through intermediaries, although tourism providers (hotels, airlines, etc.) can sell their services directly. This has put pressure on intermediaries from both on-line and traditional shops.

It has been suggested there is a strong correlation between Tourism expenditure per capita and the degree to which countries play in the global context. Not only as a result of the important economic contribution of the tourism industry, but also as an indicator of the degree of confidence with which global citizens leverage the resources of the globe for the benefit of their local economies. This is why any projections of growth in tourism may serve as an indication of the relative influence that each country will exercise in the future.

Space tourism is expected to "take off" in the first quarter of the 21st century, although compared with traditional destinations the number of tourists in orbit will remain low until technologies such as a space elevator make space travel cheap. Technological improvement is likely to make possible air-ship hotels, based either on solar-powered airplanes or large dirigibles. Underwater hotels, such as Hydropolis, expected to open in Dubai in 2006, will be built. On the ocean tourists will be welcomed by ever larger cruise ships and perhaps floating cities.

Some futurists expect that movable hotel "pods" will be created that could be temporarily erected anywhere on the planet, where building a permanent resort would be unacceptable politically, economically or environmentally.

2

TOURISM TODAY

A look at a travel brochure these days, shows a tendency by travel writers to speak in superlatives. "Grand colonial architecture", "sparkling beaches", "amazing monuments" and so on; and yet, for a country like India, all these adjectives and more, are totally appropriate. However, for a country bursting with tourism opportunities, we have been slightly slow on the uptake, as far as promoting these destinations goes. A point highlighted by the First Planning Commission way back in 1955, which ranked tourism on their priority list of industries - lower than even the development of light-houses! At that time, the average number of tourists who came knocking at our door, was around 15,000.

A HISTORICAL PERSPECTIVE

Post-Independence, while critical issues like agriculture, infrastructure and power supply hogged the limelight, travel and tourism received step-daughterly treatment, as it was deemed a 'luxury' - affordable by only a few.

Not much has changed over the last four decades, and it seemed every time the industry gained some form of momentum despite the closed and protected economy, there was something lurking in the shadows to clip its wings. The introduction of FERA put a serious crimp in foreign investment in the country and the Emergency was yet another deterrent to the tourism movement. A look at the Five Year Plans shows that in the Third Plan (1961-1966) tourism got approx 4.001 crores, which was 0.11% of the total Plan outlay.

In the Eighth Plan, (1992-1997) it was Rs 272 crores - still 0.11% of the total plan outlay.

At this time, policy makers, industry representatives and opinion makers equated tourism with foreign visitors. To their way of thinking, it was the foreign visitor who occupied hotel accommodation, filled airline seats, frequented bars and restaurants and used recreation facilities. Plus, given the foreign exchange (forex) shortage, the foreign tourist was looked upon as Daddy Big-Bucks - with an almost endless supply of crisp foreign currency.

And while key aspects of Indian tourism came to be tailored to the foreign visitor, the price mechanism too, came to be tied to overseas costs. Hotel rates, food and beverages in hotels, handicrafts, etc, were priced at a level much higher than the economic standards prevalent in the country at the time. No way could our rupee-toting lads compete. Thus, for our fellow countrymen, travel was restricted to places of pilgrimage or going to one's native town to visit the family once a year. However, other South East Asian countries were on the ball soon enough when they realised the potential of tourism.

Hong Kong, Singapore and Thailand dug in the infrastructure, developed detailed tourism plans and marketed them in glorious technicolour across the world. Ironically, today, Indian outbound tourism provides a sizeable chunk of tourist inflow into these countries.

SOMETHING IN THE AIR

From the mid-80s to the early 90s, the Indian corporate world underwent a transformation. The Old Guard - Tatas, Birlas and Godrej - saw the emergence of the newer dynasties on the block - Reliance, Essar and Mahindra. As new factories opened and the corporate kingdoms spread across the country, so did the need for roving executives, with suitably generous travel and entertainment allowances. And thus was born the corporate traveller. Airlines and hotels didn't take long to work out that the man with the tie and briefcase was the man with the corporate expense account! Airlines introduced business or club class and the hospitality sector set up executive floors - complete with butlers - geared to cater to this booming segment.

The outbound segment (as we know it today) was still in its nascent stage. The "have- suitcase-will-travel" high lasted only for so long, as the reality of getting sponsor letters from friends and family overseas set in, and the forex restrictions of USD$ 500 as one's basic travel quota (BTQ) once every two years, made travelling abroad more than a little difficult. Naturally, this being the land of opportunity, the grey market for forex boomed - practically every large general store in well- to-do neighbourhoods had an extra drawer for their greenbacks. Low customs allowances meant that bringing items into the country from your travels - assuming you went to some place where US$500 would get you anything - meant the little man in a white uniform welcomed you on your return to the

Homeland, and rubbed his hands in glee. "Red channel please" was the helpful direction he gave you as you wearily pushed your trolley towards a long and tortuous queue!

The Yuppies of the 90s

The tourism industry began to swing in the mid-90s, with the liberalisation of the economy, and with India ratifying the agreement to set up the WTO unit in India. Foreign investment in industry, foreign investment in airlines and foreign media got the country excited about the world "out there" and the guy with 50 channels at his disposal, found bikini-clad motivation on his 21 inch screen, to get out of his armchair and check out new destinations. The alphabets 'MBA' next to a young person's name opened up the road to five-figure salaries, six-figure bonuses and stock options. Young people were raring to go where they parents hadn't been and they had the means to do it! And, more surprisingly, the Indian traveller began to get excited about touring around his own country and the trend for domestic tourism was firmly set. The last decade of the last century alone, saw an increase by more than 100 million travellers in the domestic tourism segment - from 63.8 million visitors in 1990, to 176 million in 1999.

The Number Crunch

On a broader scale though, finding accurate figures and statistics is something of a problem even today, and in the absence of a centrally appointed and vigilant monitoring body, one can only make estimates. Immigration figures based on disembarkation cards are unreliable as they make little distinction between visitors coming only to India or backtracking from Nepal or other neighbouring countries. Also, a large number of arrivals stay with family or friends and do not contribute much to the forex kitty.

Forex earnings have been accepted by the tourism industry, as being the surer criterion of the quality and number of tourists a country is attracting. A study by

FICCI, in 1994, showed that the overall forex earnings from tourism had been static around US$ 1.2 - 1.4bn. In 1989, our earnings in forex were Rs. 2103 crores, which rose to Rs 3,990 crores in 1993. But if one were to take into account the devaluation that the rupee had been facing against the dollar at the time, then the net dollar earnings had virtually remained stagnant. Tracking tourism in the domestic sector is even more difficult as this is still an unorganised sector, with individuals making their own arrangements or availing of the services of small outfits. The tourism industry began to swing in the mid-90s, with the liberalization of the economy, and with India ratifying the agreement to set up the WTO unit in India. Foreign investment in industry, foreign investment in airlines and foreign media got the country excited about the world "out there" and the guy with 50 channels at his disposal, found bikini-clad motivation on his 21 inch screen, to get out of his armchair and check out new destinations.

Here and Now

Post-September 11, the tourism industry in India has shown resilience with Indian travellers opting to look inwards to domestic tourism or to explore other destinations such as Australia and New Zealand. The Kargil conflict, the current Iraq war and the new flu on the loose in South East Asia, have also dealt serious blows to the global tourism industry. Despite this litany of international crises, today, it is an accepted fact that tourism is the fastest growing industry in the world; a creator of wealth and business opportunities, an income multiplier, a catalyst for employment and preserver of the environment. An investment of Rs 10 lakhs in tourism, creates 89 jobs, as against 45 in agriculture, and 13 in manufacturing for the same investment.

The current budget has finally granted the tourism industry "infrastructure" status, and an increase in plan outlay to Rs 225 crore. The international airports in the four metros are to be upgraded to world-class standards and six comprehensive tourism circuits will be developed to help promote tourism. The lack of a centralised government apex body to give it the tourism industry focus and direction, is still a cause for serious concern. At present, the central ministry of tourism's functions are limited to marketing India overseas and providing meager financial support to state governments for the creation of tourism facilities. Most of the important issues relating to tourism are deciding elsewhere. The Ministry of Civil Aviation controls aviation policy as well as the administration of airports. The Ministry of Home Affairs/External Affairs decides the visa regime, and the Ministry of Finance supervises the fiscal policy for investment in the tourism sector and of course the all- important tax structure. It is left to the private sector to run between the ministries to bring about any radical reforms. The classic Indian bureaucratic runaround - the death-knell to an industry on the move!

Future-wise

The more significant findings of the many reports done for the international travel and tourism industry show that the focus of the industry is gradually shifting from Europe and N America to east/South Asia and the Pacific. A research forecast by the World Travel and Tourism Council pegs tourism industry growth at 4.5% over the next ten years. Turkey is expected to be the fastest growing travel and tourism economy over the next 10 years at a rate of 10.2%, while India will have a growth of 9.7%. This buoyant outlook also reflects a possibility of the creation of nearly 7 million jobs over the next 10 years.

3

ECOTOURISM : THE PROSPECTS AND PROBLEMS

Ecotourism is the fastest growing sector in the International Tourism. The problem of ecolabeling to market tourism products. The absence of co-coordinated effort and guidelines to support standardisation of facilities. Ecotourism practices ultimately lead to sustainability of the environment. It is the future of modern day tourism. As tourism is emerging only, it can be monitored to attain its natural growth by having various discussions with the stakeholders all over the world.

The eco-tourism urgently needs proper guidelines & directions of international standards to sustain its natural growth. In each country many products are developed without any general standards, to suit their own interest. This will lead into major problems in the future. As ecolabeling is becoming a very important marketing tool in selling of tourism products all over the world, a conscientious effort from all the concerned in developing management and marketing of ecotourism products is the need of the hour. The ecotourism products should be diverse as each country has its own needs and requirements, but it should have a pattern.

The various standards introduced by numerous organisations in conceptualising, developing and sustainably managing and marketing ecotourism products should have a common direction. The chances of ecotourism practitioners all over the world over to come together and interact together to solve their management problems should be made frequently and more effectively through various organisations. It should be planned regionwise, ountrywise as well as globally, both at micro level and macro level during these interactions. The numerous problems arising during the ecotourism development and management should be brought to the notice of all the concerned and serious discussion and interactions followed, will be of great help to all. The experiences at micro level lead to answers to the questions of macro level.

ECOTOURISM AS THE FUTURE OF MODERN DAY TOURISM

As the future of tourism depends on sustainability ecotourism has all the prospects to become very popular among the travellers. Mass tourism and tourism in general damages the mother nature in many ways. More travellers in future will opt for ecotourism.

An awareness should be created among the travellers in opting a tour, which is sustaining mother nature, supporting local community, their culture, traditional ways of life and not exploiting them in any way. Only then the damages created by mass tourism should be reversed.

The ultimate aim of tourism should be while attaining mental and physical happiness by experiencing varied environments, way of life style, cuisine, culture etc without causing much damages to the visiting population and contributing to the economic, mental, physical characteristic of them. Thus ecotourism will benefit both the visitors as well as the host community.

Thus ecotourism should be the role model in popularizing the responsible tourism and fair trade in tourism. Ecotourism should help the visitors for a learning experience of a diverse environment, ambience causing minimum damages to mother nature and its various components.

Need versus Greed

Like all business activity, tourism is centered around economics, more money with less expenses. But careful strategies are essential to control the needs of the people than their greeds. Once measures are taken to look after the needs, then sustainability could be attained. On the other hand, if the greed of the people became prominent, the end result will be disastrous like killing a goose laying golden eggs. Thus ecotourism practitioners all over the world has to come together and evolve a methodology, look after the needs and not greeds for the sustenance of themselves as well as mother nature.

Ecotourism as a Philosophy and way of Life

Practitioners of serious ecotourism has to develop a separate mind set other than normal tourism professionals as ecotourism is a way of life in itself. A serious ecotourism practitioner has to look into the possibilities of always choosing for the right things. Their practice has to be routine for day to day life conducting of business in a ecotourism resort. They are the honorary emissaries to function as a role model for the sustainable ecotourism practices.

They should also try their best to promote the philosophy to all others. Thus preaching and practice should go together. Successful ecotourism practitioners are always not prophets of doom, but are glittering rays of hope for the betterment humanity as well as mother nature.

As tourism is becoming the biggest economic activity in the world in the 21 century, ecotourism practices and principles has more relevance than ever. Let us hope by working together, we could hope for a better world where all are equally important.

PROBLEMS AND PROSPECTS FOR INVESTMENT AND BUSINESS

The initial euphoria following the partition of India in 1947 had seen the establishment of several industries in Khulna, and the setting up of the Chalna Anchorage, which later became Mongla port. The sentiment then was that Khulna would be the counterpart of Calcutta as a center of commerce and industry. But by the 1960's, the euphoria had subsided as construction of Farakka barrage began in India. The barrage was being built no more than 16 km upstream of the place where the mighty Ganges River enters Bangladesh, and its purpose was to divert its waters to keep the Calcutta (at present Kolkata) port navigable.

Moreover jute, which had been the "Golden Fibre" and goods produced with it, that were the principal export commodities of this region began to lose ground to cheaper and more durable synthetics, in spite of the fact that jute, because of its bio-degradable nature, is more environment-friendly than synthetics. The downfall of jute was accompanied by the implementation of the Coastal Embankment Project (CEP), which enclosed the entire southwest coastal region of Bangladesh within about 30 polders with 1566 km of high earthen embankments and 282 sluices.

The CEP proved beneficial for about a decade and a half, but man's intervention in the Acts of Nature was also building up during that period. As the saline tides were denied entry into the polders in order to keep them free of salinity for year-round cultivation of food grains, the tides began to deposit their load of silt on the riverbeds. Gradually the riverbeds silted up and rose until they became higher than the land within the polders, causing at first seasonal drainage congestion, which later became permanent water logging within the polders. The waterlogged area gradually expanded until it stood at over 100,000 hectares by 1990.

This degradation of Khulna's hinterland had both harmful and beneficial effects. Harmful because it rendered thousands of small and marginal farmers jobless, and they began to migrate to the city to add to its congestion and degradation of environment. The beneficial effect was that the farmers who lost their lands to water logging began cultivating at first merely fish and later on shrimps and prawns. The world's demand for frozen shrimps and prawns kept on increasing and is increasing still. The result was the establishment of over two score plants for processing shrimp, which revived the diminishing importance of Khulna as an industrial and commercial center.

During the same period, that is, from the mid-1980's till date, jute is also having a two-pronged revival. One is that its bio-degradability is finding favour in a world that has become more environment conscious than ever before, and secondly, coordinated multinational research has resulted in finding more uses for jute. So now the closed jute mills are reopening one by one and export of jute goods are increasing year by year. Moreover, the government is in the process of privatization of state-owned enterprises, which will make many jute mills and other industries available for private investment. There is also the feeling of a revival in South Asian inter-state cooperation, which kindles further possibilities for Khulna for being close to India.

But by far the most important attraction in this coastal region is the Sundarban, which is the single largest block of mangrove ecosystem that exists in the world today, though its tourist potential has never been exploited through sheer negligence and lack of initiative. Here also, private initiative has shown the way, and there is the potential for tourism to expand more speedily, especially eco-tourism, both of the natural as well as of the cultural variety.

Thus tourism is destined to flourish in the Khulna region, calling for investments in the hospitality industry, transport and many other related fields. Khulna can be a hub for tours and excursions into the Sundarbans as well as the numerous historical sites that represent the culture of this part of the world. And for all this, Khulna and its hinterland is one of the most promising areas for investment in Bangladesh.

Thus jute, shrimps and prawns and tourism give promise of good returns from investment, and opens up a world of opportunity for the economic prosperity of the inhabitants, which in turn will enable the local markets for manufactured goods to grow.

But the problems of salinity and shortage of fuel and energy will still remain. In order to solve the salinity problem, there is already a provision in the proposed Ganges barrage project to ensure year round supply of a minimum 250 cubic metres per second (cumecs) of fresh water to the Gorai, which will push the saline front to the downstream of Khulna city. By further providing 125 cumecs to the Mathabhanga, from which the Kapotakhi and Bhairab get their water, the saline front can be pushed farther downstream.

Another requirement is to extend the Natural gas pipeline from Sirajganj to Khulna or at least to Bheramara, and build power generating units using gas. Coal is also an option for power generation, but it will be foolish to burn it off without deriving additional benefits from coal. Huge coke ovens can be set up at mines to produce coke and other by-products. These by-products including coal tar and gases can be used as raw materials for innumerable organic chemical industries. Coal burning must be prohibited, and coke may be burned whether in iron smelting furnaces or in cooking stoves. This will also save the country from air pollution.

There is a huge potential in the shrimp industry. At present we are in culture and freezing only, and that too in an under-developed stage. Further development will require new technology, which can be acquired easily. By stepping one level higher, we can advance to Fish and Shrimp canning. In that sector there is plenty of scope for joint venture, which will be needed to acquire technology. Shrimp and fish wastes can also be used as raw materials for many small-scale industries.

With the development of the shrimp industry, there will be a huge demand for shrimp feed, which can also be used as poultry feed. There is urgent necessity for establishing feed industries in the Khulna region, from which both shrimp and poultry sectors can benefit.

There is also a prospect for developing earthenware and ceramic products, as roofing and flooring tiles are being exported to Italy and other countries of Europe for the last few years. There is much scope for development of such an industry, as there is an abundance of skilled labour in this region. Thus it is seen that Khulna and its hinterlands holds a lot of promise to courageous and imaginative investors, and general improvement in the lives and livelihoods of the people.

PROSPECTS FOR TOURISM

IT is apparent that Northeast India as a whole needs a big push or a kick-start to put the economy on the path of development. Looking East provides an opportunity to overcome problems of distance from markets. Tourism provides a marketable product which does not depend on raw materials from outside. In a comparable situation of economic doldrums in the '80s, Mexico stepped out of the traditional models of economic growth to depend on tourism as an important input. This strategy showed remarkable results. Outlining the experience, Mexico's planning minister summed up that tourism was relevant because -

- Agriculture and manufacturing are location specific, but tourism can be promoted and developed almost anywhere. It is therefore an ideal tool for decentralized regional development.
- It provides infinite product possibilities - anything under the sun if properly packaged and marketed - such as culture, heritage, nature, sun and beaches, cruises, business, conventions, spirituality, adventure, sports, ethnicity and so forth. The benefits are more spread out and not centred around urban areas as in the case of most industries.
- Being a personal service it is hard to automate and is therefore labour intensive.
- The foreign import component of investment in tourism is very low. In Mexico as a whole it was

estimated to be 6-8% as against 35-45% for the automobile industry. In the case of the Northeast the component would be even more negligible. The tourist expenditure within the country is almost always equivalent to cash. It therefore has an advantage over traditional exports in respect of immediate cash flows.

- The multiplier effect of tourism is very high. The ripple effects are widespread and the benefits are shared by an incredibly large number of service providers, like lodgings, food and beverages, handicraft, local transportation, guides, shopping, entertainment, photography. In the total range of services, many of the service providers are not visible at all.

These are only some illustrative examples and all the observations are relevant to the Northeast. The employment intensity of tourism in the Indian context was demonstrated by an oft-quoted sample survey of the Ministry of Tourism. According to this survey, for every million rupees invested, at 1985-86 prices, the comparative employment generation in some of the sectors were as follows - agriculture 44.7, manufacturing 12.6, mining and quarrying 2.6, railways 0.9, other transport 13.8, tourism 47.5, and hotels and restaurants 89.0.

Another recent survey by the Ministry shows the impact of tourism on local level employment - about 96% of the total income of artisan households in Kerala and 90% in Rajasthan comes from tourism related income. The study also indicates that 'tourism plays a vital role in enhancing the standard of living of the artisan families... As regards folk artists, their average per capita income during the peak season is nearly four times that in the lean season. ...Share of female employment is the highest in the lower income segment of the artisan households.'

The tourism potential of the Northeast has not been fully exploited. The Ministry of Tourism calls the region a 'paradise unexplored'. Global tourism has been booming and future projections show that this trend will continue. The new generations of travellers who are 'money rich and time poor' are increasingly looking for unique experiences. More and more people are looking at tourism as less of a journey and more of an experience - a phenomenon being called the emergence of the 'experience economy'.

For these new and growing breed of tourists the Northeast with its variety and uniqueness holds immense attraction. The rich natural beauty and its diversity, exotic cultural and ethnic mosaic, flora and fauna and the serenity of the virgin, unexplored ecosystems provides possibilities of a totally different experience for the tourists.

The rationale for a trade led growth strategy for the Northeast integrated to the 'look east' policy has been well explained. The landlocked Northeast, it is explained, is ideally placed to link India with ASEAN both in a geographical and commercial sense. The Northeast also has strong cultural and historical linkages with the East, which could be exploited to forge economic cooperation.

So far as tourism is concerned, such an approach comes out of India's tourism experience of the last decade. This was a decade of good growth thwarted by continuous crisis - the Gulf war, the nuclear tests and subsequent economic sanctions, the Kargil war, terrorist attack on Parliament, the Gujarat earthquake, the

Afghan war and the Iraq war, just to mention a few. The infamous 'advisories' issued by the national governments in Europe and USA - the countries from where most of the tourists come - adversely affected the tourism flow to India. Globally, in the first three years of the new millennium, tourism saw many ups and downs. The wars and the 9/11 incidents, as well as the SARS, adversely affected tourism growth. Nevertheless, in almost 50 years since the World Tourism Organisation started keeping statistics, tourism growth has shown negative results only three times and two of them came during the first three years of the new millennium.

One key lesson learnt during this time was that in periods of crisis, regional tourism and domestic tourism is the mainstay of the industry. Unfortunately, Indian tourism depends heavily on the long haul tourists of the West. Whereas globally the ratio of interregional to regional tourism is 20:80, in case of India it is almost exactly the other way round. The marketing strategy of the Ministry of Tourism is now identifying new markets for tourism and this search is aligned with the 'Look East' trade policy.

Such a policy shift is particularly relevant and important for the Northeast. Because it is situated far away from the main entry points of tourists, the Northeast is at a disadvantage in attracting foreign tourists from the West. This is reflected in the negligible tourist flow to this region. In 2002, out of about 5.8 million visits to the states (by 2.75 m tourists), the Northeast received only about 22000. If the figures of Sikkim are excluded, all the other seven states of the Northeast accounted for only 12000 visits.

Looking to the East is fortunately a natural marketing option for the Northeast. By 2020 the Asia Pacific region will be the second largest tourist generating market in the world. The world tourism projection shows that by 2020 this region will generate 405 m of the total 1561 m tourists. These countries have continuous geographical land links with the Northeast. China is already vigorously developing tourism in its southern provinces to take advantage of this outbound tourist market of the region. These areas have cultural, historical and ethnic links with the Northeast. The tourism marketing strategy of the Northeast should focus on these links to establish a natural flow of people within the region, including the Northeast.

In such a strategy it will be of crucial importance to develop access to this region. Presently in the western tourist dominated scenario, access to the Northeast is seen as a constraint. While air access will have to be developed as a sine qua non of a tourism development strategy, fortunately, the Asian Highway Project is looming in the horizon as a great opportunity for the region. The Asian Highway, if properly planned and integrated, can completely change the tourism scenario of the region. It proposes to cover 90,000 km in 25 countries, of which 40,000 km will be international routes and 50,000 km regional routes. ESCAP, which is spearheading the project, recognizes the excellent tourism potential of the Asian Highway. It has already undertaken a survey to identify the potential and possible bottlenecks so that timely action can be taken to remove them.

Here is a golden opportunity for the Northeast to exploit. The plan of action for the Northeast with the objective of using the Asian Highway as its link to the East, could be, among others -

- The international route touches only a part of the Northeast. Therefore, integrated feeder communication links should be developed through the national and state planning processes, in consultation with ESCAP. This will require quick coordination among the states and identification of suitable implementing agencies.

- A comprehensive tourism potential survey should precede the planning of routes to form the feeder to the Asian Highway. Among other things, the routes planned should be able to serve and promote the most important tourism destinations.
- Tourism cannot be developed in a vacuum. It requires social and economic infrastructure for proper growth. As a first step to planning, a survey of the infrastructure gaps should be undertaken. Thereafter, the projects should be prioritized for their overall importance to the trade led growth strategy. A major component for tourism should be the development of wayside amenities along the Asian Highway and feeder routes. In Japan a concept of community based tourism and wayside facilities called 'Michi-no-eki' has proved immensely successful. Under this scheme, the facilities are community run in partnership with the private sector. The centres not only provide facilities, they also work as outlets for local handicraft and handloom products and showpiece local culture, cuisine etc. Such involvement leads not only to better economic benefits for the people, but also ensures better visitor experience.

If the very high expectations of the 'look east' policy unleashing economic opportunities through tourism is to become a reality, the Northeast must first make an assessment of its own comparative advantage and then plan strategy based on such assessment. The South Asian growth quadrangle of Bangladesh, Bhutan, India and Nepal (BBIN) will also directly touch the Northeast. The Asian Development Bank (ADB) has explored these growth possibilities with its South Asia Subregional Economic Cooperation (SASEC) initiative. Under this initiative, the main tourism strengths of the region have been identified as (i) sustainable ecotourism and (ii) the Buddhist circuit.

In both areas the advantage of the Northeast is apparent. The SASEC concept of the Buddhist circuit is in fact very comprehensive. It goes beyond the traditional circuit of places where Lord Buddha lived, meditated, attained enlightenment and parinirvana.

It covers places of living Buddhism like Ladakh, Sikkim and Arunachal (Tawang). Art, culture and archaeology of Buddhism are also integrated into the total Buddhist circuit concept. A significantly large number of tourists from the Asia Pacific region are Buddhists and, therefore, these attractions may open up interest in the Northeast.

What needs to be done? Unfortunately what is obvious is not always immediately perceived. This seems to be the case with tourism in the Northeast. Despite such obvious advantages, tourism has not played an effective role in the economic planning of the region, nor does its growth inspire any confidence.

A look at the statistics shows that the unique resources of tourism have not been properly exploited. India itself is far from realizing its true tourism potential. But the figures for the Northeast compared to the national figures, are insignificant. The arrival figures of tourists both domestic and international make this abundantly clear.

	1999	2000	2001
Arunachal Pradesh	1008/48	9932/2044	6349/323
Assam	14336/604	891433/5954	1010651/6171
Manipur	97523/277	105167/429	76527/183
Meghalaya	159730/1971	169929/2327	178697/2390
Mizoram	27139/216	28221/235	28771/152
Nagaland	21041/119	13272/451	9946/920
Sikkim	138785/8554	143105/10409	203306/31028
Tripura	246507/335	231902/0	254912/0
All India	190671014/ 5832105	22106941/ 5893542	234200935/ 5427366

The total number of approved hotels and the room capacity also shows the poor state of infrastructure.

	No. of approved hotels	No. of rooms
Arunachal Pradesh	1	10
Assam	17	714
Manipur	-	-
Meghalaya	5	254
Mizoram	1	30
Nagaland		
Tripura		
Sikkim	4	133

It is quite possible that the figures suffer from deficiencies in statistical compilation. So far as hotels are concerned, it is likely that most of the accommodation is in the unorganized sector and does not come under the purview of government. In either situation one cannot escape the conclusion that the state of affairs is far from satisfactory.

There is much to be done. If tourism development is not taken up with some urgency and in a planned manner it is quite possible that instead of tourism providing an economic push, in a liberalized atmosphere, the region may suffer from a reverse flow. In tourism, as elsewhere, if the goods cannot meet the competition, the outflow may overtake inflow. Some of the areas in which action is to be taken to make tourism an effective tool of development have already been mentioned. By way of illustration we can mention a few initiatives urgently needed at the macro level.

Unfortunately, despite its comparative advantage in this area, tourism is not perceived as an important economic activity. The first task of the governments should be to create awareness about the place of tourism in general and of sustainable tourism in particular, in the socio-economic planning of the region. But such awareness creation efforts can start only when the governments themselves are convinced of tourism's importance and provide it due priority in the planning process.

Most of tourism planning in the region appears to be ad hoc. It is essential to move away from such an ad hoc approach to draw up definite plans of action, charting out the future directions clearly. Every state must bring out a pragmatic tourism policy, not couched in general terms but clearly defining an implementable action plan. It should indicate the government's commitment to sustainable tourism, the place assigned to tourism in broad development planning, the role of government and other key players. The policy should identify the organizational pattern to implement the policy and a system of monitoring and accountability.

A tourism policy would remain on the wish list of the tourism department alone unless it reflects total government commitment. Tourism being a multidimensional activity, depends on the involvement of many other agencies for its success. Other departments like roads, culture, forest and so on, can play an important role in the development of the total tourism product. For achieving maximum coordination, institutional arrangements should be put in place.

Domestic tourism plays a key role in Indian tourism. Against the average ratio of about seven domestic tourists for every foreign tourist in the total picture internationally, the ratio for India is about 100:1. In absolute terms the figure of total domestic tourists is about 300 million against three million foreign tourists. The Northeast has a insignificant share of this huge number of tourists who contribute to employment and income generation in other states. Movement of domestic tourists will gradually improve the image of the place and the demand created will lead to development of essential infrastructure. This process will then facilitate movement of foreign tourists.

Tourism planning for the Northeast states, whether aimed at the domestic or the foreign tourist, would be most attractive and cost effective if based on an integrated NE perspective. The attractions of the different states, rather than competing, should supplement each other and enhance the total attraction of the region. Unfortunately this vital necessity of projecting the totality of NE tourism suffers from two fundamental inadequacies: First, poor internal communication between the states. The road communication is arduous and time consuming. Air communication has of late improved, but is not yet tuned to tourism requirements. Coordinated planning of tourism for the NE is possible only when internal communication by air becomes efficient and reliable.

Second, the lack of an organizational setup. There is no organizational setup that can harmonise action for projecting NE tourism as a whole. Prospective tourists who wish to visit and sympathetic entrepreneurs who want to market the NE find it exasperating to draw up an integrated schedule for the whole region. There is too much of dependence on the government and too little incentive for the private sector to enable them to play an effective role. If tourism in the NE has to grow, a common platform of all the states, involving the government and non-governmental agencies, should be immediately formulated.

These are only a few illustrative areas where action has to start on a priority basis. The action agenda is long because the Northeast has a lot to catch up with. Human resource development, creating institutional arrangements for people's participation, looking at ways to harness greater resources for tourism, creating public-private partnerships are some of the issues which will demand attention as tourism grows.

'Even a five thousand mile journey must start with the first step,' says an old Chinese proverb. There is a long journey ahead for the Northeast as it tries to look eastward. A beginning has to be made soon.

TOWARDS A NEW TOURISM POLICY

The tourism industry is a composite of service providers which includes travel agents, tour operators, air, rail and sea transportation operators, guides, hotels, guest houses and inns, restaurants and shops selling handicrafts, souvenirs, clothing footwear, leather items and other objects of interest to the tourists. The common factor about these service providers is that all are involved in meeting the requirements of international and domestic tourists. These service providers are generally in the private sector. Public sector institutions such as the national or state departments of tourism are involved in planning, development and management of tourism-related service providers. In many cases they even provide direct services to the tourists.

Left to itself, the industry will develop naturally, but not necessarily, optimally on a sustainable basis. If the industry is properly planned, developed and managed at all levels of government in partnership with the private sector, it will strengthen the country's cultural structure and natural heritage and lead to positive economic results including enhanced employment and income opportunities especially in rural areas.

The 1982 Tourism Policy was drafted in a different socio-economic milieu in an environment of an economy with strict licensing procedures. Foreign investment in the economy was not anticipated, development of new technology was not envisaged and there was no focus on balanced development of various regions. The Policy did not differentiate specifically the roles of the government and the private sectors and there was no emphasis on the latter's role in the development and promotion of tourism.

In the post-liberalisation period various developments in the tourism sector have taken place. The sector has been accorded the status of export house and various incentives like income tax exemptions, interest subsidy and reduced import duty are available to the hotel industry, travel agents, tour operators and tourist transport operators. Several incentives have been made available for attracting private investment in tourism projects including those under the Liberalised Exchange Rate Management System (LERMS).

The economic reforms introduced by the Centre are integrating India into the global economy and making Indian industry internationally competitive. Foreign direct investment and technical collaborations form a major platform of the economic reforms. With a view to attracting investment in this sector the hotel and tourism-related industry has been declared as a 'high priority industry' for foreign investment. It is now eligible for automatic approval of direct investment upto 100 per cent of foreign equity.

Non-Resident Indian (NRI) investment is allowed upto 100 per cent automatically. In a fast-changing world, the relationship between suppliers and users of technology, agreements have to be recognised. To promote technology upgradation in the hotel industry, approvals for technology agreements are now available automatically subject to the fulfillment of certain conditions. Applications for automatic approvals for foreign investment or technology agreements and management contracts can be made to the RBI for according such approvals and the entrepreneurs can approach authorised dealers for release of foreign exchange.

Tourism Boom

There has been a global tourism boom in the recent times. Tourism has already achieved the distinction of being the world's largest export industry. India had received just over 16,800 international tourists in 1951. The arrivals increased to 1.7 million in 1990 and further to 2.64 million in 2000. The growth rate between 1990 and 2000 has been 4.46 per cent per annum. A higher growth rate of 6.4 per cent has been achieved in the year 2000 over the previous year. However, India's share in world tourism arrivals has remained virtually stagnant at 0.38 per cent from 1995 onwards. India with about 42 per cent share in the arrivals is the major receiver of international arrivals in the South Asia region in the year 2000 and yet its growth rate lags far behind that of many countries in the region. The tourism receipts of India went up from US$ 2583 million in 1995 to US$ 3168 million in 2000 showing an annual average growth rate of 4.17 per cent as compared to the world's average growth rate of 3.2 per cent during this period. However, in 2000 India's growth rate of 5.3 per cent compares very poorly with many of the neighbouring countries such as China (15 per cent), Hong Kong China (10.7 per cent), Malaysia (27 per cent), Thailand (12.5 per cent), Macau (25 per cent), Iran (28.4 per cent) and Pakistan (14.5 per cent).

There has been a phenomenal growth in domestic tourism in the country during the last one decade. The domestic tourist visits increased from 63.8 million in 1990 to 210 million in 2000.

Potential

Tourism provides enormous opportunity for employment generation. According to an estimate the travel and tourism industry would have directly generated 9.3 million jobs in India. The travel and tourism industry includes activities such as accommodation, transport, catering, entertainment, recreation and other travel-related services. The travel and tourism economy which expresses the impact of travel and tourism and its flow-through effect across the wider economy would have generated 17.4 million jobs in India. Travel and tourism jobs are rapidly generated at relatively low cost, are concentrated in small business and local communities, provide significant opportunities for women and young people, offer education, training and skills development and protect and revitalise traditional arts and crafts.

Focus

Integrated development of infrastructure including basic amenities and on-site facilities like accommodation, restaurants, entertainment and shopping facilities in identified tourist centers is a primary requirement for achieving any large-scale expansion in the tourist traffic. Poor visitor experience particularly due to inadequate infrastructural facilities, poor hygienic conditions, incidence of touting and harassment of tourists in some places and the unscientific approach to taxation policy which includes heavy imposts on hotel room rents, sales tax on food and beverages, heavy excise on liquor, prohibitive customs duty on imported tourist vehicles and taxes on interstate tourist transport are factors that adversely affect the flow of tourist traffic to the country. As a service industry, it is also necessary to achieve high standards of professionalism in providing services to the tourists.

The new tourism policy would take into account the role of Indian tourism as an engine for economic development, employment generation, social integration and promotion of its cultural image abroad. It takes into account the various barriers and constraints that it faces and find a solution to overcome them so as to be able to develop and promote tourism to greater heights.

Indian Tourism on a High

According to figures released by the Ministry of Tourism (MoT), Government of India, in April 2007, around 1.42 million foreign tourists had visited India in the first quarter of 2007 (Q1 2007). This marked a

14.4% growth when compared to the corresponding period in 2006. The foreign-exchange earned in Q1 2007 was Rs.910.24 million, a growth of 16.8% over the same period of the previous year. These strong growth numbers had raised the hope of another good year for the tourism industry in India. More significantly, India was attracting more upmarket tourists, which was in sync with the objectives of the 'Incredible India' campaign initiated by the MoT in 2002.

The 'Incredible India' campaign was a multifaceted campaign aimed at increasing tourist inflow in India by promoting India as an attractive destination. The campaign was a refreshing change from the earlier campaigns, which invariably revolved around the Taj Mahal. Moreover, unlike the previous campaigns, the positioning and communication was kept the same in all the countries. The campaign showcased the unique aspects of India's rich cultural heritage and history like yoga, spirituality, etc. Efforts to promote medical tourism and rural tourism were also intensified. As a part of the campaign, a national social awareness program called Atithi Devo Bhavah (Guest is God) was launched in 2005. This program was aimed at sensitizing key stakeholders about their responsibility toward foreign tourists.

The MoT had also spent heavily on marketing and publicity campaigns. For 2006-07, the MoT had spent Rs.2.35 billion for the marketing and publicity efforts. The marketing and publicity for 'Incredible India' campaign in overseas markets had cost Rs.534.9 million in 2006-07. Analysts opined that this global campaign had helped to boost the Indian tourism industry. Foreign-exchange earning from tourism had jumped from Rs.141.95 billion in 2002 to around Rs.296.0 billion in 2006. The 'Incredible India' campaign had also won various awards for advertising excellence. According to the World Travel and Tourism Council, Indian tourism was expected to grow annually at 8.8% till 2015, which was one of the highest growth rates in the world. Foreign-exchange earnings are expected to cross US$12 billion by the end of 2012.

However, some experts were skeptical and believed that there were still many challenges that prevented India from realizing its full potential. These included poor connectivity, high taxes, visa problems, unsanitary conditions, and shortage of affordable, good quality accommodation. According to experts, building the necessary tourism infrastructure was critical to future success. They opined that India should have developed the infrastructure prior to launching such a high-profile marketing campaign. Some even felt that the future of the industry was more dependent on solving the infrastructure problems rather than on having costly campaigns.

Campaigns are Only Part of the Challenge

Against the historical growth of 6.2% in the foreign tourists visiting India annually, the CAGR since '02 has accelerated to 16%. This growth has been attributed to the strong economic growth and resultant foreign investment opportunities in India, enhanced connectivity and development of infrastructure (spends for which doubled in 2004-7 from 01-04), occupancies are at a historical high while number of rooms in India is rising at a CAGR of 6.1%; increased investments by international players and PEs in hospitality sector.

Previously, India tourism campaigns varied across countries, and projected the uni-dimensional attraction of the Taj Mahal. The Incredible India campaign, first initiated in 2002, has, in a significant departure from earlier tourism ministry campaigns, promoted India uniformly, as a destination offering a wide variety of experiences encompassing culture, spirituality, cuisine etc.

Overseas surveys have indicated that while interest in visiting Asian countries is burgeoning, basic information on India as a destination is limited. The campaign is targeted at bridging this gap and creating desired perceptions through a concerted effort.

Further, critics pointed out that 'marketing' India is only one part of the challenge, and in order to truly build a brand that inspires trust and sustains confidence, it is more crucial to deliver as promised. Given visitor concerns over security, visa issues, supply-demand gaps in tourism travel and accommodation infrastructure etc, the campaign hence would run the risk of losing credibility in the long run. Industry still has a long way to go

Prem Subramaniam, Director, Uttaranchal Infrastructure Development Company & head, CII -Tourism Committee The Incredible India campaign aggregated stunning visuals of India which helped alter a potential traveller's perception of India as a destination. However to be able to evaluate the true impact of the campaign, one would need to look at the outcomes in slightly greater detail. First if there is an increase in leisure travel, there must be a corresponding increase in entrance collections to ticketed attractions, in shopping expenditure at emporia, in collections of taxes for tourist vehicles and in all economic activity of the visitor. There is unfortunately inadequate data in this regard.

What seems to be evident is that there is a surge in business travel. This has caused a shortage of room inventory at gateway and business related cities, our airports are unable to cope with the increased number of flights, and the impression of India not representing good value seems to be growing stronger.

The campaign to engage stakeholders including sensitizing taxi drivers at Delhi is laudable but needs to be continued on an ongoing basis at all tourist locations. The campaign is not supported by adequate product development and development of alternate propositions that lead a potential visitor to seamlessly move from an expression of interest or curiosity to making a booking and returning as a satisfied customer. This will require a more integrated holistic approach and the campaign is only one element of this exercise.

Just getting a visa can be a problem if one were to take the example of the founder of Easy Jet who was in Mumbai. So the campaign has to be supported by easier entry formalities and it will be better to redress all the issues which impact on tourist inflows. Many of these issues are outside the ambit of the Ministry, but nevertheless influence tourism. The campaign has been a useful beginning but there is still a long way to go to realize our full potential.

Potential of Indian Tourism

India has significant potential for becoming a major global tourist destination. The country witnessed foreign tourist arrivals of 2.75 million in 2001.

- Travel and tourism is the second highest foreign exchange earner for India, and the government has given organisations in this industry export house status. The industry is waking up to the potential of domestic tourism as well, with an estimated 4.7 billion domestic trips in 2001. Tourism spending within India in 2001 was US$ 22 billion.

- There is considerable government presence in the travel and tourism industry. Each state has a tourism corporation, which typically runs a chain of hotels /motels and operates package tours, while the central government runs the India Tourism Development Corporation. Divestment of these state-run tourism corporations have either already taken place or are in process.
- Incoming foreign tourist arrivals have shown a 6% compounded annual growth rate over the last 10 years. The government has realised the potential and has advanced several incentives to promote infrastructure growth in the tourism sector.
- Current investments are likely to see hotel room capacity increase by 20% over the next three years, with several international hotel chains entering the hotel industry. Similar growth is anticipated in air travel capacity.

Policy Initiatives

- The New Tourism Policy released in May 2002 has outlined the following policy initiatives for the tourism sector:
- The new policy is built around the 7-S Mantra of Swaagat (welcome), Soochanaa (information), Suvidhaa (facilitation), Surakshaa (security), Sahyog (cooperation), Sanrachnaa (infrastructure) and Safaai (cleanliness).
- The new policy envisages making tourism a catalyst in employment generation, wealth creation, development of remote and rural areas, environment preservation and social integration. The policy also aims to spruce up economic growth and promote India's strengths as a tourism destination that is both safe and at the same time

exciting.

- The policy proposes the inclusion of tourism in the concurrent list of the Constitution so as to enable both the central and state governments to participate in the development of the sector.
- No approval is required for foreign equity of up to 51 per cent in tourism projects. Enhanced equity is considered on a case-to-case basis. NRI investment is allowed up to 100%.
- Approvals for Technology agreements in the hotel industry are available on an automatic basis, subject to the fulfilment of certain specified parameters.
- Concession rates on customs duty of 25% for goods that are required for initial setting up, or for substantial expansion of hotels.
- 50% of profits derived by hotels, travel agents and tour operators in foreign exchange are exempt from income tax. The remaining profits are also exempt if reinvested in a tourism related project.
- Approved hotels are entitled to import essential goods relating to the hotel and tourism industry up to the value of 25% of the foreign exchange earned by them in the preceding licensing year. This limit for approved travel agents/tour operators is 10%.
- Hotels located in locations other than the four major metro cities are entitled to 30% deduction from profit, for a ten-year period.
- The expenditure tax has been waived in respect of hotels located in the hills, rural areas, places of pilgrimage or specified place of tourist importance.

Government of Meghalaya Tourism Department

Tourism development is as significant to Meghalaya, as it has been in the other more progressive States of India where it has grown into a promising industry. In this context, Tourism can, therefore, be considered to be the gateway to economic development of the State. Meghalaya offers enormous potential for employment and economic growth by utilizing the natural attractions like landscapes, mountains and peaks, beaches, rivers, waterfalls, flora and fauna. It also applies to a multitude of man-made attractions like monuments, places and unique rural and city environment.

To overcome the over-growing unemployment, the Government has attached more importance in the tourism industry. Meghalaya has an edge over other tourist centres in the Northeast as it has unique blend of different cultures, congenial climatic conditions and better infrastructures for setting up of tourism related activities. During the last twenty years, Government has made several attempts to develop Industries, encourage agricultural and other related activities in efforts to create employment. Unfortunately, the impact has not been as desired as there is no viable industrial base and even in the Tourism Sector; infrastructure so developed has been in an unorganised manner without any concise plan and sense of direction.

The Meghalaya Tourism Policy - 2001 has been formulated to attract more tourists from India and abroad and at the same time allow benefits to reach the grassroots of the populace thereby mitigating innumerable interlinked problems being faced presently.

Objective of the Policy : In the context of the above, the overriding objectives of the Tourism Policy will be to :-

i. Create self sustainable jobs for the local youth of the State;

ii. Generate substantial revenue for the State exchequer;

iii. Project a friendly tourist image to the world at large and make the State one of the best tourist destinations of the country by capitalising on the State's natural assets; managing them properly and creating a consistent competitive advantage;

iv. Promote local interests through strategic alliances with investors;

v. To be the number one Indian destination by per capital market share of visitor's expenditure;

vi. Create a business climate which will attract outside investment;

vii. Encourage domestic tourism (inter State) with a view to provide to the people of the country as well as the State especially those living in rural areas to understand geographical and cultural diversity of the State as well as the aspirations and viewpoints of others so as to bring about a greater national integration and cohesion.

viii. Offer opportunities to the youth not only for employment but also for taking up activities of nation building character like sports, adventure and the like;

ix. Bring socio-economic benefits to the community and the State terms or faster economic growth, larger employment opportunities, better income generation and foreign exchange earning, balanced development of backward areas and weaker sections, higher tax revenue to the State and cause sustainable human development.

x. Preserving and enriching our cultural heritage in all its manifestations and causing accretion and strength, rather than damage to our social and cultural values;

xi. To create suitable environment for development of basic infrastructure facilities for tourism including Communication and transportation links.

xii. To promote and protect the interest of the people of Meghalaya by making various incentives available for setting up of hotels, health resorts, amusement parks etc.

xiii. To encourage traditional artisans and the handicraft sector.

xiv. To include ail Circuit Houses and Dak Bungalows under different Meghalaya Government Departments within and outside the State for providing facilities to Tourists in co-ordination with the concerned departments.

Definition and Eligibility

New Unit : New units means a tourism unit, which commences execution/operation of the project on or after January 1997 with prior approval in writing from the Director of Tourism, Government of Meghalaya.

Eligible Units : Only projects approved by the Department of Tourism after 1997 would be eligible for incentives and concessions.

Incentive : Incentives shall be available for new units as well as to the existing units undergoing expansion modernisation and diversification.

Investment Subsidy : 20% of the capital cost of investment on land, building, plant and machinery subject to a ceiling of Rs. 25.00 lakhs shall be provided for all tourism related activities including drawal of Water Supply.

Maintenance And Up Keep Subsidy : 20% on the cost of maintenance and upkeep of the equipment needed for the goifer, adventure tourism and water sports subject to a maximum of Rs. 5.00 lakhs per year shall be allowed for a period of 5 years.

Publicity Subsidy : 10% of the cost incurred for publicity shall be eligible for subsidy upto ceiling of Rs. 2.00 lakhs per annum for a period of 5 years.

Sales Tax Exemption : All new units shall be exempted from payment of sales tax wherever applicable for a period of 5 years from the date of commencement of commercial operation.

Subsidy on Power Generating Set/Power : Subsidy on captive power generation set including non-conventional energy generation set including drawal of line shall be 50% of the cost of the set subject to a ceiling of Rs. 5.00 lakhs. Subsidy on power shall be granted as per provisions laid down in the Meghalaya Industrial Policy 1997 on the subject.

Subsidy on Telephone Connection : Fifty percent subsidy on one time investment on telephone connections.

Exemption From Stamp Duty : An exemption of 75% of the applicable stamp duty will be provided to assist entrepreneurs in executing deed(s) for financial assistance from Bank/Financial Institutions.

Subsidy on the Cost of Feasibility Studies And Projects Reports : Subsidy will be provided at 100% for meeting the cost for preparation of feasibility/project report subject to a maximum of Rs. 25,000.00 provided that the report is of a Registered Reputed Agency approved by the Government. However, Project estimated for Rs. 1 crore and above shall be eligible for 1% of the total cost subject to a maximum ceiling of Rs. 1 lakh.

Interest Subsidy : A subsidy on interest payments to bank/financial institutions will be provided at the rate of 4% on term loans (excluding working capital loans) availed by an entrepreneur for setting of approved Tourism Units subject to a maximum of Rs. 10,000.00 per month for a period of 5 (five) years from the date of disbursement of the loan.

This subsidy will be in the form of re-imbursement of actual repayment made.

Support For Paying Guest Accommodation Scheme : Soft loans/subsidies for renovation of property which is 2/3rd of the capital cost with a maximum ceiling of rupees one lakh will be provided in Paying Guest Schemes. The Government will give necessary publicity through its various offices and ensure that commercial tariffs are not charged from the owners or such units for electricity/water use etc. The units shall not come under the purview of the local taxes such as sales tax, luxury tax etc; since the units are required to provide the facility of only bed and breakfast.

Exemption On Luxury Tax: All new units shall be entitled for exemption from luxury tax for a period of 5 (five) years from the date of commencing operation.

Definition

Tourism Units : Tourism units are commercial establishments providing public facilities/services to the tourist and will include the following :-

1. Accommodation units including hotels and restaurants, wayside facilities, apartments,

hotels, and other facilities like telephones, toilets, parking area etc.

2. Tourist resorts.
3. Amusement parks and adventure sports etc.
4. Paying Guest Accommodations.

Hotel : Hotel means a boarding and lodging unit providing adequate finished beds in double and single rooms attached with sanitary fitted toilets and bathrooms, with suitable dining, reception and public area, vehicular parking area etc.

Tourist Resorts : A Tourist Resort will be defined as thrust unit which has at least any three of the following activities/facilities :

a. Accommodation of at least 10 (ten) rooms with attached bath/toilets in urban areas and 5 (five) in the rural areas.
b. Full-fledged Restaurant with modern kitchen and geared to provide room service etc;
c. Health Club facilities e.g. Sauna Bath, Jacuzzi, Steam Bath, Gymnasium etc.
d. Water Sports e.g. white water rafting, canoeing, kayaking.
e. Beauty parlour including Barber Shops and massage facilities.
f. Children's corners including Grocho, park, Indoor Games and other recreational facilities.
g. Landscaped Gardens and Orchards.
h. Jogging tracks/nature trails.
i. Convention/Conference facilities.
j. Shopping Arcade.
k. Well-stocked Library including Video Library.
l. Auditorium.

m. Nature care facilities e.g. Yoga, Ayurvedic/Herbal Care.

n. Open Air Recreation.

Amusement Parks : It may be defined as an open area development for recreational facilities for people of all ages. It should contain various kinds of fun/joy rides, magic shows, toilets, telecommunication, first aid, adequate parking, etc. It should also contain restaurants with attached bath and toilet facilities.

Paying Guest Accommodation : The Scheme will be introduced to provide affordable and hygienic accommodation for the domestic and international tourists at important tourist centres in the State helping in supplementing the existing accommodation. The concept offers visiting tourists an opportunity to stay with a local family, experience the local way of life, discovers its rich culture and cuisine. The scheme envisages accommodation located in suitable localities with easy accessibility from the transport station/airport which in turn will involve the local people and generate employment. The rooms will be of suitable sizes with attached bathrooms with a good standard of hygiene on bed and breakfast basis. The Scheme is voluntary with units to be registered with complete details with the State Tourism Department and shall include Co-operative Group Housing Society.

Role of the Government : Tourism is a multi-sector activity and the industry is influenced by many other sectors of the country economy. The Government efforts will therefore, be directed at ensuring inter-governmental linkage and effective co-ordination. Government has to play a pivotal role in tourism management and promotion. There are several areas in which Government has to play a key role. These are :-

a. Providing public infrastructure facility including local planning.

b. Planning tourism development as a part of the other overall area development strategy.

c. Creating nucleus infrastructure in the initial stage of development to demonstrate the potential of the area.

d. Providing support facilities and facilitation services to private enterprises along with appropriate incentives.

e. Introducing regulatory measures to ensure social, cultural and environmental sustainability.

f. Ensuring that the type and scale of tourism development is compatible with the environment and socio-cultural milieu of the area.

g. Ensuring that the local community is fully involved and the benefits of tourism accrue to them.

h. Facilitating availability of trained manpower and providing training and exposure particularly from amongst the local population jointly with the industry department.

i. Undertaking research including folklore legends etc and compiling, preparing master plans, and facilitating formulation of marketing strategies.

j. Providing efficient transport and communication services.

k. Providing clean and adequate basic amenities like drinking water, toilet facilities, wayside refreshment centres, healthcare centres etc.

l. Providing aggressive publicity through all the Metropolitan cities as well as abroad and setting up of Tourist Information Centres.

m. Inter-Departmental Co-ordination.

Inter-Departmental Co-ordination will be established among the tourism related agencies/departments like Tourism, Forest, Arts & Culture etc. to work united for maintenance, conservation, development and marketing of attractive tourism products. This will be achieved through a Committee known as Tourism Advisory-cum-Co-ordination Committee comprising of :-

(i)	Chief Secretary	Chairman
(ii)	Principal Secretary/ Commissioner & Secretary/ Secretary, Finance.	Member
(iii)	Principal Secretary/ Commissioner & Secretary/ Secretary, Planning.	Member
(iv)	Principal Secretary/ Commissioner & Secretary/ Secretary, Forest.	Member
(v)	Principal Secretary/ Commissioner & Secretary/ Secretary, Art & Culture.	Member
(vi)	Principal Secretary/ Commissioner & Secretary/ Secretary, C&RD.	Member
(vii)	Principal Secretary/ Commissioner & Secretary/ Secretary, Industries.	Member
(viii)	Principal Secretary/ Commissioner & Secretary/ Secretary, Tourism.	Member
(ix)	Secretary, P.W.D.	Member
(viii)	Director of Tourism	Member-Secretary

To sum up the State Government will confine it efforts to infrastructural development, dissemination of information and co-ordination of sectoral activities to create conditions for attracting substantial private sector investment in the tourism sector. It is not the job of State Agencies to run hotels and Tourist Buses and gradually the state will withdraw its activities from such operations and hand them over to the professionals in the tourism industry. The State will also provide fiscal incentives, assist in providing suitable sites and remove bottlenecks, especially those connected with infrastructural development. The State accords high priority to manpower development and protection of the interests of the tourists. It will set up or assist in setting up training institutions and suitable systems for ensuring quality control in tourism services. It will encourage more active participation of voluntary groups and the associations of hoteliers, the travel trade and tour operators in ensuring that the tourists are provided a fair deal.

The State will ensure that its natural and cultural resources will be enhanced with the help of tourism activities and nothing that disturbs the ecological balance will be permitted.

Role of Private Sector : The private sector has always been playing a bigger role in the field of tourism. The Government Policy will, therefore, aim to encourage the private sectors in the following areas :-

1. Building and managing the required tourist facilities in alt places of tourist interest.
2. Assuring collective responsibility for laying down industry standards, ethics and fair practices.
3. Involving the local community in tourism projects and ensuring that the benefits of tourism accrue to them in right measure.
4. Undertaking industry training and manpower development for achieving excellence in quality of services.
5. Participating in the preparation of investment guidelines and marketing strategies and assisting in database creation and research.
6. Facilitating safety and security of tourists.
7. Ensuring preservation and protection of tourist attractions.

8. Endeavoring to promote tourism on a sustained and long-term perspective.

Thrust Areas : Based upon the opportunities available in the State, the following forms of tourism have been identified :-

(a) *Nature Tourism (Flora & Fauna)* - There is tremendous scope for development of tourism based on wildlife in the State particularly in Balpakram, Nokrek Biosphere reserve, Nongkhyllem and Nongdaju areas in West Khasi Hills, National parks and Game sanctuaries should be developed in coordination with the Forest Department and requisite facilities should be developed at or near such areas.

(b) *Adventure Tourism-* Comprising of trekking, caving, watersports, hang gliding bungee-jumping, mountain trekking, climbing etc and abseiling activities. This type of tourism should be promoted in close coordination with recognized adventure associations.

(c) *Cultural and Socio-cultural Tourism (Fairs and Festivals)* - Cultural Centres are proposed to be developed in the major districts of East Khasi Hills, West Garo Hills and Jaintia Hills. Promotion of major fairs and festivals will be effected in both domestic and international markets.

(d) *Health Resort Tourism* - The State as a whole is acquiring a reputation for alternative medicine and also for producing natural healer. Efforts will therefore be made to promote this type of tourism through the development of healthcare infrastructure.

(e) *Golf Tourism* - Meghalaya and Shillong in particular have tremendous potential for development of several golf courses. The temperate climate also is a comparative advantage for promoting this form of tourism.

(f) *Conferencing and Convention Tourism* - The salubrius climate and beautiful natural setting are a comparative advantage, which could make Shillong in particular an important convention centre.

(g) *Sports Tourism* - Once the studies are completed, Shillong, Jowai and Tura can become venues for one day international cricket tournaments and other sports such as badminton, tennis and so on. The temperate climate makes the State attractive for such events.

(h) *Casino Tourism* - This form of tourism is vital to overcome the constraints facing tourism development in the State, as it will have wide appeal especially in Muslim dominated countries such as Bangladesh, Malaysia and Indonesia. However, an international airport at Umroi is a prerequisite if this project is to succeed.

(i) *Travel/Transportation and Communications* - To reach the tourist destinations, considerate upgradation of State and National Highways and roads leading to the places of tourist interest are needed. The Government will actively pursue and facilitate developing of the existing airports in co-operation with the National Airport Authority.

It is hoped that the current policy of the Ministry of Civil Aviation and Tourism encouraging charter flights will continue so that such destinations can be serviced regularly in the near future in Meghalaya.

The Government will encourage transport services for tourism purposes and also cruises without any restriction on fares or any monopoly rights. It will take up the development of selected jetties and river ports for the smooth operation of boat services. Entrepreneurs in the private sector would also be encouraged to provide such facilities.

The passenger tax will be restructured to encourage larger tourist movement. The Government will continue to provide interstate transport permits and such other facilities as may be necessary.

(j) *Arts & Crafts promotion Tourism* - The Tourism Department in association with the Art and Culture Department and other State agencies will hold annual festivals and exhibitions for promoting specific destinations. Visitors' Reception Centres will be set up at five or six places in the State to provide recreation as well as to encourage local cuisine and village arts & crafts. The funds for these purpose will be provided by the State Government.

Implementing Agency

1. The Directorate of Tourism will register all tourism and tourism related units.
2. The Directorate of Tourism preferably the Meghalaya Tourism Development Corporation Ltd. will create and provide the tourism related infrastructure and prioritize as far as possible.
3. The Directorate of Tourism in collaboration with Director of Industries, Commercial Banks/ Financial Institutions will scrutinize sanction and disburse subsidies to tourism units.

4. The Department of Tourism shall work out the criteria for accredition of certain Categories of Hotels/Restaurants within the State of Meghalaya.

TOURISM INDUSTRY POISED FOR BIG LEAP: EXPERT

Bangalore, June 12: The Indian Tourism Industry, which is still evolving, was poised to reach a greater height, thanks to the emergence of technology, said Mr Deep Kalra, Founder and CEO, MakeMyTrip.Com, India's top online travel company.

Speaking after opening company's Karnataka office here, he said Indian Tourism Industry, which had a potential of over USD 10 billion to 15 billion, was contributing about six per cent to the national GDP. With its robust growth of over six to seven per cent annually, the industry would be among top 10 in the world in the next 10 years.

He said except Kerala, Goa and Rajasthan, the potential value of hospitality was yet to be tapped elsewhere in the country due to constraints in infrastructure availability.

The revolution made in the telecom industry and the emergence of Mobile, Broadband, Credit Cards and Venture Capital funds had made the industry in the country to achieve robust growth. Taking advantage of the emerging technology, MakeMyTrip.Com was launched in 2000 for the booming 'USA to India' travel market and hit early success and then launched India operations in 2005 with over six years of profitability in real time bookings of flights, hotels, holidays and car rentals in United States, he added.

Mr Kalra claimed that his company made one million trips recently and became country's top online travel company. To maintain its market leadership and reach further height, it had received USD 18 million venture capital from two firms including US-based Softbank Asia Infrastructure Fund (SAIF). The fund would be utilised to expand operations and create infrastructure across the country, he added.

Replying to questions Mr Kalra said Karnataka was emerging as the biggest market for international and domestic travel after Maharashtra, Gujarat, Punjab, and New Delhi, growing at 25 per cent annually and was expected to be worth Rs 2,500 crore over the next three years.

Thailand, Malaysia, Singapore and Bali were the favourite international travel destinations from Bangalore. Bangaloreans are also displaying an increasing interest in off beat destinations like Kenya, Vietnam, Cambodia, South Africa and Eastern Europe, he added.

MakeMyTrip.Com, a market leader in online travel domain, has several firsts to its credit including providing a lowest airfare guarantee, introduce online bookings for hotels, cash back offer for travel products ranging from air ticket to international holidays.

The site also maps hotel locations from reference points like city centre and major local attractions. While addressing the needs of the growing travel community in the country, it sells over 5,000 flight tickets, 1,000 hotel rooms and more than 50 holiday packages every day, he added.

TOURISM POLICY

The State new Tourism Policy was released on 27-9-2001. The mission statement of the Tourism Policy is to evolve a pragmatic policy designed to ensure optimum utilization of rich tourism resources of the state to generate employment specially in rural areas, to develop a ready market for the rich and varied handicrafts, to preserve varied bio-diversity, natural historical, cultural and cultural heritage of the state by scientific methods and to accelerate contribution of tourism industry in socio - economic development of the state by making tourism a truly People's Industry in Rajasthan. The copy of the Tourism Policy placed at Annexure - 3.

Tourism was declared as an industry in 1989 and with the issue of notification dated 7-11-2002, the condition of issuing separate notification granting benefits to Tourism Industry has been deleted and now benefits to Tourism, would be available at par with the Industry.

Fairs - Festivals and Cultural Programmes

The Fairs and festivals of Rajasthan are the example of State's lively cultural heritage. Through the organization of these fairs and festivals and cultural programmes, attracting tourist makes tourism promotion. They have a great appeal for tourists. Department by organizing the world known annually fairs and festival, tends to promote the prosperous cultural heritage of State. The list of Fairs and Festivals being organized by Department in 2003-2004 is placed at Annexure-6.

Tourism Publicity - Promotion and Marketing

In order to facilitate dissemination of information about tourist places, department annually publishes brochures, folder, booklets posters etc of tourist places. The literature published is being distributed in the country and abroad, so that the tourist can gain precise information. It is also being circulated to the tourism trade related personalities and organisations. Tourist can have these literatures available through the Tourist Reception Centres / Tourist Information Centres run by the department.

For tourism promotion and Publicity and aggressive marketing, following efforts are being made at the department level:

1. Printing of Tourism Publicity Literature
2. Advertising
3. International Conferences
4. Film, Photos, VHS, CD's etc.
5. Exhibitions
6. Seminar & Conferences
7. Hospitality
8. Library
9. Souvenirs.

For making expenditure under above head, Tourism Information and Publicity (TIP) Rules have been formulated. Copy enclosed at Annexure-7

Against the budget provision of Rs. 651.00 lacs available in the current plan for Tourism promotional activities, an amount of Rs. 217.00 lacs have been utilized till Nov, 2003.

Apart from above department has been making efforts for wide promotion - publicity & aggressive marketing of the states tourist places and products. Department participates in the various international and national exhibitions, seminars and conferences. In the previous year, department has conducted Rajasthan Road Shows in the southern region of country in Coimbatore, Chennai and Kolkata, which have been most successful. The shows at Coimbatore and Chennai were duly co-ordinated by the local Rajasthan Sangh, in which thousands of people participated and greatly appreciated the programme. Department has represented Rajasthan in overseas this year at WTM, London, TAAI, Malaysia and PATA, Singapore and for tourism promotion has participated in different International / national level conferences, seminars, exhibitions etc. Apart form that Road Shows were organized in U.S.A. also.

For increasing tourist arrivals and wide promotion & aggressive marketing of tourism in the state, Department has made efforts through Print Media. In the year 2003-2004, Department has released several advertisement in the prominent magazines and newspaper for tourism promotion and publicity.

In the year 2003-2004 Department participated in various exhibitions, trade fairs, conferences, seminars etc and was awarded for best exhibition and best tourist literature. The prize won by the department in this year is as below:-

Awards won by the Department for Best Tourism Literature and excellent exhibition

Event	Date	Prize
TTF, Kolkata	14-17 Aug, 2003	Best Pavilion of Rajasthan
ITTM, Bangalore	19-21 July, 2003	Runner for Best Pavilion
ITTM, New Delhi	26-28, September, 2003	Group Participation

TOURIST ASSISTANCE FORCE

Though TAF (Tourist Police) was started in State from 01-08-2000, for the safety, security and assistance to the tourist, department made efforts to resolve the problems experienced by tourist and to protect them from anti-social element, so that they had hassle free stay in the State. Presently the force has been deployed at Jaipur, Udaipur, Jodhpur, Jaisalmer, Pushkar (Ajmer) and Mt. Abu. In the cfy, a budget provision of Rs. 35.00 lacs has been sanctioned and till Oct' 2003, Rs. 15.74 lacs have been spent on the same.

Land Bank

The State Govt. with an objective for easy establishment of Tourist Units has launched an innovative scheme of Land Bank. Under this scheme, such Govt. Land / Nazool properties which are being selected for establishment of Tourism units by the department be transferred to Land Bank for further disposal at level of DoT and RTDC. Such selected property would be available for disposal in the "Land Bank" established in RTDC, so that entrepreneurs can invest in tourist units in the State. The disposal of the properties of Land Bank would be by open two-stage bidding sanction. In the first stage, bids will be evaluated on the basis of bidders experience in hotel industry, its financial standing and management capability etc. In the second stage, financial bids will be invited from the short listed bidders of the first stage and thereafter the property would be awarded as per the decision of the committee, which shall be communicated to the successful bidder.

General Administrative Department has transferred 29 Nazool properties located in 10 district to the department for further development of these as tourism units. RTDC is the executing agency for disposal of such properties. In the first stage, disposal of Tizara Fort in Alwar is being done, for which NIT has been released in newspapers.

Apart form above Panchayati Raj Department has transferred 7 highway facility centre to the Department for disposal of these properties through Land Bank by the Department for Tourism Development. RTDC is the executing agency for the disposal of these properties. NIT have been released in newspaper for disposal of these properties.

DOT/RTDC Rules, 1997, would dispose off these properties as per the provisions of Rajasthan Tourism Disposal of Land Properties.

Rajasthan Institute of Tourism and Travel Management

Rajasthan Institute of Tourism and Travel Management (RITTMAN), Jaipur was registered on 29th Oct, 1996 under Rajasthan Society Registration Act 1958 (Rajasthan Act No. 28, 1958). The registered office of this society is Paryatan Bhawan, Govt.Hostel, M.I. Road, Jaipur. The objective of the society are as below:

1. Human resource development for the acitivities related to the Tourism Department in the State of Rajasthan.
2. To provide latest information related to tourism.
3. Human Resource Development of manpower working in tourism agencies in State, Govt. entity and Private Sector.
4. To ensure better facilities tourist through effective management keeping in view the incorrect opportunities in tourism cantor in the State.
5. Conducting progress of foreign languages for Shopkeeper, Guide, Chuffers, Hoteliers and Tourism personnel.
6. Training programmes for Guides.
7. Organization of workshops, seminar, conference for developing tourism in Rajasthan.
8. Providing consultancy, survey, research for State

Govt. entity & Private sector independently or in joint collaboration with other agencies.

9. Providing graduates for bright future of tourism & travel sector.
10. Regulation of any other activity, which is, directly or indirectly which related to the promotion of Tourism in Rajasthan.

In the year 2003-04 at the important centers of State, Local level guide training programmes was conducted by RITTMAN, in which 2199 unemployed youths were given technical training for employment. Apart from above Training Programmes on Eco-tourism was conducted at Bharatpur. Workshop on maintenance of religious tourist places at Shrimahavirji was organized.

Workshop and Seminars of Rural Tourism, Religious Tourism, Paying Guest House Owners, Travel Agents and Tour operators and lesser-known destination is also proposed.

Apart from above, foreign language & computer training programe of DoT/RTDC employees, foreign language training programme for Guides, Refreshers courses for elephant riders (Mahawats) and State Level Guide is also proposed. A budget provision of Rs. 25.00 lacs is available in RITTMAN for the cfy 2003-2004.

Incentives available for establishment of Tourism Industry in Rajasthan

1. New Tourism Units such as Hotels/Lodging Houses
   a. Exemption in Luxury Tax:- 100% exemption of Luxury Tax for a period of 7 years.
   b. Exemption in Stamp Duty:- 50% exemption in stamp duty for a period of 7 years.

c. Other Incentives:-

(i) 50% exemption of entertainment tax for seven years;

(ii) 50% exemption of electrical duty for seven years;

(iii) 50% exemption from conversion charge; and/or

(iv) 50% exemption from mandi tax for seven years.

d. Interest Subsidy to tourism Units such as Hotel, Motel etc.:-

5% Interest subsidy and wage /employment subsidy would be made available to eligible investor during the operative period of the scheme. An additional interest subsidy of 1% shall be made available to SC/ST Entrepreneurs.

Note:- State Government has declared Tourism as Industry. The above exemptions are available between the period of 1-7-2003 to 31-3-2008. The prescribed authority under the new Rajasthan investment promotion policy shall grant these exemptions 2003 issued by the Department of Industries.

2. Allotment / Conversion of land to Tourism Units

a. Under the Rajasthan Land Revenue (Conversion of agriculture land for non agriculture purpose) rule 1992 no land use conversion charges will be paid for establishment of tourism units up to the land of 2000 sq. mts. subject to the condition that 100% unskilled workforce will be employed from the local area.

b. Under Rajasthan Land Revenue (Industrial area allotment) rule 1959 allotment of Govt. Agriculture Land up to 4 bigha in Rural Area on payment of 25% of the reserve price of the prevailing market price in the concerned area subject to the condition that 100% unskilled workforce will be employed from the local area.

c. For Heritage Hotels in Rural Areas no lands Conversion Charge are taken. In urban areas conversion charge are levied under the provisions of Rajasthan urban improvement trust rules 1974 on built up area only.

d. For Tourism units conversion / allotment of land is being done under Rajasthan Land Revenue (Industrial area allotment) rule 1959 and Rajasthan Land Revenue (Conversion of agriculture land for non agriculture purpose) rule 1992 on Industrial rates.(Other than point no. A & B above)

e. Under Rajasthan Development Trust (Urban Land) rule 1974 - rule 15 & 15B tourism projects to be establish in Rajasthan, the land will be allotted on rates and basis of following investment:-

Department of Tourism

S.N.	Cost of Investment	Rate of allotment
a.	Upto an investment of Rs. 5.00 Crore	200% of the concerned area residential reserve reserve price
b.	An investment of more than Rs. 5.00 Crore and upto Rs. 25.00 Crore	125% of the concerned area residential
c.	An investment of more than Rs. 25.00 Crore and upto Rs. 50.00 Crore	75% of the concerned area residential reserve price
d.	More than an investment of Rs. 50.00 Crore	60% of the concerned area residential reserve price

New Multiplex Cinema Halls, Drive in Theatres/ Cinemas

a. Films which have been 75% picturized in Rajasthan and having U-Certificate are 100% exempted from Entertainment Tax (including additional Entertainment Tax) for one year from the date of its first exhibition

b. For new Multiplex Cinema Halls, Drive in Theaters/Cinemas in Rajasthan are exempted from Entertainment Tax for 3 years from the date of Commencement of their commercial exhibition as follow:

   1. 75% for First Year,
   2. 50% in Second year s
   3. 25% in Third Year

State Capital Investment Subsidy Scheme for Tourism Development - 1993

Tourism units such as hotels / motels etc are eligible for subsidy upto 15.00 lacs or 15% of the eligible investment. And for heritage hotels 20% or Rs. 20.00 lacs of the eligible investment whichever is less. The scheme was in operation upto 31.3.99. In the year 2002-2003 a sum of Rs. 122.70 lacs was dispursed under the scheme for the previous cases. In the cfy 2003-2004 a provision of Rs. 55.00 lacs has been made.

Accommodation Facilities

In Rajasthan sufficient accommodation facilities are available for tourists comprising of one star to five star category classified Hotels, classified Heritage Hotels, other Hotels, Dharamshalas / Inns, Rest Houses, Rajasthan State Hotel Corporation and Rajasthan Tourism Dev. Corporation Hotels and accommodation units and Paying Guest Houses.

Due to the departments promotion and encouragement, the Heritage Hotels have become a great attraction for foreign tourists, as it owes past (royal) orignal work along with the latest amentities. Rajasthan has been the pioneer in context of launching Heritage Hotels in the country. In India, among the total 33 heritage hotels of Rajasthan is providing a royal hospitality to the guests.

At the cities of tourism importance in the State viz. Ajmer, Alwar, Bharatpur, Bikaner, Bundi, Jaipur, Jaisalmer, Jodhpur, Mt. Abu & Udaipur, the department has launched Paying Guest Scheme. Its main objective is to make tourist aware with the Rajasthan's Culture and lifestyle. Under this scheme, about 306 Guest Houses are being operated in above mentioned cities, and is being mainly acquired by foreign tourists.

Guest Hospitality and Familiarization Tour

The world's renowned Tourism writers, photographers, Journalist, TV Team, Travel Tour Operators, Actors and Tourism trade related personalities are being invited for the Fam Tour conducted by the Department. They are being made to travel around State as Department Guests and are provided information relating to the fairs and festivals being celebrated in the State, so that through their travel experiences, articles and photos, tourism industry can get a boost to attract maximum for tourism in the State.

Training Institutes Operating for Human Resource Development in Tourism Sector

- Institute of Hotel Management, Jodhpur and Jaipur
- Food Craft Institute, Ajmer
- Food Craft Institute, Udaipur

Execution of Development Works

Keeping in view the tourist arrivals at different tourist places locate in the State, Tourism Department undertakes several development works. The different development works being executed / financed mainly are as below:

1. Works of Centrally Sponsored Scheme (CSS), which are being executed / financed are as per below:

   Presently under CSS works amounting to Rs. 300.00 lacs have been got done under Mewar Complex Project. This amount was received from GOI to the State Govt. in 1999-2000. Thereafter in the year 20001-2002, GOI restricted utilization of this amount, due to which works couldn't be completed. Due to the untiring efforts of the State Tourism Department, GOI has recently in Aug-2003 has lifted restriction on the use of the rest amount of Rs. 208.00 lacs, in compliance of which financial and administrative sanction has been issued & NIT has also been called. A detail note on Mewar Complex Project is placed separately at Annexure___.

   Apart from above in the FY 2003-2004, Rs. 100.00 lacs scheme has been sanctioned by GOI for establishing Swiss Tent, with a view of providing high standard accommodation facilities to the tourists coming at world renowned Pushkar Fair.

   Under another scheme, for the facilitation of pilgrims in Ajmer, a scheme of Rs. 74.00 lacs has been sanctioned for up gradation of existing Vishram Isthali at Ajmer, the first installment of Rs. 10.00 lac had been received in September, 2003. This work has to be got done through UIT,

Ajmer as proposed and is expected to be completed by March 2004.

Alongwith this the State Govt. has also allotted 80 Bigha land free of Dargah Committee for constructing a new Vishram Isthali. GOI has preliminary sanctioned this project for complete funding. The department is making effort for issue of its financial sanction at the earliest.

2. Works under CSS which are executed through CPWD / other agencies of GOI.

   Under this scheme GOI for integrated development in the State has sanctioned Jaipur-Jodhpur-Bikaner-Jaisalmer - Shekhawati - Jaipur Circuit Project in March, 2003. Though department has sent a total of 81 Projects of Rs. 35.35 crores to GOI under this scheme, among which GOi has sanctioned a total of Rs. 644.00 lacs for 8 projects. The work would be executed by CPWD with corodination of Secretary, Tourism, Rajasthan. Presently Architect consultant for these projects have been nominated, and whoc are preparing detail action plan / report. It is assumed that thework would be got completed by March, 2004.

   Similarly GOI through ITDC is undertaking following works at various important tourist places:

   1. Light and sound show at chittorgarh fort.
   2. Light and sound show at Khumbhalgarh Fort.
   3. Integrated development of Pushkar Ghat.

3. The development works are also being executed by the tourism department on the basis of joint venture of GOI and State Govt. Presently the

no. of such types of works is 68, comprising of Rs. 1549.59 lacs as GOI Share and Rs. 1039.82 as State Share. In the cfy for these works proposed GOI share is of Rs. 300.00 lacs and state share amounts to Rs. 136.00. The details of these works placed at Annexure-___.

The department is pursuing Planning and Finance Department since July, 2003 for sanctioning this, but till date the share has not yet been released by the FD, due to which completion of the work is not accelerating.

Department is also trying to allocate provision of such pending projects under this category, in the forthcoming RE, so that all the works are completed in the cfy.

4. Cent per cent State Govt. Financed Dev. Projects.

   In the cfy under State Plan a total of Rs. 260.00 lac provision is available, among which for CSS Projects Rs. 136.00 lacs has been as State Share and Balance for utilisation on other works, details placed at Annexure- ___.

   The proposal for releasing above share was sent to the Planning & Finance Department in July, 2003, but the funds have not yet been received.

Initiatives by the Department since Last One Year

1. *Web Portal* : The Department has for the first time got prepared its own Web Portal, so that domestic and foreign tourist can have online information about Rajasthan Tourism.
2. *Tizara Fort*: The Project Report for the renovation, reconstruction and commercial use of Tizara Fort has been prepared. Tender quotations have also been received. Its disposal is under consideration.

3. *Jal Mahal Project*: Tenders have been received from the private entrepreneurs for investment in the development of Jal Mahal, Jaipur. The highest bidder would provide annually Rs. 2.52 crore and Rs. 125 crores will be invested on this project in the next 4 yrs.
4. *Rope-way*: For establishing Ropeway at Mt. Abu and Udaipur Project report was got prepared and tenders were invited. Due to the Hon'ble High Court stay order, it had delayed the execution of above. For Udaipur stay order has been vacant and tender quotations have been received.
5. *Golf Tourism*: Today Golf Tourism has been pivot in the field of Tourism. It makes tourist to stay form more at a place The expertise is being hired for preparation of Project Report for making international standard Golf Complex in Rajasthan.
6. *Charter Flights*: Due to the untiring efforts of the Department, at Jaipur Airport inflow of International Charter Flights has begin. Between Nov, 2003 - April, 2004 daily charter flights of FINNAIR are being operated. An attempt is also being made for initiating similar international flights.
7. *Adventure Sports Tourism*: It is the important dimension of Tourism Sector. Recently department has organised adventure sports activities at Jaipur and Kota. For identification of adventure sports tourism sited in the State, Project Report is being prepared.
8. *Development and Construction of approach roads to tourism sites*: Through the initiative of Tourism

Department, PWD has constructed / upgraded 114 roads for easy accessibility to the important tourist places.

9. The draft of Rajasthan Tourism Regulation, facilitation and Heritage conservation Act has been prepared.
10. For the wide publicity of Rajasthan Tourism, new brand "Rajasthan - simply colourful" has been adopted and which has gain well appreciation.
11. New buildings of Institute of Hotel Management, Jodhpur and Food Craft Institute, Udaipur have been constructed.

Due to the above initiatives and aggressive marketing programmers, there has been significant increase in development of Tourism in Rajasthan and tourist arrivals.

CONCLUSION

The State has a long way to go before it can complete with tourism facilities of nationally and internationally popular destinations like Rajasthan, Himachal Pradesh and Goa. The entire State, in a way can be called backward in terms of tourism facilities of national and international standards and the provision of modern tourism facilities prevailing in other States and countries especially South East Asia.

The State Government will have to co-ordinate the efforts of other concerned Departments and concentrate in infrastructural development in selected areas as well as provide special incentives to the private sector to set up tourism facilities of international standards. More than the Tourism Department, the other State Agencies which provide basic amenities like electricity, water supply, roads etc. will have to play a significant role in bringing about faster development of tourism. As outlined in the policy for tourism development, a major role is to be played by the hoteliers, tour operators, travel agencies and others who provide services in the Tourism Sector, The role of the State in providing infrastructure and co-ordinating development efforts will be performed through a small and compact administrative set up as already incorporated.

The State Government is hopeful that the tourism industry, investors, tourists and the general public will respond whole-heartedly to the approach and policy of tourism development in the State and help in bringing about integrated and healthy tourism development.

4

TOURISM INDUSTRY: A STUDY

Businesses manage a world of information about sales, customers, inventory, demographic profiles, mailing lists, and so much more. At the very core of this information is a geographic location, an address, a service boundary, a sales territory, and a delivery route that can be illustrated and interactively managed on a map. GIS software is reshaping the business world. From multinational corporations to entrepreneurial start-ups, from hardware stores to hospitals, companies of every kind are introducing geographic analysis to solve business problems.

In the process, they're making better decisions, delivering better service, and finding new market opportunities. Businesses are using GIS technology to find solutions for marketing, site selection, asset management, risk analysis, regulatory compliance, delivery routing, customer service, demographic analysis, and much more. GIS enables businesses to better understand and evaluate their data by creating graphic displays using information stored in their databases. But a GIS does more than just display data; it enables users to interactively and dynamically analyze and manage the information linked to those locations. And by simply updating the information linked to a map, the map automatically reflects those changes. It is this analytical capability of the GIS which strongly supports the need for existence of such system for business planning. GIS allows the creation of map displays simply by pointing and clicking. GIS lets users visualize and analyze information in new ways, revealing previously hidden relationships, patterns, and trends. Business people in marketing, advertising, insurance, and retail are already using GIS to analyze markets, optimize media campaigns, pinpoint the best store locations, and model demographic spending patterns.

The present paper emphasis the power of GIS in support to the Tourism industry, wherein a customized package was developed in assisting a Tourister in selecting Hotels, to suit his requirements, and to suggest the tourister his needs such has nearest shopping center's to his hotel, or nearest place of Worship, or areas of interest closer to his hotel. The case study was made with respect to Chennai city, incorporating the spatial database of the city as point data, As Shape file (not to Scale), and associated attribute data pertaining to the spatial data was created on MS-Access. A easy interface for the user was customized where in the user can query on the datasets to retrieve tabular and spatial information. Provision was also made for hosting the information on the web, such that the Client can view the information and query using ArcExplorer 3.0 software, provided the spatial database should be hosted using Internet Map Server. The primary software used was ArcView3.2 GIS under windows environment.

TOURISM IN INDIA - ANOTHER CASE OF MISSED OPPORTUNITIES

Internationally, tourism occupies a very important place in the economies of several countries. Among the world's largest industry, it is forecasted to grow 4 per cent annually till 2010. It currently contributes about 11.6 per cent to the global GDP and employs about 9.4 per cent of the global labour force.

However, in India, the industry has largely remained ignored, performing well below its potential, despite the fact that India has a unique heritage and culture and a wide gamut of tourism attraction it has to offer to the world. Surprisingly, despite the winds of liberalization blowing across the country, tourism seems to have been the least affected. Even now, setting up a resort means getting as many as 72 clearances from different authorities! Will the tourism industry in this country be yet another victim of missed opportunities? Will the tremendous potential, and the resultant benefits to the economy that it has to offer, go unexplored? And just what is the potential like?

According to figures put up by Confederation of Indian Industries (CII), an apex body representing Indian industry, by the year 2020 India could have 40 million tourist arrivals, constituting 4 per cent of the world travel. Currently, the country gets 2.4 million international arrivals or 0.4 per cent of the world travel. The report goes on to state that the industry could end up employing about 50 million people, as against 20 million now -- 10 million directly and another 10 million indirectly. At today's prices the travel and tourism economy could grow as big as Rs.10 lakh crore or 7 per cent of the GDP, as against Rs 6 lakh crore now or 5.6 per cent of GDP. Foreign exchange earnings could grow ten times, from the current US $ 3 billion to about US $ 30 billion!

Speaking to domain-B, Mr. Ravi Bhoothalingam, president the Oberoi Group and head of the tourism committee at the CII said, "Looking at the tremendous potential the tourism industry offers, it is time the government pays some attention to the needs of the industry, lest it may turn out to be another case of "opportunity lost", which will be very sad." According to him, the travel and tourism economy in India accounts for 5.6 per cent of the GDP, supports 5.8 per cent of the total employment in the country and generates 10.8 per cent of the total exports from the country.

In spite of this, the capital investment that goes into the industry is a paltry 6.4 per cent of the GDP compared to the world average of 11.8 per cent. The government's support to the industry has fallen well short of expectations and budgetary and other allocations to the sector have been 1 per cent of public spending, as against global average of 6.8 per cent. Despite this partisan approach on the part of the government, tourism in the country has registered a fairly impressive growth rate over the last few years. Says Mr. Bhoothalingam, "We, at CII, have come out with a 17 point agenda, which needs to be incorporated into the new tourism policy on the anvil if the country wants to avail the benefits the sector offers."

One of the most vociferous demands is to declare tourism an "infrastructure industry", which will help it attract low cost funds, so important to keep any industry globally competitive. Despite being the largest net foreign exchange earner and the second largest gross foreign exchange earner, after the IT industry, tourism as a segment continues to find itself ignored by the government. Insufficient aviation seating capacity, pathetic road and airport conditions, poor rail infrastructure, inadequate economical hotel accommodation and relatively high level of taxation continue to be the bane of an average international traveller. According to the World Travel and Tourism

Council, an international association of the tourism industry, "Tax paid by tourists in India, is the highest in the world. Indian hotels charge about 40 per cent tax compared to other Asian countries where the tax rate varies between 3 per cent and 6 per cent." It is not surprising therefore that repeat visits of international travellers to India are few and far in between. The Indian government however stays unmoved. Strange and very criminal considering that India, as a nation, remains starved of foreign exchange and an adequate support to tourism could go a long way in bolstering its forex reserves. Needless to say that forex "Earned" in this fashion is "India's own" and not borrowed!

Procedural hassles in getting visas and poor infrastructure (including roads which are pot-holed, dusty and narrow to say the least) are some of the major problems that need to be attended to. Against present requirement of about 130,000 hotel rooms, India offers just about 60,000. Says Mr. Bhoothalingam, "The biggest shortfall is in the three star category. Our archaic land laws, which make land acquisition a very cumbersome process, are doing precious little to solve this problem. They render the cost of putting up a hotel very high. There is a big gap between five star and lower categories of hotels. The government needs to create separate zones and then give liberal floor space index or FSIs for setting up two and three star hotels. This will dramatically and drastically change the economics of the hotel industry."

The industry is also worried about airline seat capacity. Against a demand of 10 million seats in the international segment the supply is just about 5.3 million and in the domestic segment against a demand of 19 million supply is just about 9.79 million. According to Mr. Bhoothalingam, the demand-supply gap will get compounded with the outbound traffic growing so fast. He adds, "Our airports are bursting at the seams. We not only need more airports, but also mush better roads. The Cochin airport is a fine example of private enterprise. Privatisation is the only answer and we have to move towards open skies. The government must accept that aviation is no longer a luxury --- it is the basic need of a growing economy."

Visa facilitation is yet another process, which needs to be rationalized urgently. Stringent eligibility requirements and cumbersome procedure put off many visitors from visiting India. One of our major policy restrictive to the growth of tourism is "reciprocity", under which we give visas to citizens of only those countries which give to Indians. Countries like Bhutan, Nepal, Singapore, Seychelles, Maldives, Thailand, Turkey, Taiwan and Indonesia give visas on arrival without reciprocity as a condition. Thailand has a visa-on-arrival policy for over 140 countries and there is no reciprocity in every case. Suggests Mr. Bhoothalingam, "We should abolish visa requirements for main source markets such as USA, European Union and Japan. For other countries it should be visa-on-arrival. Finally we could have a third list of countries which could qualify for strict visa requirements." The government may however cite security concerns as prime reason for very strict visa requirements.

Advantages of tourism are plenty. It remains confined not just to urban agglomerations, but spreads its benefits deep and wide into the rural countryside providing significant gains for the economy. Further, by its very nature tourism is conducive to protecting the environment.

According to figures provided by the CII, an additional 1 million visitors can help generate revenues of Rs. 4,300 crore annually. For every Rs. 1 million of investment, tourism can help create 47.5 jobs, manufacturing 12.6 jobs and agriculture 44.7 jobs.

With just 2.4 million arrivals (0.4 per cent of the world list of international arrivals) in fiscal 2000, India finds itself ranked a poor 43rd in the world list of international arrivals, despite the fact that it boasts of some of the most exquisite sites and locales, with some of the best monuments to see. Countries far smaller in size such as France (62 million arrivals -- ranked 1st), Spain (41 million arrivals -- ranked 3rd), Hungary (21 million arrivals -- ranked 8th) and Poland (19 million arrivals -- ranked 9th) are way ahead of India. Even a country as small as Sri Lanka, despite the ethnic conflicts plaguing it for the last 12 years, is ahead of India with about 4 million international arrivals.

It is time therefore that the government pulls up its socks and pushed tourism ahead. Else, it will be one more case of missed opportunities.

The Booming Tourism Industry

The year 2004-05 saw tourism emerging as one of the major sectors for growth of Indian economy, the foreign exchange earnings increased from Rs. 16,429 crore to 21,828 crore up to December.

Similarly in the last year, tourism industry registered a growth rate of 17.3% in foreign tourist arrivals, which has been the highest in last 10 years. Foreign exchange earnings grew at an even higher rate 30.2%.

India's tourism industry is thriving due to an increase in foreign tourists arrivals and greater than before travel by Indians to domestic and abroad destinations. The visitors are pouring in from all over the world: Europe, Africa, Southeast Asia and Australia. At the same time, the number of Indians traveling has also increased. Some tourists come from Middle East countries to witness the drenching monsoon rains in India, a phenomenon never seen in desert climates.

Domestic tourists are also fueling the industry's revival. Many of them escape from the summer heat on the plains to resorts in the Himalayan Mountains. One of the major beneficiaries this year is Kashmir, where a cease-fire between India and Pakistan has reduced violence, if not completely, at least enough to help revive the state's sagging tourism industry.

Among the most favoured tourist destinations in India, Kerala for its scenic beauty, Agra for Taj Mahal, Khujraho for its sculptures and temples, Goa for its beaches and some pilgrimages are the most important.

Interesting feature of this growth is that it has come even as global tourism has dropped, due to the September 11 terrorist attacks in the United States, the outbreak of Severe Acute Respiratory Syndrome in East Asia, and the Iraq war. Even the disastrous tsunami didn't affect India's tourism industry, as tourist arrivals in India rose 23.5 percent in Dec 2004 and tourist arrivals crossed 3 million mark for the first time in 2004.. The disaster was expected to have a negative impact on India's tourism in terms of large-scale cancellations of tourists to India but nothing of that sort was seen.

Reasons for this Boom

There could be several reasons for the buoyancy in the Indian tourism industry. First, the upward trend observed in the growth rate of Indian economy has raised middle class incomes, prompting more people to spend money on vacations abroad or at home. Also, India is booming in the information technology industry and has become the IT center. Aggressive advertising campaign " Incredible India" by the government has also had contribution in changing India's image from that of a land of snake charmers, and sparking new interest among overseas travellers.

Tourism Contribution to the Indian Economy

It is not hidden that tourism is among India's important export industries. Even with comparatively low levels of international tourist traffic, tourism has already emerged as an important segment of the Indian economy. Tourism also contributed to the economy indirectly through its linkages with other sectors like horticulture, agriculture, poultry, handicrafts and construction. Foreign exchange earnings from tourism during 2003-04 were US $ 3,533 million (Rs 16,429 crore). Besides being an important foreign exchange earner, tourism industry also provides employment to millions of people in India both directly and indirectly (through its linkage with other sectors of the economy.) It is estimated that total direct employment in the tourism sector is around 20 million.

Measures Taken for Tourism Promotion

Recently, Indian government adopted a multi-pronged approach for promotion of tourism, which includes new mechanism for speedy implementation of tourism projects, development of integrated tourism circuits and rural destinations, special capacity building in the unorganized hospitality sector and new marketing strategy. A nation wide campaign, for creating awareness about the effects of tourism and preservation of our rich heritage & culture, cleanliness and warm hospitality through a process of training and orientation was launched during 2004-05. The aim was to rebuild that sense of responsibility towards tourists among Indians and re-enforces the confidence of foreign tourist towards India as a preferred holiday destination. More than 6500 taxi drivers, restaurant owners and guides trained under the programme.

Government also took several other initiatives to promote Indian tourism industry and increased the plan allocation for tourism i.e. from Rs 325 crore in 2003-04 to Rs. 500 crore in 2004-05. Road shows in key source markets of Europe, Incredible India campaign on prominent TV channels and in magazines across the world were among the few steps taken to advertise Indian tourism. In addition a task force was set up to promote India as prominent health tourism destination. However, in order to attract more visitors, India still needs to upgrade its airports, roads and other infrastructure to global standards. Even with the recent surge, tourist arrivals are just a mere percentage of those in such popular Asian destinations like Bangkok and Thailand.

Recent Development in Tourism Industry

India Tourism office at Tokyo won two International Awards in Tour Expo held at Daegu in Korea for excellent tourism promotion. Indian Pavilion won the Best Booth Design Award as well as Best Folklore Performance Award competing with major players in tourism such as China, Japan, Thailand, Malaysia and Canada. The theme of pavilion was the Buddhist pilgrimage in India. Multi promotional activities undertaken by Tokyo office drew a large crowd to India Pavilion, which added colours to the entire travel show. The Korea's leading newspapers published on the front page the Incredible India booth's photographs highlighting various aspects. The live Yoga performance and Indian traditional snacks at the pavilion were enjoyed very much by the visitors.

TOURISM INDUSTRY : CURRENT STATUS AND FUTURE POTENTIAL

Tourism as an activity or as a phenomenon has been existing since the olden days. The quest travel often quoted as the "travel bug" is apart of human psyche. A result of this psyche is the birth and growth of the all encompassing "tourism industry". Goa has long been identified as a major tourism destination in India and the world over. The "flower children" of the 1960's ended up at the pristine and virgin beaches of Goa thus giving the first indications of what was to become of Goa as a tourist destination. Last year i.e., 2004-05 season witnessed a tourist inflow of the magnitude of 2.4 million (Tourism Statistics: Govt. Of Goa) which included more than 300,000 international tourists and 2,100,000 domestic tourists. These figures are being seen in the last few years with the growth in the immediate past three years being in the range of 9% to 27%. This kind of phenomenal growth in a short span is certainly not without its share of issues as far as tourism is concerned. Growth is an essential part of life and tourism industry is no exception. However planning for growth is a prudent activity if one desires to harness its full potential.

Many people have researched destination growth and Miossec(1976) identifies a five-stage pattern in the growth of a destination. The destination witnesses these stages slowly and each stage is indicative of the changes that occur both in the tourists' perception of the destination as well as in the nature of the reaction of the local community to tourism activities at the destination.

Britton (1982) has argued that the international tourism industry, due to the commercial power held by the foreign enterprises, imposes on peripheral destinations a development mode that reinforces dependency on and vulnerability to, developed nations. This would be seen in different intensities at different stages of the destination's growth path.

Pearce (1989) observes that tourism is encouraged as a means of increasing the inflow of foreign funds into the economy or pursued for political purposes and not as an end in itself. It is perhaps this focus on tourism as a means that is creating the myopia that destination development activity is suffering from.

Honey-pot Areas in Tourism in Goa

Tourists like to travel and explore different places, people, cultures, traditions etc., and experience them. This penchant for travel in fact is the backbone of tourism so much so that Smith (1995) calls it "geography in action". Given this nature of tourism it is but natural that most destinations try to showcase their products and product potentials for the tourists so that visitation can be increased. In most resource-intensive destinations where the natural resources of the destination are the most visited attractions, the development takes place rapidly in the early stages of destination development. In fact Butler (1980) identifies the stage as the stage of involvement wherein the local and outside investment is seen for the growth of the destination. Further stage of development witnesses the loss of local control on investment n tourism as larger investment needs are felt by the destination to accommodate a larger inflow of tourists. In such a situation investments generally find their way to areas that have high resource interactive attractions, thus creating a honey-pot situation where the attraction is the main reason for which tourists come and related activities are planned around it. Over a period of time this leads to either haphazard growth due to ad-hoc decision-making and ad-hoc development or saturation or both. In all the above cases destination resources get depleted in terms of quality as there is tremendous pressure on their capacity to service the tourists. In fact Jeffries (1971) indicates that resources by themselves are not products at a destination but need to be developed in quite different ways in answer to the needs of quite different markets. This shows that one needs to showcase the tourism resources at a destination in a manner that is conducive to tourists form a viewpoint of creating a good experience for them. This is possible only when there is an optimum utilization of the resource base. With honey-pot areas this rarely happens as the resource gets degenerated and results in a negative experience for the tourists. Though honey-pot areas at a tourism destination generate higher revenues the concomitant depletion of the natural resources around the area negate the economic benefits arising out of it.

Tourism Experience Development

Creating tourism experiences for tourists is the central theme of any tourism destination stakeholder. This has to be borne in mind when the developmental platform of tourism is debated. The need for proper planning as far as tourism product development or tourism attraction development could never have been more emphasized than in the process of creating experiences for tourists. One of the most desired experiences for tourists is to get the feel of being welcomed at a place, which she visits. If such experiences are designed then the tourist would certainly involve herself with the experience and create a better tourism experience for herself as well as for others around her.

Currently Goa has seen a huge rise in the tourist inflows in the past three years and this is a good indication for the economic benefits to the industry in particular and to the general public at large. However one needs to look more deeply at this issue because there is more to economic benefits than meets the eye.

One needs to look as to who benefits and how the benefit percolates in society. Foster (1985) says that "the search for, and developing and launching of new products is essential for the long term survival in tourism. The slow rate of change in demand for tourism products disguises this necessity". This statement indicates that there is a dynamic activity that is necessary, which can look at the product development process effectively throughout the destination.

The Future

The increase in tourism arrivals heralds with it the imminent need for increased resource usage. This is evident from the requirement of increased beds per tourist in terms of hotels in all categories. At the current level of Tourist arrivals in Goa in 2004 of 24,48,959 the total bed requirement is 39,183 beds. If we fit a trend to the tourist arrivals then the tourist arrivals for the year 2016 are projected at 42,80,000, which needs a phenomenal increase in bed requirement of 69,400, which is almost twice the amount for 2004. This is only one area of resource development need and one can imagine what kind of resources are needed in terms of basic resources such as water, electricity, garbage disposal, land, roads etc.

Furthermore one needs to look at the kind of resources on the primary demand side of tourism such as increased demand on attractions, natural as well as man-made. Viewed from this point one is compelled to take a hard look at the honey-pot areas such as Calangute, Baga, Candolim, Palolem etc., and then incorporate the tourism attraction demand from tourists in future. This would certainly lead to the development of hinterland areas of Goa and most of this would be in the realms of Heritage and Culture. This is where the destination managers and stakeholders need to come together to create strong policies that are conducive to better tourism experience creation. Till recently tourism has been viewed as an economic activity that creates and distributes wealth at the destination. One needs to look deeply into this phenomenon and realize what impacts this has on the phenomenon of tourism itself. Most people call the traditional approach as the demand side approach in the sense that tourism is looked at from the benefits of demand for tourism. However the supply-side aspect is not taken with equal vigour. There are many organizations and stakeholders who are eager to market their product to the tourists but not many of them would get together and spend time, efforts and money in designing the tourism products that are offered to the tourists. The future of Tourism in Goa will certainly depend on how this is created. Economic benefit dispersion and resource generation, maintenance and dynamic evaluation alone will help Goa retain its pristine nature and benefit both the hosts as well as the guests.

Tourism dependent economies generally create products and services keeping in mind the tourists. However it would be prudent to view the local economy and population as the main demand sector and tourism as an add-on economy. The reason for this is the involvement of all sections of the local economy. Tourism products created and distributed to the tourists have a built in risk factor of competition, market backlash by way of tourism activities not occurring in the region due to exogenous factors. If the tourism products are a part of the local economy then there is lesser fluctuation as far as the demand is concerned and hence price stability is relatively ensured. This in itself is a great relief for investors who seek a stable business environment to enable them to take better investment decisions. This in turn would lead to a sense of stability for investors thus boosting their confidence in terms of bringing in new investments to bolster the supply side of a destination.

Robustness of a Tourism Destination

A tourism destination is as robust as its weakest link or weakest spot. As such creating a destination growth path that includes growth and stability of resource utilization is the need of the hour. At current levels of resource strength Goa will reach saturation point in terms of Carrying Capacity in the year 2018. This is indicative of how fast the tourism scenario is growing in comparison with the resource development process. Unless priority is given to the development of resources there is no hope for Goa to keep creating better tourism experiences for the tourists.

The level of resources needed for tourism development is large and individual organizations may not be able to marshal them. Since most of the firms that are functioning at a tourism destination are small and medium enterprises it becomes all the more imperative that larger investments come in from the state itself or are outsourced through other means such as joint ventures, alliances, specifically created organizations that have access to larger funds, etc,.

In terms of creating an image for the destination and in terms of ensuring that the effects of tourism are spread throughout the destination strong cooperative environment needs to be created. Co-operation can exist in the form of alliances, joint ventures, Co-operatives for specific purposes etc,. Most resource specific activities could use these forms to foster the growth and development of tourism as well as that of the resource.

One such example is of the heritage tourism in Portugal, which is created out of a strong co-operative organization to rejuvenate the hinterland tourism. Rural tourism is fostered through this Co-operative organization caller TURIHAB and its success in restoring cultural and heritage tourism is quite astounding. One can safely say that the future of tourism in Goa will depend a lot on how the different stakeholders of the destination will co-operate and build a significantly strong Goa from the viewpoint of tourism.

CONCLUSION

Goa Undoubtedly is one of the most important destinations of India. International and domestic tourists have a special place for Goa in their hearts and it might be difficult for Goa to sustain that place in future unless it organizes itself for the delivering better tourism experiences to those visiting its wonderful locales. The forms of intervention to achieve this have to be designed by the stakeholders themselves and the future certainly is in the co-operative domain as well as in the development of tourism throughout the destination rather than at honey-pot areas.

5

TOURISM POLICY OF INDIA: AN EXPLORATORY STUDY

The objective of this lesson is to assess the impact of Tourism Policy on the tourism sector and make a preliminary study of the possible impact such policy imperatives might have on the socio-economic fabric of the country. The study, commissioned by EQUATIONS, Bangalore, utilised a methodology involving a historical preview of the evolution of Tourism Policy since 1982, and an exploratory assessment of the impact. The study material included documentation available at EQUATIONS and relevant publications of the Union Government.

The impact assessment of the sectoral policies on the specified sector suffers from a serious methodological problem. Briefly, it may be argued that the development of a sector is not solely dependent on the factors within the sector: it is influenced by the general socio-economic environment, the political system and the overall policy framework.

Thus the study integrates within itself the dynamic aspects of historical changes that are taking place at the macro-economic level. Similarly, Tourism Policy would not have evolved on its own without being influenced by the general tenor of macro-economic policy. Tourism policy thus has a socio-political grounding as much as it has a macro-economic colouring.

The 1980s witnessed the era of liberalisation initiated by the Congress Government at the Centre. The process of liberating the Indian economy from the shibboleths of 'license-permit Raj' culminated in the initiation of the structural adjustment programme in 1992.

"Objectives, Thrusts and Macro-economic Dimensions of the Eighth Plan" endorsed by the National Development Council, clearly outlines the context within which the structural reforms were initiated: "The need to restructure our systems of economic management has become an imperative if India is to emerge as a vibrant and internationally competitive economy in the 90's. Systems of control and regulation, developed for good reasons in the past have outlived their utility and some positively (sic) stand in the way of further progress. Such dysfunctional systems have to be overhauled in the light of emerging realities.

" The process of structural adjustments has brought about far reaching changes in the Indian economy at a breath-taking pace. The impact of these changes over the tourism sector need to be studied in a dynamic context. Nevertheless, the above should not be taken as ignoring the fact that sectoral policy does have a direct and unambiguous impact over the concerned sector.

Tourism Policy, as a statement of intent by the Government, would form the reference point for action and criticism. Any initiative by Government in Tourism by way of legislation or direct investment is envisaged within the framework of Tourism Policy. The debates in Parliament had taken recourse to the received policy of the Union Government while making references to particular cases. The backdrop of a policy always serves as a guideline for further executive and legislative initiatives. It would be cynical to regard these policy statements as mere exercises in eloquence and additions to the already existing volumes of wishful thinking.

Furthermore, Policy statements by Government should be viewed in their evolutionary stance. It would be a negation of the democratic content of our political system to view a Policy statement as a static and rigid formulation, at a point in time, applicable for years to come. Thus, since 1982, various initiatives undertaken by the Government need to be perceived as additions or modifications to the received Policy.

While it may be argued that these changes in the policy are only marginal and superficial from the viewpoint of equity and social justice, it would be an oversimplification to view the latest policy statement as nothing but the "nth" version of the Policy formulated in 1982. Recognising the all-pervading inertia that looms large in matters governmental, one is often tempted to deny the scope for lobbying which makes possible the desired modifications in the policy corpus. In short, policy, as a body incorporating proactive intentions, is amenable to periodic reviews and possible modifications.

The issues stressed in the preceding paragraphs provide the framework within which Tourism Policy needs to be considered. In brief, there is more to policy in tourism than is found in the Tourism Policy. Perhaps, the links within a macro-economic framework need no special mention.

MAJOR POLICY INITIATIVES

The first ever Tourism Policy was announced by the Government of India in November 1982. It took ten long years for the Government to feel the need to come up with a possible improvement over this. Thus the National Action Plan for Tourism was announced in May 1992. Between these two policy statements, various legislative and executive measures were brought about.

In particular, the report of the National Committee on Tourism, submitted in 1988 needs special mention. In addition, two five-year plans - the Seventh and the Eighth - provided the basic perspective framework for operational initiatives.

The Seventh Plan advocated a two-pronged thrust in the area of development of tourism, viz., to vigorously promote domestic tourism and to diversify overseas tourism in India. While laying stress on creation of beach resorts, conducting of conventions, conferences, winter sports and trekking, the overall intention was to diversify options available for foreign tourists.

The Tourism Policy, 1982 was more an aggressive statement in marketing than a perspective plan for development. Its main thrust was aimed at presenting India to the foreigners as the ultimate holiday resort. With a view to reach this destination, the following measures were suggested by the Policy:

1. To take full advantage of the national heritage in arriving at a popular campaign for attracting tourists;
2. To promote tourist resorts and make India a destination of holiday resorts;
3. To grant the status of an export industry to tourism;
4. To adopt a selective approach to develop few tourist circuits; and,
5. To invite private sector participation into the sector.

The Planning Commission recognised tourism as an industry by June 1982. However, it took ten years to make most of the States to fall in line and accord the same status within their legislative framework. At the beginning of the Eighth Plan (1992-97), 15 States and 3 Union Territories had declared tourism as an industry. Four States had declared hotels as an industry.

The National Committee on Tourism was set up in July 1986 by the Planning Commission to prepare a perspective plan for the sector. Within the broad framework of the Seventh Plan, the Committee had to evolve a perspective plan for the coming years.

The Committee, headed by Mr. Mohammed Yunus, submitted its recommendations in November 1987. The list of Members was as impressive Mr. S.K. Mishra (Secretary, Department of Tourism), Mrs. Kapila Vatsayan, Mr. K.L. Thapar, Mr. Rajan Jaitley, Mr. A.B. Kerker, Mr. R.K. Puri and Mr Pran Seth. The Committee in its Report recommended that the existing Department of Tourism be replaced by a National Tourism Board. It suggested that there be a separate cadre of Indian Tourism Service to look after the functioning of the Board. It also submitted proposals for partial privatisation of the two airlines owned by the Union Government.

By September, 1987, the Central Government declared more concessions for the sector: these included tax exemption on foreign exchange earnings from tourism (a 50% reduction on rupee earnings and a 100% reduction on earnings in dollars), a drastic reduction in tariff on import of capital goods, and concessional finance at the rate of 1 to 5% per annum.

The Tourism Development Finance Corporation was set up in 1987 with a corpus fund of Rs. 100 crores. Until then, the sector was financed on commercial lines by the Industrial Development Bank of India, Industrial Credit and Investment Corporation of India and other commercial banks.

The National Action Plan for Tourism, published in May 1992, and tabled in the Lok Sabha on 5 May 1992, charts 7 objectives as central concerns of the Ministry:

- socio-economic development of areas;
- increasing employment opportunities;
- developing domestic tourism for the budget category;
- preserving national heritage and environment;
- development of international tourism;
- diversification of the tourism product.,
- and, increase in India's share in world tourism (from the present 0.4% to 1% during next 5 years)

As per the Action Plan, foreign exchange earnings are estimated to increase from Rs.10,000 crores in 1992 to Rs.24,000 crores by 2000 AD. Simultaneously, the Plan aims at increasing employment in tourism to 28 million from the present 14 million. Hotel accommodation is to be increased from 44,400 rooms to 1,20,000 by 3 years. Other provisions in the Action Plan include a discontinuance of subsidies to star hotels, encouraging foreign investment in tourism and the setting up of a convention city for developing convention tourism. The Action Plan envisages the development of Special Tourism Areas on lines of export processing zones. Special Central assistance is to be provided for the States to improve the infrastructural facilities at pilgrimage places. It proposes to set up a National Culinary Institute, and projects a liberalised framework for recognition of travel agents and tour operators.

The Eighth Plan document makes a special mention that the future expansion of tourism should be achieved mainly by private sector participation. The thrust areas as enumerated in the Plan include development of selected tourist places, diversification from cultural related tourism to holiday and leisure tourism, development of trekking, winter sports, wildlife and beach resort tourism, exploring new source markets, restoration of national heritage projects, launching of national image building, providing inexpensive accommodation in different tourist centres, improving service efficiency in public sector corporations and streamlining of facilitation procedures at airports.

The Eighth Plan aims at luring the high spending tourists from Europe and USA. It also envisages a 'master plan' to integrate area plans with development of tourism. This is envisaged to ensure employment opportunities for the local population. In April 1993, the Government announced further measures aimed at export promotion. The existing Export Promotion of Capital Goods Scheme (EPCG) was extended to tourism and related services. Against the existing 35%, the tourism sector would now pay an excise duty of 15% only on capital goods import, subject to an export obligation of 4 times the cargo, insurance and freight (CIF) value of imports. With an obligation period of five years, this came as a boon to the hotel industry. The cost of construction had also come down by 20%.

In addition to the above policy pronouncements by the Union Government, our planners had envisaged the possibilities of developing specific regions on a zonal plank. Special area programmes like the Hill Area Development Programme and the Western Ghats Development Programme form part of the overall national plan.

The Eighth Plan document stipulates that the strategy in such designated special areas is to devise suitable location-specific solutions, so as to reverse the process of degradation of natural resources and ensure sustainable development. This approach perhaps needs to be integrated into the project of special tourism areas, now being made popular by the Government. Administrative Control and Developmental Compromises The federal principles enshrined in the Indian Constitution require that the tourism sector be treated as a State subject.

As such, the Department of Tourism (under the Ministry of Civil Aviation and Tourism at the Centre) undertakes certain promotional and developmental activities with a view to enhance the sectoral potential. The Department has certain regulatory functions to perform involving the hotel industry, travel agencies and tourist operators. Over the years, there has been considerable erosion of powers so far as State Governments are concerned. The sustained campaign for privatisation in all the policy documents has left limited space of operation for the States.

The public sector is increasingly being perceived as an agent of inertia than of change and hence the pressure for a hands-off policy. On the other hand, the Union Government has been usurping the powers of the State with some pretext or the other. Promotion schemes, designed at the Centre, are transferred for implementation at the State level. The special Central Assistance, for example, granted for the development of infrastructure at the pilgrim centres, carries with it a pre-defined scheme and mode of execution. Furthermore, there are occasions when the Centre forces the State Governments to extend certain subsidies and concessions to the sector. The terms of such concessions would have been fixed by the Centre and the States would have no choice but to fall in line. For example, during the State tourism minister's conference in December 1991, the States were urged to freeze water and electricity rates for 10 years. They were also asked to exempt certain hotels from local and state taxes for 10 years. Seventeen circuits and destinations were identified under the National Action Plan for development through Central assistance and investment by the States and the private sector.

The centres were identified by the Centre and the States were asked to do the needful. There were also times when the federal division of power resulted in operational contradictions. For instance, by 1989, many foreign hotel chains like Hilton, Hyatt, Penta and Kempinski had applied for licenses for investing in India. However, the revenue departments of the respective States failed to locate and allocate land for the construction of hotels. The scheme, thus, fell flat. Curiously, the Union Government was not hesitant to make use of Constitutional provisions when it suited its interests. As has been stated earlier, the Yunus Committee had suggested the creation of the Tourism Board on lines of the existing Railway Board. (Perhaps, it was the brainchild of Mr. K.L. Thapar, then adviser to the Planning Commission, in charge of Transport and Tourism Sector.

Being from the Railway Service, it is not surprising that Thapar thought about a 'Tcurism Board'). To begin with, the empowered committee of secretaries challenged the idea of creation of a Board. It was said that the Railway Board as an independent entity was created for historical reasons. It would be difficult for tourism to be looked after by a Board, because legally the sector would come under the Industrial (Development) Act. It was also found that such a Board would not be viable financially. In 1991, the think-tank on tourism created by Minister Madhavarao Scindia rejected the idea of a Board in toto. It was emphasised that the Board cannot be in charge of a sector that is basically under the jurisdiction of the States! Scope for Federal Interventions The previous section highlights the dubious ways by which the Centre attempts to hijack initiatives at the State-level. This is achieved essentially by threatening to curtail Central assistance or by cajoling through promises of more financial aid. It is common knowledge that the resource-base of the States is very narrow, making them vulnerable at the negotiating table.

However, States have the freedom to resist the Centre's strong- arm tactics, provided State assemblies stand-by the interests of the States. For instance, State legislatures may refuse to freeze water and electricity rates on grounds of revenue generation. In that event, the concerned Chief Minister or the Minister of Tourism may convey the intensity of resistance that he is confronted with, and thus refuse to comply with the Centre's diktats. It is heartening to realise that the States have often exercised their power of self-determination and consequently refused to toe the line drawn by the Centre.

This offers enough scope for possible interventions at the federal strata of our political system in matters of policy formulation. Privatisation and its Implications According to the Approach Paper to the Seventh Plan, " there is a vast potential for development of tourism in the country. Tourism should be accorded the status of an industry. Private sector investment will have to be encouraged in developing tourism and public sector investments should be focused only on development of support infrastructure". Thus the seeds of private initiatives were sown during the Seventh Plan. The Government took the matter of privatising the tourism sector seriously by 1988. It was during the tenure of Mr. S.K. Mishra as Tourism Secretary that the talk of inviting private investment into the sector began.

The Government permitted foreign equity participation up to 5 1 %in tourism projects. Foreign charters were allowed to operate in the country for the first time. Foreign companies were allowed to repatriate their profits to the extent of 3%. The structural adjustment programme, initiated in June, 1992, paved the way for privatisation in almost all sectors of the economy. The Annual Plan (1992-93) document emphatically enunciated the Government's position vis-a-vis tourism: "(T)he future growth of tourism will have to be achieved mainly through private initiative.

The State will contribute to tourism by planning broad strategy of development, provision of monetary and fiscal incentives to catalyse private sector investment." The process of privatisation brought in its wake big investments and private involvement at various levels. As an offshoot, environmental considerations were thrown to the winds and there were instances of large scale human rights violation. The self- correcting nature of policy made provisions for stricter controls in this regard. More seriously, privatisation meant alienation of the majority of our population and their deprivation.

Employment generated in tourism is generally seasonal and ill paid. The private sector- induced pockets of tourism had the potential of turning into centres of pollution, drug trafficking and prostitution. Industry Status Granted to Tourism The Seventh Plan proposed that tourism be declared an industry. However, it took time for the States to implement this, even though they agreed in principle. The smokeless industry had the advantage of generating maximum value-added, because of low-cost inputs.

The Tourism Policy Statement carried certain provisions in favour of the hotel industry. It stated that there should be provision for depreciation in the balance sheets of hotels. Being an export industry, hotels were to be given excise concessions. The provisions of the Monopolies and Restrictive Trade Practices (MRTP) Act were relaxed for hotels, because any hotel with 300 or more rooms would have incurred an investment of Rs. 25 crores. The document also hinted at lower tariffs for power and water and regulations for easy import of equipment. As a follow-up, hotel and shipping were added to the list of 27 industries exempted from Section 22 A of the MRTP Act.

The consequences of declaring tourism as an industry need to be studied in detail. It is not possible to capture its implications in an exploratory work like this. However, it is obvious that the private sector has primarily benefited to a great extent by this measure. Importing Modifications to Policies We have earlier stated that the arena of policy formulation should be self-evaluating and self-correcting. In the case of Tourism Policy, this has proved to be the plus point. As an illustration, the Policy statement of 1982 made no mention of infrastructure development.

The successive governments at the Centre failed to create proper tourism infrastructure, thus resulting in loss of traffic. This lacuna was corrected in the National Action Plan. However, much of this change was due to intensive lobbying by such agencies like the Indian Association of Tour Operators (IATO), the Travel agents

Association of India (TAAI) and the Indian Hotels and Restaurants Association (IHRA). It is for the voluntary agencies and pro-people forces to exploit the avenue of lobbying at various levels. The environmental implications of tourism development did not form part of the 1982 Policy. The consequences are too obvious to be written about. However, the NAP, 1992 did carry specific provisions for environmental protection and harnessing.

From Policy to Cartooning Policy statements may also lead to justifiable flights of fantasy. Two examples would illustrate how policies were used to justify stands taken by the politicians: a. Shri Devi Lal, the then Deputy Prime Minister wanted a 50% discount for farmers at Five Star Hotels run by India Tourism Development Corporation.

The scheme had teething problems since it was not easy to distinguish a farmer from amongst the clients who visit such hotels. However, on his insistence, the so-called CHAUPALs recreated a village ambience to the amazement of foreign tourists, who took a liking for them. b. Pursuing the objective of the Seventh Plan to diversify overseas tourism to its logical conclusion was what prompted A&. Jagdish Tytler to float the idea of casinos. It was an attempt to provide some entertainment for foreigners during the evenings. It was said that Indian classical music would not provide much needed entertainment for foreign guests because the artistes spend a lot of time tuning their instruments! Folk dances get over in an hour. So much for our much touted cultural diversity.

It is embarrassing to believe that the consultative committee attached to the Ministry of Civil Aviation and Tourism had endorsed the idea. Conclusion Broadly, our successive policy pronouncements in the realm of tourism falls within the "liberalising" framework of the macro- economic policy environment. The Finance Bill, 1988, had assured 50% tax exemption on foreign exchange earnings in the sector, and a further 50% exemption if re-invested. In effect, it amounts to 100% tax concession. Luxury hotels enjoy exemptions of all kinds with a view to encourage tourism earnings. These tax exemptions coupled with provision of soft loans to the sector led to a boom in the tourism related private investment.

The Economic Survey 1991-92 aptly summarises the ultimate aim of such incentives for private sector participation: " The Government has tried to expand the economic space in which the people can exercise their initiative and ingenuity. It hopes to do more to expand their opportunities, to enhance their potential. But what shape the economy takes ultimately depends on what the people make of it. In that sense, the future is in their hands." We should not forget that tourism is an industry which emerges in the context of unresol ved socio-economic structural issues, such as land distri bution patterns or the take over of traditional occupations by modem mechanised capital. Tourism happens to be a source of livelihood for millions in India and aggressive privatisation does not ensure social and economic safety nets. In the face of the unhindered entry of international capital and successive alienation, perhaps, it is difficult to agree that "the future is in our hands"

SCENE OF NORTH-EAST

North-East India is a paradise for tourists. Its enchanting hills, dancing rivers, roaring waterfalls, thick and dark forests, heavy rains during monsoon, innumerable varieties of flora and fauna, countless species of wild animals and plants, mysterious clouds, melodious folk music, thrilling dances and festivals, variety of many delicious dishes, handlooms and handicrafts, and above all its green landscape used to attract people from different parts of the world since time immemorial. Assam, one of the constituent states of the region, an embodiment of the natural beauty and grace, a true representative of the region, has been at the centrestage of tourist attraction. The recorded history tells that since the days of Hieu-en Tsang, the great Chinese traveller, who came to Assam during the reign of Kumar Bhaskar Burman (594-650 AD), Assam has been fascinating millions of people by its aura of myths, mystery, music, mountains, nay, all the gifts of nature. The ungrudging blessings of nature have made tourism in Assam essentially nature-centric, despite the fact there are historical and religious places of tourist attraction.

Tourism has generated employment in different parts of the country. Besides creating opportunities for tourist guides, conducted tours, establishment of hotels, and so many other avenues in the tertiary sector, tourism can be a major source of employment in Assam. It is argued that every domestic tourist can generate direct and indirect employment of three persons, and this can be higher (seven) in the case of inflow of every foreign tourist. It is also projected that every one million rupees invested in tourism, 47.9 direct jobs can be created, besides, of course, creating more avenues for indirect employment. Yet paradoxically it attracts very few tourists. Why? What can we do about it?

Tourism Potential

Existing Places of Tourist Attraction

As stated already, tourism in Assam is essentially nature based, therefore, natural parks and sanctuaries, rivers, lakes, warm water springs, forests, wild life, are the principal components of tourist attraction. These places can be grouped together under four categories: (a) nature-related, (b) historical, (c) religious and (d) others.

Nature related

Places in alphabetic order	Distance from Guwahati in km	Speciality
1. Bhairabkunda	137	A beautiful place at the border of Arunachal Pradesh
2. Bhalukpung	205	A beautiful place by the side of river Jia Bhoroli, famous for angling and water sports
3. Chandubi	64	A natural lagoon, beautiful picnic spot
4. Dibru-Chaikhowa	490	70 km from Dibrugarh, national park, the habitat of elephants, buffaloes, famous for wild horses
5. Haflong	355	One of the hill stations in Assam with unsurpassed sylvan beauty
6. Jatinga	364	Near Haflong, North Cachar district, a beautiful hilly place, where birds behave in a mysterious way, the local people call that the birds commit suicide here on certain specific days
7. Kaziranga	217	Internationally famous national park, the home of great Indian one-horn rhinoceros, tigers, elephants, buffaloes, deer, wild ducks and geese, breeding place of pelicans, habitat of reptiles and monkeys more particularly golden langurs and host of other species

Contd...

Places in alphabetic order	Distance from Guwahati in km	Speciality
8. Manas	176	Situated in the foothills of the Himalayas, one of the magnificent national parks in the country, the Manas river flows through it, famous for the tiger project, a habitat for various wild animals
9. Orang	150	A wild life sanctuary, known as a miniature Kaziranga
10. Pabitara	65	A wild life sanctuary
11. Potasoli	173	38 km from historic town of Tezpur, near the picturesque river Jia Bhoroli, famous for eco-camp set up jointly by the Department of Forest and Assam Anglers Association

Source: Directorate of Tourism, Guwahati

Wildlife

An attractive feature of the Assam's forestry is its colourful wildlife. Some of species are exclusive to the state. Assam is famous for as the home of one-horned rhinoceros. Some of the endangered species found in the state are hollock gibbon, the stamp tailed macaque, the capped langur, the golden langur, the pigmy hog, the clouded leopard, the golden cat, the white winged wood-duck, and the like. All these can make Assam as one of the best destination of the tourists. There are five National Parks and eleven wildlife and bird sanctuaries for protection and preservation of wildlife in the state. The five National Parks - Kaziranga, Manas, Nameri, Orang and Dibru-Saikhowa covers an area of 1561.14 sq km. The total area covered by eleven wildlife and bird sanctuaries is 492.97 sq km. The Assam National Park Act, 1968 was enacted for the preservation and protection of flora and fauna in the wildlife parks and sanctuaries. The Assam Forest Protection Force Act, 1986 was enacted for better protection and security of the forest produce. However, the state of affair in the Forest Protection Force is sad. This is testified to by the fact that the endangered species like rhinoceros are the regular victims of human lust and there is hardly any visible preventive measure to stop such acts of poaching. The forest guards are still with outdated equipment to counter the poacher with sophisticated arms.

Religious

Places in alphabetic order	Distance from Guwahati in km	Speciality
1. Barpeta	137	Famous for a Vaishnava monastery
2. Batadrawa	134	Birth place of Shri Sankardeva, the Vaishnava reformer, saint and a great literary figure
3. Hajo	35	Sacred place for Hindus, Muslims and Buddhists
4. Kamakhya		An important religious place of the Hindus within the city of Guwahati, on the top of Nilachal hill, attracts thousands of devotees and other tourists every day by its natural grandeur
5. Madan Kamdev	35	Vast archeological ruins of fine erotic sculpture
6. Majuli	326	The largest river island in the world, centre of Vaishnava culture, seat of many satras which are known as the centres of Assamese art, dance, drama, music, a safe heaven for various migratory birds

Contd...

Places in alphabetic order	Distance from Guwahati in km	Speciality
7. Surya Pahar	162	Situated on a hill surrounded by innumerable statues of Durga Devi, Ganesha. Surya, Chandra, Buddha

Historical

Places in alphabetic order	Distance from Guwahati in km	Speciality
1. Digboi	523	Famous for the first oil refinery in Asia, war cemetery of World War II
2. Sibsagar	369	Seat of the Ahom rule, famous for royal palaces, monuments, temples and massive ponds
3. Tezpur	137	Ruins of an ancient capital of the Mahabharata time, famous for the love story of Usha-Anirudha

Source: Directorate of Tourism, Guwahati

Others

Guwahati: Situated on the bank of the mighty river Brahmaputra, it is a fast growing metropolis. Though unplanned, it is the gateway to the North-East India. It is well connected with the rest of India by rail, road and air. The airport, known as Gopinath Bordoloi airport, is being upgraded to an international one. The places of worth visiting are: the famous Shakti temple of mother Goddess Kamakhya on the Nilachal hills, the ancient Siva temple Umananda situated on the Peacock island in the middle of the river Brahmaputra, the

Navagraha temple, Srimanta Sankardeva Kalakshetra, Balaji temple, Science Museum, Vaisisthashram (founded by famous sage Vaisistha amidst grand natural beauty), the State Museum, the State Zoo-cum-Botanical garden, the Saraighat Bridge, the Lachit Barphukan Park etc.

Potential to Attract Tourists of Diverse Interests

The above list shows that there is an ample scope for tourism to grow as an industry in with it diverse endowments of tourist interests. The following are the existing and potential variety of tourism:

Nature Tourism

Assam and its six neighbouring states of the North-East are known for their bio-geographic richness (Coopers and Lybrand Report, 1996, p. 49). With its dense forests, uneven topography, flora and fauna, the majestic Brahmaputra and its tributaries, wild life sanctuaries like Kaziranga, Manas, Pabitara, Dibru-Saikhowa, Bhalukpung, Pabitara and similar others, and many rare species of animals, Assam offers basically nature-centric tourism. From one end to the other, the state offers to the tourists so many places of natural beauty with wide variety of wildlife that very few places in the world can compete with it. Nature tourism understood in terms of wildlife sanctuaries constitutes the core of tourism in Assam. The tourists, both domestic and foreign, are likely to find these places attracting, nay alluring, provided a well-definite programme of action is evolved.

Tea Tourism

Tea was first discovered in Assam in 1823 by two intrepid British adventurers, Robert and Charles Bruce and since then tea has become an integral part of Assam's economy. Each of these lush green tea gardens in Assam (about 1000 in number) is a treasure house of exotic beauty of nature with colourful people and their enchanting songs and dances, sprawling bungalows, and residential facilities. Many of these tea gardens have polo fields and golf courses. There are as many as 30 air strips and helipads maintained by the tea garden management. These facilities can form into an attractive package for tourism. The road communication to most of the tea gardens is fairly well maintained, and the rest houses and bungalows with modern facilities located there are generally kept ready for visitors and guests. Therefore, coordination with the management of the tea gardens can effectively do a lot in promoting tea tourism in the state. It may be noted that tea tourism is a recent concept, its potentiality, remains unexplored.

Eco-tourism

Eco-tourism is also a new concept, developed around the idea of travelling to places of natural beauty, moving around and staying with the places of nature for a couple of days. It has the twin objectives of conserving environment and improving the welfare of the local people. Countries like Kenya, Costa Rica, South Africa have already successfully promoted eco-tourism. Kerala presents a unique success story of eco-tourism in our country. On this similar line, Assam has immense scope for eco-tourism, as its natural scenario and climatic condition resemble those in Kerala. The state is virtually free from industrial pollution. Its green forests, blue hills, enchanting rivers are the basis on which an eco-friendly tourism can be developed. For that a host of matters to be properly addressed, including: (a) development of good approach road to the spots of tourist attraction, (b) creation of infra-structural facilities like good quality tents with provisions for food and other logistics, (c) river cruising and water sports, bird watching towers etc. These facilities are likely to attract eco-tourists. It may be noted that eco-tourism is yet to come to the take-off stage.

Cultural Tourism

Assam is a conglomeration of various ethnic tribes and groups each having a distinct language, culture, way-of-life, festivals, songs and dances. Most of these people have their spring festivals. Songs and dances, display of colourful dresses, tasting of innumerable varieties of both vegetarian and non-vegetarian dishes mark these festivals. Sankardev Kalakhetra, Guwahati, has been organising, in recent years, spring festivals, on the line of the desert festival of Rajasthan, the Rangali Utsav in the month of April in which the various colourful shades of Assam are presented. This could be as big an attraction as the Pushkar Mela in Rajasthan.

Pilgrim Tourism

Assam has many ancient temples and shrines, some of which like Kamakhya date back to pre-historic time. As stated already Kamakhya is one of the most revered religious places in the country. An average of 1000 visitors visit the Kamakhya temple every day throughout the year. It becomes a centre of attraction in the month of June when it celebrates the Ambubchi mela. At that time more than hundred thousand pilgrims come for pilgrimage from different places of India. Situated on a hill top Kamakhya is also a very beautiful place that attracts many tourists. There are other religious places where visitors often come from different parts of the country. But most of the places do not provide adequate facilities to the tourists and pilgrims, for which these places of religious importance fail to attract a large number of tourists.

Adventure Tourism

The enchanting blue hills and speedy rivers of Assam provide an enormous scope for the development of adventure tourism. Recently, some of the adventure sports activities like rock-climbing, trekking, para-sailing, water sports, river rafting and angling are promoted by the Department of Tourism. There is an annual angling competition held at Bhalukpung-Potasali side every year in November in which Indian and foreign tourists participate. But other areas of adventure tourism like hang gliding are yet to grow. Assam has a number of ideal places like Nilachal hills (where the Kamakhya temple situated) in the city of Guwahati and the hills around Kaziranga. Since most of the tourists come to the state through Guwahati and visit Kaziranga, there is an enormous scope for hang gliding.

Golf Tourism

There are about 10 golf courses located mostly within the compact areas of tea gardens. The Oil India maintains a very good golf course in the industrial town of Duliajan. These offer a unique opportunity to develop golf tourism in the state. Most of the courses are located near to air-strips and helipads maintained by the tea garden management. In recent years, domestic and foreign tourists are coming to play golf in different golf courses, and a good number of them use these air-strips and helipads. Golf tourism can be integrated with eco and tea tourism. One has to recognize that some tourists may more than one interest and may like to combine various aspects of tourism described above.

Status of Tourism

In a recent statement, Mr M P Bezbaruah, Union Tourism Secretary, said that the inflow of foreign tourists in India has registered a 6 per cent growth in 2000-01. The absolute figure is 2.7 million people from abroad. Foreign tourists fetched $3 billion to the Union exchequer making tourism the second highest net foreign exchange earner in the country.

However, Assam does not present a happy picture. Only 0.22 percent of the foreign tourists visiting India last year made Assam their destination. Table below presents the inflow of both domestic and foreign tourists to Assam:

Table : Tourist Inflow to Assam 1995-2000

Year	Indian	Foreign
1995	348,532	2,575
1996	327,260	5,885
1997	842,656	4,194
1998	939,721	3,843
1999	964,939	5,218
2000	1,001,577	5,959

Source: Directorate of Tourism, Assam

It is noteworthy that the tourists visit Assam throughout the year. But the peak period starts from October when the rainy season comes to an end, the climate becomes more pleasant and the national parks like Kaziranga are opened for the visitors. The peak period continues till April when the national parks are closed due to rain and other accompanying problems. The figures stated in Table 8.1 include only those who those who visited the places listed in the directory of Tourism and stayed at tourist lodges of the State Tourism Department, hotels, inspection bungalows and Kamakhya Temple's accommodation. The revenue earned for last four financial years are stated in Table below.

Table : Revenue Earned from Tourists (Rs '000)

Year	Directorate of Tourism	ATDC@	Total
1996-97	3,688	NA	3,688
1997-98	2,743	1,972	4,715
1998-99	3,105	1,979	5,084
1999-2000	3,172	3,226	6,398

Source: Directorate of Tourism, Assam

It is evident from the two Tables that there has been some increase in tourist traffic as also in the revenue earning from tourism despite the fact the law and order situation in the state has not been satisfactory and insurgency activities are rife. These data, however, do not present an idea about the spillover revenue and employment generation in the state. They also do not indicate an idea about the income and employment generated in the tertiary sectors associated with tourism.

What has Ailed Assam's Tourism?

Despite the fact that Assam has the potentiality of developing tourism in a big way, the statistics shown in Tables 8.1 and 8.2 do not present a happy situation. The reasons are manifold.

Absence of a Tourism Policy

The Government of India has a policy to develop tourism into an industry and a target to achieve in respect of attracting foreign tourists, who constitute an important source of hard foreign currency. As a result, process tourism has become the second largest foreign exchange earner. It has taken steps to revise the National Tourism Policy, 1982 and to redraft the draft policy of 1993 to envision global tourism based on four S - Swagat (welcome), Suvidha (facilities), Soosna (information) and

Suraksha (security). It is said that Assam has a policy on tourism prepared in November 1987. Unfortunately, it is not available in any of the offices connected with tourism. It appears that there was an attempt in November 1987 to formulate a tourism policy and then in December 1992 an exercise was done to frame certain rules on tourism. It appears that these steps did not bring forth any concrete result. The media, in the recent time has been giving adequate publicity highlighting the importance of tourism in the economic development of the state. Most of the newspapers in both English and Assamese, have been publishing a good number articles in frequent intervals highlighting various aspects of tourism and its potentiality in the sustainable development of Assam. Ideas on this matter are generated through media, but these are yet to be crystallized and institutionalized, as result tourism remains in the domain of ad hocism.

Restricted Area Permit (RAP)

The RAP to the North-Eastern region was enforced in 1955 in the backdrop of alleged missionary involvement in the Naga rebellion. Under this a foreigner intending to visit North-East including Assam had to undergo a long arduous procedure of obtaining permission from the Home Ministry. With RAP in force till May 18, 1999 it was an uphill task for any foreign tourist to visit Assam and other places in the North-East. Unfortunately, the ghost of RAP still continues to loom large and the efforts to disabuse the false apprehension in the mind of the foreign tourists are minimal.

Insurgency

Assam, and for that matter almost whole of North-East has been experiencing violent movements, some of which are secessionists in nature, since 1953 when A Z Phizo fired the first salvo of armed struggle against Indian Union. The foreign and the domestic tourists consider it risky to visit this part of the country, in view of the prevailing law and order situation. The general impression has been that any foreign or domestic tourist could be a soft target of the insurgents. Therefore, they are reluctant to undertake an adventurous journey to Assam and North-East. Contrary to this general impression, however, there is not a single instance of harassment, not to speak of threat to life to any domestic or foreign tourists visiting the region since the outbreak of the Naga movement. But the general impression about the deteriorating law and order situation is enough to ward off any tourist. On the top of this, Manas sanctuary, undoubtedly one of the most beautiful natural parks in the country has been virtually under the control of the Bodo militants for which it is still not considered to safe to visit the place. Recently, Manas has been opened for the tourists, but it will take time to ward off the long-standing impression of the tourists about the sanctuary.

Lack of Infrastructure

To attract tourists, there must be dissemination of information, infrastructural facilities like good hotels and tourist lodges, affordable and reliable communication network, clean and hygienic food and accommodation, availability of water sports equipment, and the like. Most of the places of tourist attraction are not by the side of the national highways, and approach roads are in bad condition. This is a strong discouraging factor, which works against a good inflow of the tourist. It appears that the potentialities for developing tourism to a stable source of revenue are not matched by proper policy and strategy.

Lack of Coordinated Efforts

There is a palpable lack of coordination among several agencies like Department of Tourism and Department of Archaeology in handling the demands of the tourists in places of both historic and religious importance.

There is virtually no coordination between various public industries and private sectors like tea industry, oil and coal on one hand, and the Department of Tourism or Assam Tourist Development Corporation (ATDC), on the other, in the efforts towards developing eco and tea tourism. Similarly, there is no tangible and effective coordination between the twin bodies of Assam tourism, that is, the Directorate of Tourism and ATDC on one hand, and road and river transport system run by both Government and private sectors on the other. Therefore, stagnation has been the striking mark of the status of tourism in Assam.

Absence of Tourist Guides

Assam virtually does not have any trained guides placed in important places of tourist attraction. Consequently, as the tourists arrive at such a place there is hardly anyone to satisfy the inquisitiveness of the tourists. The Department of Tourism initiated a programme to train tourist guides.

The effort did not yield good result as most of the trainees left the job. Some of them found other means of livelihood while others found it to be less paying because of the poor inflow of the tourists to the state. It is a chicken-and-egg syndrome which can be resolved by the state government by adopting a two-front strategy - (i) tourist guide training programme for a very limited number of youths, and (ii) setting a target of inflow of the tourists.

Recent Steps

Assam Tourism Development Corporation (ATDC) was set up in June 1988 under the Companies Act of 1956 with the objective to boost tourism in the state. It took over most of the tourist lodges, tourist bungalows, hotels, guest houses, entertainment projects etc., all the means of transport which had been under the control of the Department of Tourism, Government of Assam, and many other functions performed by the said Department to market tourism in the state. Since then it has been making efforts in coordination with the Directorate of Tourism to promote tourism. It prepared an agenda to start as many as 25 new projects. Some of these have been already commissioned and some are in the process of completion.

It is expected that ATDC will be able to reduce bureaucratic bungling standing on the way of promoting tourism in the state. It is not out of context to refer to the fact that the ATDC has been earning profit during the last two financial years (See Table below) although its track record was not quite satisfactory. But if the recent phenomenal trend (profit from Rs 1.1 million to Rs 2 million, which accounts for 82 per cent increase) is maintained, it can definitely fulfill the objectives of the MOA (Memorandum of Association) of 1988.

Table : ATDC's Net Profit (1994-95 to 1999-2000)

Financial Year	Net profit in Rs
1994-95	700,000
1995-96	400,000
1996-97	1,100,000
1997-98	300,000
1998-99	1,100,000
1999-2000	2,000,000

Source: ATDC, Guwahati

Table below presents the ATDC's turn-over per employee for the last six years. It indicates that the ATDC is not a liability and has the potentiality of contributing to the economy of the state. The slump registered in two years (1997-98 and 1998-99) has been overtaken by the significant growth in 1999-2000.

Table : Turnover per Employee

Financial year	Amount in Rupees
1994-95	21,000
1995-96	38,000
1996-97	43,000
1997-98	34,000
1998-99	37,000
1999-2000	51,000

Source: ATDC, Guwahati

Table 8.5 gives an idea about the projects undertaken by the ATDC. It shows that its physical performance is not satisfactory. Out of 113 schemes carried over for last six years it has been able to complete only 45 schemes. It means that average two schemes have been completed in each financial year.

Table : ATDC's Physical Performance

Financial year	No. of schemes sanctioned (cumulative)	No. of schemes completed (cumulative)
1994-95	56	38
1995-96	61	40
1996-97	68	42
1997-98	79	42
1998-99	93	44
1999-2000	113	45

Source: ATDC, Guwahati

To attract tourists, Assam tourism has been organising tea-tourism and Rongali Utsav in the state as a part of its publicity campaign. These two mega events have been included in the national calendar of festival to get favourable response from both domestic and foreign tourists. These are very recent innovative steps, which are likely to succeed in attracting tourists, both domestic and foreign.

During the last four years, the ATDC and the Directorate of Tourism have participated in various fairs and festivals like Travel and Tourism Fair in Kolkata and Mumbai, India International and Tourism Expo in New Delhi, Hyderabad Fair, Darjeeling Tea Festival, International Fair at Udaipur, Investment Festival in Jaipur, Surajkund Craft Festival in Haryana, Kullu Festival in Himachal Pradesh etc. in the country. These two bodies also participated in international festival in Berlin in 1988 and 1999. It is premature to comment on the impact of such participation in terms of significant increase in the tourist inflow to the state.

Assam tourism had produced documentary films, colourful brochure, and stickers, besides creating a website assamtourism.com.development as a part of the publicity campaign.

Strategy for the Future

It is generally believed that tourists, both domestic and foreign, visit different places in search of specialities, which include a variety of things, such as, beauties of nature, architecture, peace of mind and fulfilment in religious places, new and different variety of food, culture of the people and uncommon adventure. In the midst of so many varieties, tourists make certain common demands, and these are (i) clean, hygienic and comfortable living accommodation; (ii) good transport system to take them from one place to another; (iii) decent shops particularly catering to ethnic art, clothes, artifacts, and (iv) entertainment representing cultural heritage of the place (Report of the Advisory Committee on Industries, Vol. I, Assam, 1996, p. 22).

The Annual Report of the Ministry of Tourism: 1999-2000 also states that tourists invariably seek "a pleasant and delectable experience on their trips". The most desired tourism product, the Report states, should consist of (a) an environment of peace and stability, (b) an assurance of safety and security, (c) an affable host society, (d) an industry and a government that provides the requisite service with a smile, (e) absence of extortion and hostility, and (f) accessible tourist attraction (p. 6).

Assam is richly endowed by nature to become a spotlight of tourism, but mere having a good number of attractive tourist spots is not enough unless all the minimum requirements stated above are not readily available.

The issue of promoting tourism, through which a major source of national revenue can be created and generated, cannot be handled in isolation. A multi-front strategy has to be developed to elevate it to the status of industry. The following points are advanced in this direction:

a. *State Policy for Tourism*: A policy of tourism for the state of Assam has to be evolved on the line of National Policy of Tourism, which incorporates broad policy guidelines to attract both domestic and foreign tourists. The general principles recently announced by the Union Ministry of Tourism around four `S' should form the core of the policy of Assam tourism.

b. *Fixation of Targets*: Certain targets should be fixed in respect of tourist inflow, infra-structural development, commissioning of new projects, annual revenue to be earned and employment to be generated.

c. *Publicity Drive*: Information about tourism in Assam should be made available in the embassies in New Delhi and diplomatic offices in major Indian cities. Colour pictures of large size depicting the natural beauty of Assam and its rich culture should be displayed in the national and international airports and the basic information about places of tourist attraction and the facilities available should be kept in special corners in the airports. The website created by Assam tourism should be updated giving all the details of information on tourism. It is pertinent to mention that Assam has to market tourism aggressively. "One will have to go out and sell, instead of waiting for the customers to come and buy" in a market of stiff competition. (Assam Beyond 2000, p. 64). Information about tourism in Assam should be made widely available including one on the internet.

d. *Infrastructure*: All the infrastructure connected with tourism such as good road communication, good hotels and safari resorts, water sports, tents and other logistics for eco-tourism should be developed. In Guwahati there are a few good hotels. But in other places of tourist attraction there should be good hotels and safari resorts with decent living conditions, if not five-star hotel standard. It is reported in the media that hotels and restaurants have been earning significant revenue in recent years. This tertiary sector needs greater attention.

e. *Facilities for the Tourists*: Tourism is known as a 'hospitality service' and it should ensure all possible facilities (Suvidha) to the tourists, who are to be treated as honoured guests. Apart from infrastructure, tourist information, travel services and trained guides are needed in Assam. The Government of Assam should initiate a tourist guide-training programme for a limited number of youths and upgrade the tourist information centres.

f. *Cultural Programmes*: There should be provision for musical entertainment to the tourists staying in the hotels and tourists bungalows in important tourist places like Kaziranga and Guwahati, so that the evenings become delightful and the tourist can be enriched by the cultural contours of the region.

g. *Communication Network*: Although most of the tourist places are not very far from the airports, the condition of most of the roads including the national highways is not satisfactory. The approach roads to most of the tourist spots are in deplorable condition. Absence of good roads to the places of tourist attraction is a discouraging factor. Efforts should be made to coordinate with the PWD (Roads) to improve the condition of the approach roads to the tourist spots on priority basis. Secondly, each tourist spot should have at least a PCO for facilitating the tourists to maintain their contact with the rest of the world. In this connection, it may be noted that the river Brahmaputra offers a scope for an eco-friendly river transport. The Techno-Economic Feasibility

Study (1998-99) sponsored by the Union Ministry of Tourism confirms the viability of such a venture. The massive volume of water can be properly used to take tourist from one place to another by luxury cruisers. For example tourists might like to choose the river route to travel from Guwahati to Tezpur by a luxury cruisers.

h. *Coordination with Various Bodies and Agencies*: The Directorate of Tourism, the ATDC, Department of Archaeology, tea garden management and the civil aviation should strive for coordinated efforts to promote tourism. The Directorate of Tourism and the ATDC have mutual coordination and frequent meetings but they do not have proper coordination with other related organizations and bodies. This is serious matter, which should be addressed for the promotion of tourism in Assam.

i. *Fiscal Incentives*: The Government may offer fiscal and other incentives to the private entrepreneurs to take up a host of tourist related services like setting up hotels and restaurants, to purchase vehicles etc. by making provisions for soft loan and reducing tax rates. It may encourage the local youths to set up tents with modern facilities and to make available other related equipment for water sports in areas selected for eco-tourism. In other words, transport, accommodation, and other logistics of tourism should be left to the private sectors making the way for a healthy of privatization of the tertiary sector associated with tourism.

j. *Tourism Package for the North East*: Tourism in Assam cannot be viewed in isolation. Assam is the gateway to North-East, which, as stated already, itself is a reservoir of natural beauty with great variety. Many tourists visiting Assam would like to visit Shillong, Cherapunji in Meghalaya and a number of places in Arunachal Pradesh like Tawang, Bomdila, Tezu and Meo. There may be an integrated approach to promote tourism in the region with an attractive package of nature, eco, tea, adventure tourism. The Union Tourism Ministry has given 'special attention' to develop an integrated approach to eco and adventure tourism. On the similar line and with the active support of the Ministry, the Department of Tourism in collaboration with the ATDC can chalk out a plan of action to develop eco-tourism along with adventure and tea tourism in the state. To that end also there is the need to have a regional approach involving all the states of the region. The North-Eastern Council should come up to play an integrated role in this regard. It will be easy to have coordination with Meghalaya, but it will be a difficult task to have coordination with Arunachal Pradesh where the inner line system is in operation.

In this connection it may be mentioned that the Annual Report of the Ministry of Tourism stipulated 25 travel circuits in the National Action Plan for Tourism, one of which is Guwahati-Kaziranga-Shillong-Tawang (p.3). The Ministry is preparing a master plan for the development of Bhalukpong-Tawang travel circuit. Such steps need an effective coordination among the states of the region.

k. *Role the Media*: The media has been playing a significant role in recent years in promoting tourism. Most of the local newspapers are publishing articles and write ups giving coverage to the prospect of tourism in Assam, the places of tourist attraction with coloured photographs. But only a few national dailies have so far given coverage to tourism in Assam. The Directorate of Tourism and the ATDC should take steps even by purchasing space in the national dailies focusing on the attractive places of Assam at least once in a year just before the onset of the peak period of tourism in the state.

l. *Spring Festival*: The Department of Tourism and ATDC may organize spring festival on the line of the desert festival in Rajasthan in the historic town of Sibsagar on the courtyard of the Rangghar. This is in addition to what is at present being done in Sankardev Kalakhtra, Guwahati. The festival should be made enchanting with the presentation of songs and dances of the region, enjoyable with various dishes, and colourful with the display of various folk dresses and handicrafts. Conducted tours can be arranged from Sibsagar during that time to Dibru-Saikhowa and Digboi, both are important places of tourist attraction. The project to commission sound and light programme in front of historically important buildings in Sibsagar narrating the history of the Ahom rule covering so many events and stories of love and sacrifice can be very attractive to both domestic and foreign tourists.

m. *Role of the Government*: The development of the human, social and economic condition of a state improves greatly where there is effective and pro-people governance. The presence of the government must be felt in the positive sense and within the framework of a welfare state.

There may be policies of high order, there may be strategies of unassailable quality, but if there is no good governance, goals set cannot be achieved. In respect of Assam a couple of pertinent points be highlighted:

- The problem of insurgency and violent political movements, which stands as the stumbling block to the development of Assam, has to be resolved at the earliest. The security scenario has to be improved to make Assam absolutely safe for all tourists. Similarly, the national park of Manas should be once again made safe for them.
- The Government of Assam has to market tourism through the ATDC.
- The tourism policy of 1987 has to be made known to the people along with the steps taken towards its implementation. People's involvement in tourism should be sought by offering incentives to them to venture wayside amenities. This may produce good results.
- Effective methodology has to be evolved and implemented to forge coordination of various departments and organizations directly and indirectly associated with tourism.
- With the upgradation of the airport in Guwahati to international standard the prospect of foreign tourists visiting the region has become brighter than before. The task of ensuring good sanitary condition around the tourist spots and the improvement of the condition of the railway and bus stations nearby the tourist spots should be urgently taken up.

- The central assistance to upgrade facilities and infra-structural development should be tapped and properly utilized. The Central allocation of assistance to the state in this regard during financial year of 1998-99 was Rs 13.76 crore and out this Rs 4.6 crore was released. It is imperative to have an effective monitoring system, so that the projects sponsored by the government are implemented on time and in right earnest. This can be accomplished only when there is transparency and vigilance.
- While promoting tourism utmost care should be taken to restrain it from degenerating into "mass tourism" which carries a host of evils capable of destabilizing the society. In this regard the 'correct approach' adopted by the Government of Sikkim may be followed.

6

INDUSTRY AND SERVICES TOURISM

OVERVIEW

Tourism in India has registered significant growth in the recent years. In 1951, international tourist arrival stood at around 17 thousand only while the same has now gone up to 3.91 million in 2005. The upward trend is expected to remain firm in the coming years. Tourism is also one of the sectors, which employs the largest number of manpower.

There has been a remarkable growth in the recent years, in foreign tourist arrivals to India due to various efforts made, including promoting India through the "incredible India" campaign in overseas markets. According to the Ministry of Tourism, during January - June 2007, total tourist inflow stood at 23,86887 as against 21,32174 in the same period last year. The total foreign exchange earnings during January- June 2007 stood at US$ 3589.83 million against US$ 3037.04 million for the same period in 2006.

Indian tourism is one of the most diverse products on the global scene. India has 26 world heritage sites. It is divided into 25 bio-geographic zones and has wide ranging eco tourism products. Apart from this, India has a 6,000 km coastline and dozens of beaches. India's great ethnic diversity translates into a wide variety of cuisine and culture. India also has a large number of villages, plantations and adventure locations.

India is home to a great variety of wildlife and its reserves are well known throughout the world. It also has one of the world's biggest railway systems opening possibilities for those interested in rail tourism. India also has excellent hospitals offering affordable medicare and traditional healthcare systems like Ayurveda. In addition to this India organizes numerous fairs and festivals, which are quite attractive to foreigners.

Tourism sector holds immense potential for Indian economy. Tourism sector has the potential to stimulate other economic sectors through its backward and forward linkages and cross-sectional synergies with sectors like agriculture, horticulture, poultry, handicrafts, transport, construction, etc. Recogonising the importance of this sector, in the recent country budget, the provision for building tourist infrastructure has been increased from US$ 95.6 million in 2006-07 to US$ 117.5 million in 2007-08.

INDIAN TOURISM AS AN ENGINE OF ECONOMIC GROWTH

According to the World Travel and Tourism Council, India' s travel and tourism (T&T) industry is expected to contribute 2.1 percent to Gross Domestic Product in 2006 (INR 713.8 billion or US$16.3 billion).

In the first half of the Annual Plan period of 2005-2006, the Ministry of Tourism has taken several initiatives in the field of infrastructure development and positioning Indian tourism as a major engine for economic growth. These include:

- Emphasis for developing the existing and new destinations to world-class standards.
- Improvement of connectivity to important destinations
- Identification of 10-15 new destinations/ circuits by each state /UT for development to world class standard with all the required infrastructure components.

TOURISM: A VERSATILE SECTOR

- *Medical Tourism*: The Ministry of Tourism has taken several initiatives, in partnership with the private sector, to promote India as a destination for medical tourism and make it a global health destination. Several promotional measures like road shows and developing publicity material have been undertaken for the same.Some of the main advantages that India has are as under:
  * It has world class doctors and hospitals
  * The cost of treatment is1/5th of costs in the west
  * Eastern healthcare wisdom along with the expertise of western medicine
- *Rural Tourism*: A concept of rural tourism has been developed for showcasing the art, crafts and culture of rural India and for creating gainful employment in villages with tourism potential. Rural tourism holds immense potential for India, where 74 per cent of the population resides in its 7 million villages.Thrust is being provided to rural tourism to spread tourism and its socio-economic benefits to rural regions.
- *Cruise Tourism*: India has a vast and beautiful coastline and hence the potential to develop cruise tourism.

- *Convention Tourism*: International convention Centres of the global standard is considered to be one of the important segments for promoting India as an attractive tourist destination in the global market. Ministry of finance has already identified New Delhi, Mumbai, Bangalore, Goa and Jaipur for opening of world-class convention centres. Several initiatives have been taken up by way of public-private partnership to develop small convention centres of high standard. India is undoubtedly a unique Conference Destination as it offers cultural and heritage sites, the exotic and mystical, excellent facilities of beach and adventure holidays which can be combined as pre and post conference tours.

Investment Opportunities

- Hotel industry
- Service apartments
- Adventure Tourism
- Health Tourism
- Convention centres
- Wildlife Tourism
- Highway Tourism
- Amusement Parks

India	INR (Billion)	% of Tot 2006	Growth*	INR (Billion)	% of Tot 2016	Growth**
Personal Travel and Tourism	935.4	3.8	6.9	2,857.1	4.0	6.7
Business Travel	260.8	-	8.3	822.1	-	7.0
Government Expenditures	41.2	1.0	7.7	119.0	1.0	6.1
Capital Investment	681.5	7.2	8.3	2,314.2	7.5	7.8

Contd...

India	INR (Billion)	% of Tot 2006	Growth*	INR (Billion)	% of Tot 2016	Growth**
Visitor Exports	302.2	3.3	10.9	1,031.3	1.3	7.8
Other Exports	121.5	1.3	14.6	984.6	1.3	17.6
Travel and Tourism Demand	2,342.7	-	8.4	8,128.2	-	8.0
T&T Industry GDP	713.8	2.1	7.2	1,881.9	1.7	5.1
T&T Economy GDP	1,827.6	5.3	7.8	5,542.3	5.0	6.6
T&T Industry Employment	10,679.6	2.4	0.8	10,591.8	2.0	-0.1
T&T Economy Employment	24,349.2	5.4	1.4	27, 015.8	5.1	1.0

Source: World Travel and Tourism Council

*2006 real growth adjusted for inflation (%)

**2007-2016 annualized real growth adjusted for inflation(%)

TOURISM- POLICIES AND SCHEMES

In order to develop tourism in India in a systematic manner, position it as a major engine of economic growth and to harness its direct and multiplier effects for employment and poverty eradication in an environmentally sustainable manner, the National Tourism Policy was formulated in the year 2002. Broadly, the "Policy" attempts to:-

- Position tourism as a major engine of economic growth;
- Harness the direct and multiplier effects of tourism for employment generation, economic development and providing impetus to rural tourism;
- Focus on domestic tourism as a major driver of tourism growth.

- Position India as a global brand to take advantage of the burgeoning global travel trade and the vast untapped potential of India as a destination;
- Acknowledges the critical role of private sector with government working as a pro-active facilitator and catalyst;
- Create and develop integrated tourism circuits based on India's unique civilization, heritage, and culture in partnership with States, private sector and other agencies; and
- Ensure that the tourist to India gets physically invigorated, mentally rejuvenated, culturally enriched, spiritually elevated and "feel India from within".

SCHEME FOR PRODUCT/INFRASTRUCTURE AND DESTINATION DEVELOPMENT

The focus under this scheme is on improving the existing products and developing new tourism products to world class standards. For infrastructure and product development, the Ministry of Tourism has been providing Central Financial Assistance to the State Governments during the 9th Five Year Plan which resulted in strengthening of the infrastructure and product development in the country.

The scheme has been restructured during the 10th Five Year Plan to meet the present day infrastructure requirements. The past experience had been that a large number of small projects had been funded under the Scheme, spreading the resources very thinly, which at times had not created the desired impact. The focus in the Tenth Plan has been to fund large projects of infrastructure or product development in an integrated manner.

Under the revised scheme, the destinations are carefully selected based on the tourism potential. Master planning of these destinations is undertaken so as to develop them in an integrated holistic manner. The master plan is suppose to tie up all backward and forward linkages, including environmental considerations. Realizing the importance of destination development, the total outlay for this sector has been increased substantially. Important tourist destinations in each State, in consultation with the State Governments, are taken up for development. This include activities ranging from preparation of master plans to implementation of the master plans. The destinations are selected in consultation with the State/ UT Governments.

The focus under this scheme is on improving the existing products and developing new tourism products to world class standards. For infrastructure and product development, the Ministry of Tourism has been providing Central Financial Assistance to the State Governments during the 9th Five Year Plan which resulted in strengthening of the infrastructure and product development in the country. The scheme has been restructured during the 10th Five Year Plan to meet the present day infrastructure requirements. The past experience had been that a large number of small projects had been funded under the Scheme, spreading the resources very thinly, which at times had not created the desired impact. The focus in the Tenth Plan has been to fund large projects of infrastructure or product development in an integrated manner.

Under the revised scheme, the Destinations are carefully selected based on the tourism potential. Master planning of these destinations is undertaken so as to develop them in an integrated holistic manner. The master plan is suppose to tie up all backward and forward linkages, including environmental considerations. Realizing the importance of destination development, the total outlay for this sector has been increased substantially. Important tourist destinations in each State, in consultation with the State Governments, are taken up for development. This include activities ranging from preparation of master plans to implementation of the master plans. The destinations are selected in consultation with the State/ UT Governments.

1. *Definition of a Destination* : Destination is a place of tourist interest. For being eligible under this scheme the destination must be among the most visited sites in the State, or a recognized Heritage Monument. A group of attractions located in the same village, town or city would also qualify.
2. *Selection of the Destination* : The destinations will be selected in consultation with State Governments/UT Administrations.
3. *Finalisation of the Project* : The identification of the project, the implementing agency, and the mode of channelisation of funds would be done in consultation with the State Govt./UT Administration. The Ministry of Tourism would bear 100% of the project cost (except refurbishment of monuments which would be funded on 66:33 basis, i.e. 66% CFA) based on the project plan and estimates submitted, excluding the items which are the exclusive responsibility of the State Governments as listed in para 5. The maximum amount that could be sanctioned under this scheme would be Rs. 5.0 crores. The State Governments would have to bear the responsibility including for the items mentioned

in para 5. However for projects in the 'Protected Areas' under ASI or the State Archaeology Deptt. The implementing agency would be CPWD or any other agency to be decided by the Ministry. of Tourism. In such cases funds would be directly released to such implementing agency.

4. *Monitoring Committee* : State level Monitoring Committees would be set up under the Chairmanship of the respective Secretary (Tourism). This Committee would comprise of a nominee of the Ministry of Tourism, Government. of India and a nominee of the executing agency.
5. *Funding Pattern* : All permissible activities will be fully funded by the Ministry of tourism, Government of India. However, the State/UT Governments will be fully responsible for the following components of the project :
   i) Making the land available for development.
   ii) Implementation of rehabilitation package, where shifting of dwelling or commercial units is required. However, the Government of India would provide assistance for construction of Tourist Reception Centres including shopping complexes to house the displaced shops.
   iii) Maintenance and management of the assets created.
   iv) Any other item decided by the High Power Committee.
   v) External infrastructure like Water Supply, Electricity and Roads
6. *Permissible Activities* : The following works may be taken up under the Scheme:

i) Improvement of the surroundings of the destination. This would include activities like landscaping, development of parks, fencing, compound wall etc.

ii) Illumination of the Tourist destination and the area around/SEL Shows etc.

iii) Providing for improvement in solid waste management and sewerage management.

iv) Construction of Budget Accommodation, Wayside Amenities.

v) Procurement of equipment directly related to tourism, like Water Sports, Adventure Sports, Eco-friendly modes of transport for moving within the Tourism Zone.

vi) Construction of public buildings which are required to be demolished because of implementation of the Master Plan.

vii) Refurbishment of the Monuments. (66:33 basis, i.e. CFA of 66%)

viii) Signages.

ix) Tourist Arrival Centres/Reception Centres/ Interpretation Centres

x) Other work/activities directly related to tourism.

7. *Release of Funds* : The funds would be released to the executing agency as indicated in Para 3 above.

8. *Installments of Release* : On sanction of a work, the first installment of 30% of the approved CFA will be released. The second installment of 50% will be released on receipt of the UC of the first installment. The balance would be released on the completion of the work.

9. *Following Codal Formalities* : The executing agency shall follow all codal formalities while awarding contracts and procurement of equipment and ensure complete transparency in its transactions.
10. *Management of Assets Created* : The infrastructure and assets created will be maintained and managed by the State/UT Governments or their agencies with no financial commitment to Govt. of India except those assets created in protected areas of ASI.
11. *Prescription of the Schedule of Rates* : While executing the works the executing agency shall follow the Schedule of rates prescribed by the CPWD or the State PWD.
12. *Submission of the Utilisation Certificates* : The executing agency shall furnish through the State Government the Utilisation Certificate for release of the second installment. A Completion Certificate has also to be furnished through the State Government before the release of the final installment. In case the works are executed by a Central Agency in a 'Protected Area' the UCs would be obtained from them directly.

ASSISTANCE FOR LARGE REVENUE GENERATING PROJECTS

It is recognized that the development of tourism infrastructure projects requires very large investment that may not be possible out of the budgetary resources of the Government of India alone. In order to remove these shortcomings and to bring in private sector, corporate and institutional resources as well as techno-managerial efficiencies, it is proposed to promote large revenue generating projects for development of tourism infrastructure in public private partnerships and in partnerships with other Government / Semi-Government agencies.

Large revenue generating project, which can be admissible for assistance under this scheme, should be a project, which is also a tourist attraction, or used by tourists and generates revenue through a levy of fee or user charges on the visitors. Projects like Tourist trains, Cruise vessels, Cruise Terminals, Convention Centres, Golf Courses etc. would qualify for assistance. However, this is only an illustrative list.

Hotel & Restaurant component will not be eligible for assistance under the scheme either on a stand-alone basis or as an integral part of some other project. Besides hotel & restaurants, procurement of vehicles and sports facilities like stadiums will also not be eligible for assistance under the scheme.

Integrated Development of Tourist Circuits

Under this Central Financial Assistance scheme the Ministry of Tourism Government of India has been extending assistance to States for development of tourism infrastructure. Experience has shown that in the past funds under the CFA have been used to fund a large number of small isolated projects, spread throughout the length and breadth of the country resulting in the resources being spread very thinly. Therefore, in order to provide quick and substantial impact, during the 10th Five Year Plan, this new scheme of Integrated Development of Tourist Circuits have been taken up. The objective of the scheme is to identify tourist circuits in the country on an annual basis, and develop them to international standards. The aim is to provide all infrastructure facilities required by the tourists within these circuits. The Ministry of Tourism aim at convergence of resources and expertise through coordinated action with States/UTs and private sector.

Under this Central Financial Assistance scheme the Ministry of Tourism Government of India has been extending assistance to States for development of tourism infrastructure. Experience has shown that in the past funds under the CFA have been used to fund a large number of small isolated projects, spread throughout the length and breadth of the country resulting in the resources being spread very thinly. Therefore, in order to provide quick and substantial impact, during the 10th Five Year Plan, this new scheme of Integrated Development of Tourist Circuits have been taken up. The objective of the scheme is to identify tourist circuits in the country on an annual basis, and develop them to international standards. The aim is to provide all infrastructure facilities required by the tourists within these circuits. The Ministry of Tourism aim at convergence of resources and expertise through coordinated action with States/UTs and private sector.

Definition of a Circuit : A tourist Circuit is defined as a route on which at least three major tourist destinations are located such that none of these are in the same town, village or city. At the same time they are not separated by a large distance such that a tourist would not like to cover them in a sequence. It should have well defined entry and exist points. A tourist who enters at the entry point should get motivated to visit all the places identified on the circuit. The objective of having a tourist circuit is to increase the total number of visits to all the destinations on the circuit on one hand and to provide to the tourist the attraction of all the destinations located on the circuit.

Identification of the Circuit : The Circuit to be taken up will be identified by the Ministry of Tourism at the beginning of each year, in consultation with the State Government. While selecting the Circuit, the tourism potential of the places included would be borne in mind. It will be ensured that a circuit is identified for each State/UT in the full Plan period. A circuit could be limited to a State or it could be a regional circuit covering more than a State/UT. The identification of the project, the implementation agency, and the mode of channelisation of funds would be done in consultation with the State Government/UT Administration. However, for projects in the 'protected areas' under ASI, the implementing agency would be ASI/CPWD or any other agency to be decided by the Ministry of Tourism. The Ministry of Tourism would bear 100% of the project cost (Capital cost only, except for Refurbishment of Monuments where it would be 66:33 i.e. CFA of 66%) based on the project plan and estimates submitted, excluding the items which are the exclusive responsibility of the State Governments as listed in para 3. The maximum amount that could be sanctioned under this scheme would be Rs. 8.00 crores.

Funding Pattern : All activities agreed to by the Ministry of Tourism will be funded on 100% basis i.e. 100% of the capital cost would be borne by the Ministry of Tourism, Government of India, subject to the ceiling of Rs. 8 crores (except, for refurbishment of Monuments where CFA would be 66%). However the State/UT Governments will be fully responsible for the following components of the project.

i) Making the land available for development.

ii) Implementation of rehabilitation package, where shifting of dwelling or commercial units is required. However the Government of India would provide assistance for construction of Tourist reception centers including shopping complexes to house the displaced shops.

iii) Maintenance and management of the assets created.

iv) Any other item decided by the High Power Committee.

v) External infrastructure, like water supply, Electricity and Roads.

Permissible Activities: The following works may be taken up under the Scheme -

i. Improvement of the surroundings of the destination. This would include activities like landscaping, development of parks, fencing, compound wall etc.

ii. Illumination of the Tourist destination and the area around the SEL Shows etc.

iii. Providing for improvement in solid waste management and sewerage management.

iv. Construction of budget accommodation, wayside amenities.

v. Procurement of equipment directly related to tourism, like water sports, adventure sports, eco-friendly modes of transport for moving within the tourism zone.

vi. Construction of public buildings which are required to be displaced because of implementation of the master plan.

vii. Refurbishment of the monuments.

viii. Signages.

ix. Tourist arrival centers/reception centers/ interpretation centers.

x. Other work/activities directly related to tourism.

Release of Financial Assistance : On sanction of a work, the first installment of 30% of the approved CFA will be released, and the second installment of 50% will be released on receipt of utilization certificate of the first installment. The balance would be released on completion of the work.

Codal Formalities : The executing agency shall follow all codal formalities while awarding contracts and procurement of equipments an ensure complete transparency in its transactions.

Management of Assets Created : The infrastructure and assets created will be maintained and managed by the State Government/UT Administration of their agencies with no financial commitment to Government of India, except for those assets which are created in the 'protected areas' of ASI.

Prescription of the Schedule of Rates : While executing the works, the executing agency shall follow the Schedule of rates prescribed by the CPWD or the State PWD.

Submission of the Utilization Certificates : The executing agency shall furnish the utilization certificate through the State Government for release of second instalment, a completion certificate has also to be furnished through the State Government before the release of the final installment. In case the works are executed by a Central Agency in a 'protected area the UC would be obtained from them directly.

Monitoring Committee : A State level monitoring committee would be set up under the Chairmanship of the respective Secretary (Tourism) of the State Government. The Committee would comprise a nominee of the Ministry of Tourism of Government India, and a nominee of the executing agency.

SCHEME FOR RURAL TOURISM

Tourism growth potential can be harnessed as a strategy for Rural Development. The development of a strong platform around the concept of Rural tourism is definitely useful for a country like India, where almost 74% of the population resides in its 7 million villages. Across the world the trends of industrialization and development have had an urban centric approach. Alongside, the stresses of urban lifestyles have led to a "counter-urbanization" syndrome. This has led to growing interest in the rural areas. At the same time this trend of urbanization has led to falling income levels, lesser job opportunities in the rural areas leading to an urbanization syndrome in the rural areas. Rural Tourism is one of the few activities which can provide a solution to these problems. Besides, there are other factors which are shifting the trend towards rural tourism like increasing levels of awareness, growing interest in heritage and culture and improved accessibility, and environmental consciousness.

In the developed countries, this has resulted in a new style of tourism of visiting village settings to experience and live a relaxed and healthy lifestyle. This concept has taken the shape of a formal kind of Rural Tourism. Under this Scheme, thrust is to promote village tourism as the primary tourism product to spread tourism and its socio-economic benefits to rural and its new geographic regions. Key geographic regions are identified for development and promotion of Rural Tourism.

The implementation is done through a Convergence Committee headed by the District Collector. Activities like improving the environment, hygiene, infrastructure etc. are covered for assistance. Apart from providing financial assistance, the focus is to tap the resources available under different schemes of Department of Rural Development, State Governments and other concerned Departments of the Government of India.

Tourism growth potential can be harnessed as a strategy for Rural Development. The development of a strong platform around the concept of Rural tourism is definitely useful for a country like India, where almost 74% of the population resides in its 7 million villages. Across the world the trends of industrialization and development have had an urban centric approach. Alongside, the stresses of urban lifestyles have led to a "counter-urbanization" syndrome. This has led to growing interest in the rural areas. At the same time this trend of urbanization has led to falling income levels, lesser job opportunities in the rural areas leading to an urbanization syndrome in the rural areas. Rural Tourism is one of the few activities which can provide a solution to these problems. Besides, there are other factors which are shifting the trend towards rural tourism like increasing levels of awareness, growing interest in heritage and culture and improved accessibility, and environmental consciousness. In the developed countries, this has resulted in a new style of tourism of visiting village settings to experience and live a relaxed and healthy lifestyle.

This concept has taken the shape of a formal kind of Rural Tourism. Under this Scheme, thrust is to promote village tourism as the primary tourism product to spread tourism and its socio-economic benefits to rural and its new geographic regions. Key geographic regions are identified for development and promotion of Rural Tourism. The implementation is done through a Convergence Committee headed by the District Collector. Activities like improving the environment, hygiene, infrastructure etc. are covered for assistance.

Apart from providing financial assistance, the focus is to tap the resources available under different schemes of Department of Rural Development, State Governments and other concerned Departments of the Government of India.

Definition of Rural Tourism : Any form of tourism that showcases the rural life, art, culture and heritage at rural locations, thereby benefiting the local community economically and socially as well as enabling interaction between the tourists and the locals for a more enriching tourism experience can be termed as rural tourism. Rural tourism is essentially an activity which takes place in the countryside. It is multi-faceted and may entail farm/agricultural tourism, cultural tourism, nature tourism, adventure tourism, and eco-tourism. As against conventional tourism, rural tourism has certain typical characteristics like; it is experience oriented, the locations are sparsely populated, it is predominantly in natural environment, it meshes with seasonality and local events and is based on preservation of culture, heritage and traditions.

Identification of Villages : Each State/UT Govt. would be requested to furnish one proposal for promotion of Rural tourism. Based on the merits and after a joint inspection by the Deptt. Of Tourism, and the State/UT Govt. if required ten proposals would be identified for implementation in the country.

Preparation of Detailed Plan for Implementation of the Project : After shortlisting the proposals, the State/UT Govts would be requested to draw up a detailed plan of action. The thrust here would be to achieve convergence between the different schemes of the Govt. of India and the State Govts. It should be ensured that atleast 50% of the project should be implemented through achieving convergence of different schemes.

Assistance upto Rs. 3 lakhs would be provided to the State Govt. for engaging an expert for preparing the project report.

Assistance under the Scheme : A maximum of Rs. 50 lakhs would be sanctioned under this scheme. The activities listed under the para 5 could be taken up.

Permissible Activities : The following works may be taken up under the Scheme-

i) Improvement of the surroundings of the village. This would include activities like landscaping, development of parks, fencing, compound wall etc.

ii) Improvements to roads within the Panchayat limits. This shall not include any major road which connects the village.

iii) Illumination in the village.

iv) Providing for improvement in solid waste management and sewerage management.

v) Construction of Wayside Amenities.

vi) Procurement of equipments directly related to tourism, like Water Sports, Adventure Sports, Eco-friendly modes of transport for moving within the tourism zone.

vii) Refurbishment of the Monuments. (66:33 basis, i.e. CFA of 66%)

viii) Signages.

ix) Reception Centres.

x) Other work/activities directly related to tourism.

xi) Tourist Accommodation.

Constitution of a Convergence Committee : A Convergence Committee would be set up under the Collector to oversee the implementation of the project.

Execution of the Works : The execution of the work would be entrusted to any Central Govt./State Govt. agency and the funds would be released directly to the implementing agency by the Govt. of India as recommended by the State Govt.

Installments of Release : On sanction of a work the first installment of 30% of the sanctioned amount of CFA will be released. The second installment of 50% would be released on submission of the UC for the first installment. The balance would be released on the completion of the work.

Following Codal Formalities : The executing agency shall follow all codal formalities while awarding contracts and procurement of equipments and ensure complete transparency in its transactions.

Management of Assets Created : The infrastructure and assets created will be maintained and managed by the State/UT Governments or their agencies with no financial commitment to Govt. of India except those assets created in the protected areas of ASI.

Prescription of the Schedule of Rates : While executing the works the executing agency shall follow the Schedule of rates prescribed by the CPWD or the State PWD.

Submission of the Utilisation Certificates : The executing agency shall furnish the Utilisation Certificate through the State Government for release of the second installment. A Completion Certificate has also to be furnished through the State Govt. before the release of the final installment.

Scheme of Assistance for Large Revenue Generating Projects

It is recognized that the development of tourism infrastructure projects requires very large investment that may not be possible out of the budgetary resources of the Government of India alone. In order to remove these shortcomings and to bring in private sector, corporate and institutional resources as well as techno-managerial efficiencies, it is proposed to promote large revenue generating projects for development of tourism infrastructure in public private partnerships and in partnerships with other Government / Semi-Government agencies.

Scope of the Scheme: Large revenue generating project, which can be admissible for assistance under this scheme, should be a project, which is also a tourist attraction, or used by tourists and generates revenue through a levy of fee or user charges on the visitors. Projects like Tourist trains, Cruise vessels, Cruise Terminals, Convention Centres, Golf Courses etc. would qualify for assistance. However, this is only an illustrative list.

Hotel & Restaurant component will not be eligible for assistance under the scheme either on a stand-alone basis or as an integral part of some other project. Besides hotel & restaurants, procurement of vehicles and sports facilities like stadiums will also not be eligible for assistance under the scheme.

Promoters of Project: While considering projects for Grant-in-aid under this scheme, priority will be given to projects promoted by private sector and the projects with public private partnership. However, in some cases where private sector participation is not possible or is not forthcoming, then the proposals/ projects promoted by State Govts. State PSUs, Central Govt, Ministries/Departments like Railways, ASI and Central agencies like Port Trust and CPSEs will be eligible.

Eligibility for Assistance: Justification for providing assistance/subsidy would be ascertained on the basis of feasibility study/DPR at the stage of consideration of the project by the Competent Authority. While selecting projects, priority would be given to projects which have strong private sector participation and involve least subsidy outgo. The projects selected for assistance under this scheme would not be eligible for subsidy from other schemes of Central Government or State Governments. Similarly, the projects which have already availed subsidy/ financial assistance from any other scheme of the Central or State Govt., would not be eligible for Government of India assistance under this scheme.

Requirement of a Special Purpose Vehicle (SPV): A SPV would have to be set up by the implementing partners in case a private party is promoting the project, prior to the consideration of their project under this scheme. However, where the promoter of the project is a State Govt., State PSU or Central Agencies like Port trust or Central PSU, a separate SPV need not be required. In both the cases, a separate Project Management Group would be required and separate accounts would be maintained for the project.

The Project Management Group, where SPV has to be set up will consist of (i) MD/CEO of the SPV (ii) Project Director/Manager (iii) Finance Director (iv) A representative of the State Govt. to be nominated by them. In the other cases, the Project Management Group will consist of (i) MD/CEO of State PSUs/Central PSUs/ Statutory Body, (ii) State Tourism Secretary (where State Govt. is directly involved), (iii) Project Director/Manager (iv) Finance Director of the Central/State PSU/Statutory Body or the Director-Finance Department of State Government.

Appraisal/Feasibility Report: All project proposals under this scheme must be accompanied by project appraisal carried out by an independent public financial institution. Grant-in-aid for preparation of DPR would be admissible at 50% of the actual cost subject to a maximum of Rs.25 lakh per project. No Grant-in-aid would be admissible for preparation of Feasibility Report.

Public financial institutions, in this case, will include a public financial institution under Section 4A of the Companies Act, 1956 and any institution notified by the Government as authorized to discharge the functions of a public financial institution under this Scheme. Anyone of these institutions could also fund the large revenue generating projects admissible under the scheme.

Norms for Funding: The amount of assistance under the scheme would be released to Government agencies or PSUs, if the project is promoted by them. In case a private party is promoting the project, the assistance would be released to SPV through the financial institutions. The quantum of subsidy for the projects will normally be determined through a competitive bidding process, with a cap of Rs.50 Cr. subject to a maximum of 25% of total project cost or 50% of equity contribution of the private promoter, whichever is lower. Specific reasons will be required to be brought on record in case competitive bidding process is not adopted for determining the quantum of subsidy. The minimum equity stake of the private promoter would be 51%, wherever the private sector participation is envisaged in the projects.

The total project cost in this case will mean the total of:

i. Capital cost of the project, including cost of land, material, labour, transport, consumables, testing, commissioning, overheads, contingencies, interest during construction, insurance and supervision (including any taxes and levies);

ii. Pre-operative cost such as formulation, development, design and engineering; and

Expenses related to fund mobilization if required, such as fees for financial services and brokerage.

The assistance would preferably be credit linked and back ended and would be released in three installments. The first installment, limited to 25% of the assistance to be provided by the Ministry, will be released only after 25% of the total cost of the project has been contributed by the promoters. The second installment, limited to 50% of the assistance to be provided by the Ministry, would be disbursed only after 50% of the promoter's amount is contributed. The last installment of balance 25% of the assistance, to be provided by the Ministry, will be released after the project is fully functional.

Recovery of Government Grant: In case the project does not succeed, and there is any default by the promotees, the Financial Institution can recover its loan component and also recover the Grant-in-aid component on behalf of Ministry of Tourism.

Approval Procedures: The project proposals will be appraised by SFC/EFC depending upon the cost of the project before obtaining approval of the competent expenditure sanctioning authority.

Monitoring and Evaluation: The financial institution, which is funding the project, will be responsible for regular monitoring and periodic evaluation of project compliance with agreed milestones and performance levels. In case there is no financial institution involved in the project then an agency will be designated while sanctioning the project for regular monitoring and evaluation as stated above and the cost for the same will be met out of the scheme. Ministry of Tourism will have a separate Monitoring Group consisting of the concerned Joint Secretary & Director in charge of the scheme alongwith Financial Controller to regularly monitor and review the sanctioned projects.

Scheme for Support to Public Private Partnerships in Infrastructure (Viability Gap Funding)

Development of infrastructure require large investments that cannot be undertaken out of public financing alone. Thus, in order to attract private capital as well as techno-managerial efficiencies associated with it, the government is committed to promoting Public-Private Partnerships (PPPs) in infrastructure development. This scheme has been put into effect for providing financial support to bridge the viability gap of infrastructure projects undertaken through Public Private Partnerships.

Scheme for Support to Public Private Partnerships in Infrastructure (Viability Gap Funding)

Whereas the Government of India recognizes that there is significant deficit in the availability of physical infrastructure across different sectors and that this is hindering economic development;

Whereas the development of infrastructure requires large investments that cannot be undertaken out of public financing alone, and that in order to attract private capital as well as the techno-managerial efficiencies associated with it, the Government is committed to promoting Public Private Partnerships

(PPPs) in infrastructure development; and Whereas the Government of India recognizes that infrastructure projects may not always be financially viable because of long gestation periods and limited financial returns, and that financial viability of such projects can be improved through Government support.

Now, therefore, the Government of India has decided to put into effect the following scheme for providing financial support to bridge the viability gap of infrastructure projects undertaken through Public Private Partnerships.

Short Title and Extent

(i) This scheme will be called the Scheme for Financial Support to Public Private Partnerships (PPPs) in Infrastructure. It will be a Plan Scheme to be administered by the Ministry of Finance. Suitable budgetary provisions will be made in the Annual Plans on a year-to year basis.

(ii) The scheme shall come into force with immediate effect.

Definitions

In this scheme, unless the context otherwise requires: Empowered Committee means a Committee under the Chairmanship of Secretary (Economic Affairs) and including Secretary Planning Commission, Secretary (Expenditure) and the Secretary of the line Ministry dealing with the subject.

Empowered Institution means an institution, company or inter-ministerial group designated by the Government for the purposes of this scheme.

Lead Financial Institution means the financial institution (FI) that is funding the PPP project, and in case there is a consortium of FIs, the FI designated as such by the consortium;

Private Sector Company means a company in which 51% or more of the subscribed and paid up equity is owned and controlled by a private entity;

Project Term means the duration of the contract or concession agreement for the PPP project;

Public Private Partnership (PPP) Project means a project based on a contract or concession agreement, between a Government or statutory entity on the one side and a private sector company on the other side, for delivering an infrastructure service on payment of user charges;

Total Project Cost means the lower of the total capital cost of the PPP Project: (a) as estimated by the government/statutory entity that owns the project, (b) as sanctioned by the Lead Financial Institution, and (c) as actually expended; but does not in any case include the cost of land incurred by the government/statutory entity; and

Viability Gap Funding or Grant means a grant one-time or deferred, provided under this Scheme with the objective of making a project commercially viable.

Eligibility

1. In order to be eligible for funding under this Scheme, a PPP project shall meet the following criteria:

   (a) The project shall be implemented i.e. developed, financed, constructed, maintained and operated for the Project Term by a Private Sector Company to be selected by the Government or a statutory entity through a process of open competitive bidding; provided that in case of railway projects that are not amenable to operation by a Private Sector Company, the Empowered Committee may relax this eligibility criterion.

(b) The PPP Project should be from one of the following sectors:

(i) Roads and bridges, railways, seaports, airports, inland waterways;

(ii) Power;

(iii) Urban transport, water supply, sewerage, solid waste management and other physical infrastructure in urban areas;

(iv) Infrastructure projects in Special Economic Zones; and

(v) International convention centres and other tourism infrastructure projects;

Provided that the Empowered Committee may, with approval of the Finance Minister, add or delete sectors/sub-sectors from the aforesaid list.

(c) The project should provide a service against payment of a predetermined tariff or user charge.

(d) The concerned Government/statutory entity should certify, with reasons;

(i) that the tariff/user charge cannot be increased to eliminate or reduce the viability gap of the PPP;

(ii) that the Project Term cannot be increased for reducing the viability gap; and

(iii) that the capital costs are reasonable and based on the standards and specifications normally applicable to such projects and that the capital costs cannot be further restricted for reducing the viability gap.

Government Support

(1) The total Viability Gap Funding under this scheme shall not exceed twenty percent of the Total Project Cost; provided that the Government or statutory entity that owns the project may, if it so decides, provide additional grants out of its budget, but not exceeding a further twenty percent of the Total Project Cost.

(2) Viability Gap Funding under this scheme will normally be in the form of a capital grant at the stage of project construction. Proposals for any other form of assistance may be considered by the Empowered Committee and sanctioned with the approval of Finance Minister on a case-by-case basis.

(3) Viability Gap Funding up to Rs. 100 crore (Rs. One hundred crore) for each project may be sanctioned by the Empowered Institution subject to the budgetary ceilings indicated by the Finance Ministry. Proposals up to Rs. 200 crore (Rs. Two hundred crore) may be sanctioned by the Empowered Committee, and amounts exceeding Rs. 200 crore may be sanctioned by the Empowered Committee with the approval of Finance Minister.

(4) Unless otherwise directed by the Ministry of Finance, the Empowered Institutions may approve project proposals with a cumulative capital outlay equivalent to ten times the budget provisions in the respective Annual Plan.

(5) In the first two years of operation of the Scheme, projects meeting the eligibility criteria will be

funded on a first-come, first served basis. In later years, if need arises, funding may be provided based on an appropriate formula, to be determined by the Empowered Committee, that balances needs across sectors in a manner that would make broad base the sectoral coverage and avoid pre-empting of funds by a few large projects.

Approval of Project Proposals

(1) Project proposals may be posed by a Government or statutory entity which owns the underlying assets. The proposals shall include the requisite information necessary for satisfying the eligibility criteria specified in paragraph 3 above.

(2) Projects based on standardized/model documents duly approved by the respective Government would be preferred. Stand-alone documents may be subjected to detailed scrutiny by the Empowered Institution.

(3) The Empowered Institution will consider the project proposals for Viability Gap Funding and may seek the required details for satisfying the eligibility criteria.

(4) Within 30 days of receipt of a project proposal, duly completed as aforesaid, the Empowered Institution shall inform the sponsoring Government/statutory entity whether the project is eligible for financial assistance under this Scheme. In case the project is based on standalone documents (not being duly approved model/ standard documents), the approval process may require an additional 60 (sixty) days.

(5) In the event that the Empowered Institution needs any clarifications or instructions relating to the eligibility of a project, it may refer the case

to the Empowered Committee for appropriate directions.

(6) Notwithstanding the approvals granted under this scheme, projects promoted by the Central Government or its statutory entities shall be approved and implemented in accordance with the procedures specified from time to time.

(7) In cases where viability gap funding is budgeted under any on-going Plan scheme of the Central Government, the inter-se allocation Between such on-going scheme and this scheme shall be determined by the Empowered Committee.

Procurement process for PPP Projects

(1) The Private Sector Company shall be selected through a transparent and open competitive bidding process. The criterion for bidding shall be the amount of Viability Gap Funding required by a Private Sector Company for implementing the project where all other parameters are comparable.

(2) The Government or statutory entity proposing the project shall certify that the bidding process conforms to the provisions of this Scheme and convey the same to the Empowered Institution prior to disbursement of the Grant.

Appraisal and monitoring by Lead Financial Institution

(1) Within four months from the date on which eligibility of the project is conveyed by the Empowered Institution to the concerned Government/ statutory entity, the PPP project shall be awarded in accordance with paragraph 6 above; provided that upon application made to

it by the concerned Government/statutory entity, the Empowered Institution may extend this period by not more that two months at a time.

(2) The Lead Financial Institution shall, within three months from the date of bid award, present its appraisal of the project for the consideration and approval of the Empowered Institution; provided that upon application made to it by the concerned Government/statutory entity, the Empowered Institution may extend this period by not more than one month at a time.

(3) The Lead Financial Institution shall be responsible for regular monitoring and periodic evaluation of project compliance with agreed milestones and performance levels, particularly for the purpose of disbursement of Viability Gap Funding. It shall send quarterly progress reports to the Empowered Institution which will make a consolidated progress report once every quarter for review by the Empowered Committee.

Disbursement of Grant

(1) A Grant under this scheme shall be disbursed only after the Private Sector Company has subscribed and expended the equity contribution required for the project and will be released in proportion to debt disbursements remaining to be disbursed thereafter.

(2) The Empowered Institution will release the Grant to the Lead Financial Institution as and when due, and obtain reimbursement thereof from the Finance Ministry.

(3) The Empowered Institution, the Lead Financial Institution and the Private Sector Company shall enter into a Tripartite Agreement for the

purposes of this scheme. The format of such Tripartite Agreement shall be prescribed by the Empowered Committee from time to time.

Revolving Fund

A revolving fund of Rs. 200 crore (Rs. Two hundred crore) shall be provided by the Finance Ministry to the Empowered Institution. The Empowered Institution shall disburse funds to the respective lead financial Institutions and claim reimbursement thereof from the Ministry of Finance.

Guidelines

The Guidelines issued vide Ministry of Finance Press Release as well as OM of F. No. 2/10/04-Inf. dated 19th August 2004 stands withdrawn with immediate effect.

SCHEME FOR MARKET DEVELOPMENT ASSISTANCE (MDA)

The Marketing Development Assistance Scheme (MDA), administered by the Ministry of Tourism, Government of India, provides financial support to approved tourism service providers (i.e. hoteliers, travel agents, tour operators, tourist transport operators etc., whose turnover include foreign exchange earnings also) for undertaking the following tourism promotional activities abroad:

(A) Sales-cum-study tour

(B) Participation in fairs/exhibitions

(C) Publicity through printed material

The Marketing Development Assistance Scheme (MDA), administered by the Ministry of Tourism, Government of India, provides financial support to approved tourism service providers (i.e. hoteliers, travel agents, tour operators, tourist transport operators etc., whose turnover include foreign exchange earnings also) for undertaking the following tourism promotional activities abroad:

Sale-cum-Study Tour

In order to encourage the small and medium level service providers to go and promote Indian tourism products abroad, Ministry of Tourism, Government of India provides financial assistance to approved tourism service providers for undertaking sale-cum-study tours to foreign countries.

Terms and Conditions

1. Financial Assistance would be permissible on travel expenses by air from India to any other country and/or by air/eurorail from one country to another country abroad, in economy excursion class fare @ 75% of the fare. This would, however be subject to an upper ceiling to Rs.75,000/- (Rupees seventy five thousands only) per tour. No financial assistance is provided for travel within India.
2. One sale-cum-study tour by the tourism service provider to a particular country in one financial year is eligible for MDA assistance.
3. The tour to single country or a group of countries shall be for a minimum of two-nights stay abroad excluding journey period.
4. Assistance shall be permissible to one regular employee/Director/ partner/ proprietor of the company.
5. The assistance would be available to tourism service providers with foreign exchange earnings up to Rs.10.00 crores (Rupees ten crores only) during the preceding financial year.

6. The company shall not be under investigation or charged/ prosecuted/ debarred/ black listed by Ministry of Tourism, Govt. of India or any other Government Agency. The service provider should furnish a declaration to this effect.
7. The applicant would furnish a declaration in the prescribed format as " I hereby declare that I have not claimed/received any financial assistance for this sale-cum-study tour from Government/ Government Agency."
8. In case of more applications, priority would be given to those service providers who have not availed financial assistance in the past under MDA Scheme.

Procedure for Submission of Application

(i) The eligible tourism service provider shall obtain prior approval of the Department of Tourism, Government of India, before undertaking the tourism promotional activity/tour abroad. The application shall be submitted direct to the Additional Director-General (Tourism), Department of Tourism, Transport Bhawan, Sansad Marg, New Delhi, in the prescribed format (Annexure-I) at least 14 days in advance, along with following documents:

1. Proof of approval of the company by Department of Tourism (Copy of approval letter is to be attached)
2. Certificate of Foreign Exchange Earnings duly certified by Chartered Accountant.
3. Details of financial assistance availed during the last three years from the Government including Ministry of Commerce/FIEO and Department of Tourism.

(ii) After undertaking the tourism promotional activity/ tour abroad for which prior approval had been accorded by the DOT, tourism service provider would submit the application for MDA claim, in the prescribed format, to the Ministry of Tourism, Government of India, immediately on return to India but positively within one month of his/her return to India, along with the following documents:

(a) Details of financial assistance availed during the last three years from the Government including Ministry of Commerce/FIEO & Department of Tourism.

(b) Certificate of Foreign Exchange Earnings duly certified by Chartered Accountant.

(c) Self-certified copy of approval certificate issued by the Ministry of Tourism.

(d) Legible photocopy of passport highlighting the entries about departure from India and arrival in India and also the countries visited. In case passport does not have arrival/ departure dates regarding visits to various countries, documentary evidence such as Hotel Bills, Boarding pass, lodging pass, etc. may be submitted.

(e) Original air ticket/jacket used during the journey along with three self-certified photocopies. The following details should be given separately in a statement:

i) Name of the Traveller

ii) Ticket number

iii) Flight No.

iv) Date of Departure from India

v) Sectors/countries visited

vi) Class in which travelled

vii) Economy excursion class fare for sectors/ countries visited.

(f) Brief Report about the tour and achievements.

(g) Claim form received after one month of return to India or wherein the deficiencies in the claim as intimated are not fully completed within 30 days of the date of information given, would not be entertained and would be rejected.

Participation in Trade Fairs and Exhibitions

The Ministry of Tourism, Government of India provides financial assistance to approved tourism service providers for participation in tourism related trade fairs and exhibitions abroad.

Terms and Conditions

1) Financial Assistance would be permissible on travel expenses by air from India to any other country & by air/eurorail from one country to another country abroad, in economy excursion class fair and/or charges of the built up furnished stall, electricity and water charges etc. @75% to the service providing companies. This would, however, be subject to an upper ceiling of Rs.1,10,000/- (Rupees One Lakh and Ten Thousand only) per participation. No financial assistance is provided for travel within India.

2) A maximum of only five participations in a particular trade fair/exhibition by a tourism service provider would be eligible for MDA assistance.

3) Assistance for travel expenses would be permissible to one regular employee/ Director/partner/ proprietor of the company.
4) The assistance would be available to companies with foreign exchange earnings up to Rs.10.00 crores (Rupees Ten Crores only) during the preceding financial year.
5) The company shall not be under investigation or charged/ prosecuted/ debarred/ black-listed by Ministry of Tourism, Government of India or any other Government Agency. The service provider should furnish a declaration to this effect.
6) The applicant would furnish a declaration in the prescribed format as " I hereby declare that I have not claimed/received any financial assistance for participation in this fair/exhibition from Government/Government Agency."
7) In case of more applications, priority would be given to those service providers who have not availed financial assistance in the past under MDA Scheme.

Procedure for Submission of Application

(i) The eligible tourism service provider shall obtain prior approval of the Ministry of Tourism, Government of India, before proceeding abroad to participate in trade fair/ exhibition. The application shall be submitted direct to the Additional Director-General (Tourism), Ministry of Tourism, Transport Bhawan, Sansad Marg, New Delhi, in the prescribed format at least 14 days in advance, along with following documents:

1. Proof of approval of the company by Department of Tourism (Copy of approval letter may be attached).

2. Certificate of Foreign Exchange Earnings duly certified by Chartered Accountant.
3. Details of financial assistance availed during the last three years from the Government including Ministry of Commerce/FIEO & Department of Tourism.

(ii) After participating in the Trade Fair/ Exhibition abroad for which prior approval had been accorded by the DOT, tourism service provider would submit the application for MDA claim, in the prescribed format, direct to the Department of Tourism, Government of India, immediately on return to India but positively within one month of his/her return to India, along with the following documents:

a) Details of financial assistance availed during the last three years from the Government including Ministry of Commerce/FIEO and Department of Tourism

b) Certificate of Foreign Exchange Earnings duly certified by Chartered Accountant.

c) Self-certified copy of approval certificate issued by the DOT.

d) Legible photocopy of passport highlighting the entries about departure from India and arrival in India and also the countries visited. In case passport does not have arrival/ departure dates regarding visits to various countries, documentary evidence such as Hotel Bills, Boarding Pass, lodging pass etc. may be submitted.

e) Original air ticket/jacket used during the journey along with three self certified photocopies. The following details should be given separately in a statement:

i) Name of the Traveller

ii) Ticket number

iii) Flight No.

iv) Date of Departure from India

v) Sectors/countries visited

vi) Class in which travelled

vii) Economy excursion class fare for sectors / countries visited.

f) Original copy of receipts/bank advice etc. along with three photocopies, evidencing payment(s) made; if applicable.

g) Brief Report about the participation and achievements.

h) Claim form received after one month of return to India or wherein the deficiencies in the claim as intimated are not fully completed within 30 days of the date of information given, would not be entertained and would be rejected.

Publicity through Printed Material

The Ministry of Tourism, Government of India provide financial assistance under the MDA Scheme to approved tourism service providers for production of tourism related publicity material for distributing in foreign countries and in tourism related fairs and festivals abroad in order to promote Indian tourism products.

Terms and Conditions

1. Cost of production of publicity material like product catalogue, brochure, information handout etc., for use abroad during sales cum study tour, participation in trade fair/exhibition, MOT

sponsored buyer cum seller meet/trade delegation etc., would be permissible for assistance under MDA scheme @25% of the total approved cost subject to an upper ceiling of Rs.15,000/- (Rupees Fifteen Thousands only).

2. Assistance would be provided once in a financial year.
3. A copy of the publicity material is to be submitted along with the claim.
4. Quotations from a minimum of three printers are to be obtained and submitted along with the claim. Assistance will be allowed on the lowest quotation subject to the upper ceiling as mentioned above.
5. The company shall not be under investigation/ charged/prosecuted/ Debarred/ blacklisted by Ministry of Tourism, Government of India or any other Government Agency. The service provider should furnish a declaration to this effect.
6. The applicant would furnish a declaration in the prescribed format as " I hereby declare that I have not claimed/received any financial assistance for production of this publicity material from Government/Government Agency.".
7. In case of more applications, priority would be given to those service providers who have not availed financial assistance in the past under MDA Scheme.

Procedure for Submission of Application

(i) The eligible tourism service provider shall obtain prior approval of the Department of Tourism, Government of India, before printing of publicity material for distribution abroad. The application shall be submitted direct to the Additional

Director-General (Tourism), Ministry of Tourism, Transport Bhawan, Sansad Marg, New Delhi, in the prescribed format at least 14 days in advance, along with following documents:

1. Proof of approval of the company by Department of Tourism (Copy of approval letter may be attached)
2. Certificate of Foreign Exchange Earnings duly certified by Chartered Accountant.
3. Details of financial assistance availed during the last three years from the Government including Ministry of Commerce/FIEO & Ministry of Tourism.

ii) After distribution of the publicity material abroad for which prior approval had been accorded by the DOT, tourism service provider would submit the application for MDA claim, in the prescribed format along with necessary documents as indicated in the claim form, direct to the Ministry of Tourism, Government of India, immediately on return to India but positively within one month of his/her return to India, along with the necessary documents.

General Conditions Governing the MDA Scheme

1. For sale-cum-study tour, a tourism service provider is eligible for financial assistance under MDA Scheme for a maximum of two trips in one financial year.
2. For participation in fairs/exhibitions abroad, a tourism service provider is eligible for financial assistance under MDA Scheme to participate in two exhibitions/fairs abroad in one financial year.

3. For production/printing of publicity material, MDA would be available once in a financial year.
4. The financial benefit under MDA Scheme would be given up to a maximum of only two times to the same person in one financial year, irrespective of the number of tourism service providing companies he/she is associated with.
5. These revised MDA guidelines are in supercession to guidelines issued vide this Department's letter No. 15-TP(58)/2001 dated 21.8.2003.
6. These Revised Guidelines will come in force with effect from 16th March, 2004 and till further orders.

SOCIETY TO PROMOTE TOURISM, LAUNCHED BY MINISTRY OF TOURISM

It has been felt for a long time that marketing of India's tourism should be highly focussed, highly professional and highly innovative. Whilethe Govt. of India Tourist Offices in 18 destinations overseas have been promoting India tourism product, it is generally believed that it has fallen short of expectations. Being an extension of the Governmental activity, the Govt. of India Tourist Offices do not have the type of freedom nor the type of resources that are essential for high level publicity and promotion through electronic media and otherwise. The Ministry of Tourism, therefore, took the initiative of having a dialogue with the industry with a view of set up an organisation fully funded and driven by the leaders of hospitality and travel industry with a set of marketing professionals who could meet the objectives and take the marketing efforts much beyond the activities of the Govt. of India Tourist Offices.

After almost 6 months of consultations amongst the industry leaders facilitated by the Govt. of India, Ministry of Tourism, a society has been formed under the Societies's Registration Act to which the industry would provide funds for start up and subsequent operations.

It is a great day for the tourism in this country when all the players in the tourism sector have come together on one platform to promote and build * equity for India's Tourism overseas.

The Society will work for the following objectives :

1. To create brand equity for Indian Tourism product and related services.
2. To promote and market India overseas as a tourist destination.
3. To increase coorperation and unanimity amongst entities involved in tourism related activities in India and abroad.
4. To communicate with Central and State Government and other public bodies within or outside India to achieve the above objectives.
5. To make representations to local and Central Authorities on any matter connected with promotion of tourism.
6. To invest the money and the property of the society not immediately required for the purpose of its objects in such securities or in such manners as may from time to time be determined and subject to the approved modes of investments under the Income Tax Act, 1961.
7. To raise any moneys required for the purposes of the society upon such terms and such manner as may be determined.

8. To affiliate, aid, end to receive aid from international organisations, Govts, any other society, society, company, corporation, firm or person promoting or intending to promote any of the objects of the society and to subscribe to or aid any such society, society, company, corporation, firm or person with a view to obtain any advantage or benefit for the purpose of society and to subscribe to any fund or society as may be considered deserving from time to time.
9. To subscribe, to become a member of and cooperate with any other society, whether incorporated or not, whose objects are all together or in part similar to those of this society and to procure from and to communicate to any such society, such information as may be likely to forward the objects of the society.
10. To do all such things as may be conducive to development of tourism related trade or incidental to attainment of the above objects or any of them.

The following have signed the Articles of Association as the founding members :

1. ITC Hotels Ltd.
2. Asian Hotels Ltd.
3. Indian Hotels Ltd.
4. East India Hotels
5. C&MD (ITDC)
6. Travel Corpn. of India
7. SITA World Travel (India) Ltd.
8. Thomos Cook
9. Director General of Tourism (Honorary Member)

Each founding member of the Society will make a contribution of Rs. 15.00 Lakhs as seed money and a membership fee of Rs. 25000/- per annum. The office of the Society will be located in Ashok Hotel, New Delhi.

Membership

Anybody, corporate, firm, partnership or person who is engaged in the business of hospitality, travel and tourism or tourism related activities and approved, where applicable by the Ministry of Tourism in this regard shall be eligible for membership of the society on payment of prescibed membership fee as per the Rules and Regulations of the Society.

7

THE UK TOURISM INDUSTRY

The contribution made by the industry to employment, GDP and the balance of payments is considered. The paper also looks at the characteristics of those travelling to, from and within the UK. Other issues affecting the industry are

discussed, including funding and the Government's tourism strategy. Finally, the paper presents some statistics for the worldwide tourism industry providing an indication of its global importance.

Economic Policy and Statistics House of Commons Library

Library Research Papers are compiled for the benefit of Members of Parliament and their personal staff. Authors are available to discuss the contents of these papers with Members and their staff but cannot advise members of the general public.

Summary of Main Points

There is little doubt that the tourist industry is an important sector of the UK economy. Over 25½ million visitors came to the UK in 1999 and estimates suggest that total tourism expenditure was around £61 billion, and that total employment in tourism-related industries was nearly 1.8 million people

The tourism industry's contribution to GDP can be measured in terms of the revenue generated by tourists. Provisional figures for 1999 show that overseas tourists spent over £13 billion in the UK, a slight fall from 1998. Expenditure by domestic tourists (people who spent at least a night away from home) was estimated at £16 billion in 1999. This was a rise of 14% on the £14 billion spent in 1998. Total tourism revenue, excluding expenditure by UK tourists on day trips, contributed about 3.6% to GDP. The tourism industry is highly fragmented, with a large number of small businesses. The Government estimates that there are around 125,000 businesses in the UK industry, 80% of which have a turnover of less than £250,000 per annum. The characteristics of the industry, along with its significance to the UK economy, have led successive governments to fund a variety of bodies that exist to promote tourism both at home and overseas. There are currently five statutory tourist boards: the British Tourist Authority, the English Tourism Council and the tourist boards for Scotland, Wales and Northern Ireland. Since entering office in 1997, the Government has undertaken a wide-ranging review of tourism policy. The results of the review were published in February 1999 in the report

Tomorrow's Tourism. It set an overall target for the UK tourism industry to match the global rate of tourism growth by 2010.

Tourism is the world's largest industry and so is of vital importance to the global economy. Its contribution has risen dramatically over recent decades. The World Travel and Tourism Council (WTTC) estimate that in 1999 travel and tourism were directly and indirectly responsible for generating 11% of world GDP and 200 million jobs across the global economy.

DEFINITION

Defining the tourist industry is difficult. It is not an industry that is grouped into a single heading within the Standard Industrial Classification (SIC). The defining feature of tourism is not the product, but the purchaser, the 'tourist'. Most definitions concentrate on the services that a number of different industries, such as the travel industry; hotels and catering; retailing and entertainment provide to tourists. The internationally agreed definition of tourism says that:

Tourism comprises the activities of persons travelling to and staying places outside their usual environment for not more than one consecutive year for leisure, business and other purposes.

The information presented in this paper is taken from different sources and so coverage should always be taken into account and estimates treated as approximations of the scale of the industry, rather than precise measures. Nonetheless, there is little doubt that the tourist industry is an important sector of the UK economy. Over 25½ million visitors came to the UK in 1999 and estimates suggest that tourism expenditure was around £61 billion, and total employment in tourism-related industries was nearly 1.8 million people.

EMPLOYMENT

For reasons outlined above it is difficult to measure the exact number of jobs that are either directly or indirectly dependent on tourism. While the business generated by tourists is crucial to many hotels, restaurants, travel services and entertainment facilities, it does not account for all the business of these sectors and in some regions of the country it will make up very little of the activity.

The most commonly cited employment data ignore these problems and provide information for employment in sectors that depend on tourism for some of their business. These include employment in the following sectors:

Hotels & other tourist accommodation (SIC 551,552)

Restaurants, cafes etc (SIC 553)

Bars, public houses and night-clubs (SIC 554)

Travel agencies and tour operators (SIC 633)

Libraries, museums & other cultural activities (SIC 925)

Sports & other recreation activities (SIC 926, 927)

While these sectors will depend on tourism for some of the business, they are by no means entirely dependent on it, and will be often used by non-tourists. However this method is sometimes justified on the grounds that while it includes a certain amount of non-tourism related employment, it also excludes some which ought to be included such as employees in transport services.

CONTRIBUTION OF THE UK'S GROSS DOMESTIC PRODUCT

The tourism industry's contribution to gross domestic product can be measured in terms of the revenue generated by tourists. Provisional figures for 1999 show that overseas tourists spent over £12.6 billion in the UK, this was a slight fall from £12.7 billion in 1998.

This figure does not include payments for sea or air travel to or from the UK; the British Tourist Authority (BTA) estimate that such fare payments to British carriers totalled around £3.3 billion in 1999.

Expenditure by domestic tourists (people who spent at least a night away from home) was estimated at £16 billion in 1999. This was a rise of 14% on the £14 billion spent in 1998.

Total tourism revenue in 1999 was £31.9 million, equivalent to 3.6% of GDP. The share of GDP attributable to tourism peaked in 1996 at 3.9%.

These figures underestimate tourism's share of GDP as they exclude money spent by UK residents on day trips within the UK. The UK Leisure Day Visitors Survey collects information about day visitors, and estimates that in 1998 they spent approximately £31 billion.

If this is included then the share of tourism as a proportion of GDP rises to about 6%. This measure is of tourism's gross contribution to GDP. In fact, UK residents holidaying abroad will reduce the tourism industry's total share. The amount that UK residents spend on tourism activities abroad is effectively an import of goods and services and so acts to reduce gross domestic product.

In 1999 UK residents spent £21.7 billion whilst overseas, an increase of 12% from 1998.

If subtracted from total expenditure on UK tourist services (£31.9 billion excluding day trips), this implies net revenue of £10.2 billion, or 1.1% of GDP. In fact net contributions to GDP would be even lower than this, as this takes no account of fare payment by UK residents to overseas c arriers.Tourism's net contribution to GDP has fallen over recent years as UK residents' expenditure abroad has risen at a faster rate than total expenditure on tourism in the UK.

This will reflect a number of factors, including the less favourable exchange rate; higher real incomes; the greater availability of cheap package tours and of course the unreliability of the British weather.

BALANCE OF PAYMENTS

Previous section looked at the tourism industry's overall contribution to UK GDP. This section considers in more detail the flows of tourism expenditure into and out of the UK. The flows of tourism expenditure by UK residents abroad and by overseas visitors in the UK are treated as imports and exports and so play an important role in the calculation of the UK's balance of payments. For the purpose of national accounting these flows are recorded in the travel account. The provision of UK goods and services to overseas visitors is treated as a balance of payments credit (an export). The purchase of goods and services by UK residents while abroad is a balance of payments debit (an import). Thus every pound that visitors to the UK spend on items such as hotel accommodation, souvenirs and domestic travel makes a positive contribution to the UK balance of payments and every pound spent abroad by UK residents is a negative contribution.

Expenditure on travel to and from the UK is not included in the travel account but, where appropriate, appears in separate accounts for civil aviation and sea transport. For these purposes a visitor is someone who intends to stay in a country for less than 12 months whatever the purpose of the visit. Thus the travel account includes those travelling on business, for educational or health reasons, or to visit relatives as well as those who are holidaying.

The table below summarises the travel account in the years 1989 to 1999. The account is divided between business and leisure travel. For the purposes of the travel account, leisure travel includes all non-business reasons for travelling. Overall travel credits in 1999 were some £14.3 billion (£4.2 billion for business travel and £10.1 billion for leisure travel). This makes tourism a larger source of export earnings than, for example, exports of motor cars (£9.7 billion) and food, beverages & tobacco (£9.8 billion). However, earnings were significantly exceeded by debits of £22.5 billion (£4.4 billion for business travel and £18.1 billion for leisure travel). Thus, in 1999 there was a deficit on the travel account of some £8.2 billion (£0.3 billion for business travel and £8.0 billion for leisure travel). The account moved from surplus in the late-1970s to deficit from the mid- 1980s onwards. The deficit is mostly on leisure travel but in 1994, 1996, 1998 and 1999 there were also deficits on business travel.

TOURISM FORECASTS

All forecasts are in cash prices, but given that the BTA are expecting inflation in tourism- related activities to be around 3% per year from 1998, these estimates do imply an increase in expenditure in the UK in real terms of around 4% per annum. Tourist expenditure by UK residents, both abroad and domestically, is forecast to grow at a faster rate than expenditure by overseas visitors to the UK.

These forecasts suggest continued strong growth in overseas tourism from the UK. However forecast growth in tourism within the UK and for overseas visitors to the UK is considerably lower.

Overseas Visitors

The number of overseas visitors to the UK has more than doubled over the last 20 years. The most significant trend has been the change in the proportion of overseas visitors that came from Europe; this has risen from 55% of all visitors to the UK in 1985 to a peak of 70% in 1996. There has been a levelling off at about 68% in the last three years. In 1998 there were 25.7 million overseas visits to the UK. Visitor numbers from Europe have more than doubled from about 8 million in 1980 to over 17 million in 1999. The number of visitors from North America has increased from about 2 million in 1980 to about 4½ million in 1999; this is just under 20% of all visitors. Table 6 gives a breakdown of UK visits by their purpose.

Domestic Tourists

This section looks at the latest trends in domestic tourism. For these purposes domestic tourism encompasses all UK residents who spend at least one night away from home but remain within the UK. It therefore excludes day-trips. During 1998, UK residents are estimated to have taken about 122 million trips of one night or more away from home, lasting 438 million nights and spending £14 billion. Holidays were the main reason for trips in 1998 with 53% of trips, 65% of nights and 70% of spending all due to holidaying. A third of trips were to visit friends and relatives, but these tend to be shorter trips and cheaper, lasting only a fifth of all nights away from home and involving only 10% of spending.

Unsurprisingly the main reason for UK residents to travel abroad was for a holiday (64%). The majority of holidays taken were inclusive, i.e. package tours; these accounted for a third of all trips. People on business trips spent the most per day, £91 on average, compared to spending per day on holiday trips of £37, and £18 a day when visiting friends and relatives.

SUPPORT STRUCTURE FOR THE TOURISM INDUSTRY

The tourism industry is highly fragmented, with a large number of small businesses. The Government estimates that there are around 125,000 businesses in the UK industry, 80% of which have a turnover of less than £250,000 per annum. The disparate nature of the industry creates difficulties for both businesses and customers. For businesses, a lack of co-ordination could hamper the industry's ability to respond effectively to changes in market conditions. The presence of a large number of small businesses also affects promotional activity within the industry. Individually, the many businesses would find it difficult or impossible to fund promotional activities within the UK, let alone overseas. Furthermore, the free-rider principle applies - any given business might benefit from the advertisements of another facility in the area, and so might not consider it worthwhile to advertise their facilities, since they may not see the full benefit. For example, a hotel might benefit from the custom generated by publicity for a leisure facility in the area, and so might not feel it worth the cost of advertising themselves.

Thus, advertising and promotional activity may suffer as a result of the industry's structure. From the point of view of potential customers, such effects on the level of advertising and promotion is a disadvantage as it makes it harder to compare facilities and assess value for money. Even if information were available, it would be very costly and time- consuming to collect information on prices and attractions, in the absence of any co-ordinating body. The advent of the Internet has the potential for individual businesses to provide information to, and to take bookings from, a wider number of potential customers. However a co-ordinating body can still assist visitors by providing a central point for enquiries and by publishing guides with comprehensive details on facilities, prices, locations, standards etc.

These characteristics of the industry, along with its significance to the UK economy, have led successive governments to fund a variety of bodies that exist to promote tourism both at home and overseas. These bodies also help to co-ordinate the many small businesses within the industry by providing help and advice, encouraging higher standards and developing a cohesive strategy for the future. They also assist tourists by providing a central point for information. The Department for Culture, Media and Sport (formerly the Department for National Heritage) has overall responsibility for the industry. There are five statutory tourist boards: the British Tourist Authority, the English Tourism Council and the tourist boards for Scotland, Wales and Northern Ireland. The Northern Ireland Tourist Board was established under the Development of Tourist Traffic Act (Northern Ireland) 1948; all the others were set up under the Development of Tourism Act 1969.

The Government provides grant-in-aid to the Tourist Boards. The PQ below compares the levels of funding for 1999/2000, and expresses them in terms of expenditure per head. The English Tourism Council receives significantly less per head than the Scottish and Welsh Boards. It has been argued by previous Governments that this is because the tourist industry in England is well established and so does not need the same level of assistance as the industry in Wales, Scotland and Northern Ireland. The following sections look in more detail at the strategies and funding of each tourist board.

British Tourist Authority (BTA)

The BTA's responsibilities are:

To advise the Government and public bodies on tourism matters which affect Britain as a whole.

To encourage the provision and improvement of tourist facilities and amenities in Britain.

To help the UK trade reach overseas markets.

To work with the national tourist boards of England, Northern Ireland, Scotland and Wales to promote an attractive image of Britain.

To provide impartial tourist information.

To gather and disseminate market intelligence for the UK tourism industry.

In 1999 the BTA underwent a re-organisation of it operations. It now concentrates its marketing resources in 27 key markets, which in total generate 90% of all visitors to Britain. This is an attempt to rise the return on public investment from the current £27 for every £1 spent to a target of £30 by 2000-01.

The English Tourism Council

Following the 1998 Comprehensive Spending Review, the English Tourist Board was re-launched in July 1999 as the English Tourism Council (ETC). The role and organisation of this new body was set out in reply to the following PQ. Mr. Gordon Marsden: To ask the Secretary of State for Culture, Media and

Sport what decision he has made about the new national body for tourism in England.

Mr. Chris Smith: On 14 December 1998 we announced in A New Cultural Framework that we would establish a new streamlined, more strategic body to support tourism in England. An Implementation Team was set up in January, supported by an Advisory Group representing the industry. We have now considered its report, which was received on 9 April and of which a copy has been placed today in the Libraries of both

Houses. I am now able to announce more fully the details of the framework within which the new arrangements will operate under the leadership of a Chairman whom I will shortly appoint. The new body will be known as the English Tourism Council (ETC). Its prime role will be to provide strategic leadership to drive delivery of the national tourism strategy. It will have a parallel function as a centre of excellence supporting the industry in five key areas: research, in particular work on emerging markets and sectors; quality, including work on the accommodation schemes and also attractions and seaside resorts; overseeing systems for data collection and analysis; championing sustainable tourism, and wider access; and spreading news of innovative ideas and examples of best practice in all these areas of work. There will be a significant switch of funding so that most is available for tourism in the regions and I want to see a new system for its distribution. This will enable a greater proportion of the strategy to be delivered at regional level and will secure enhanced benefits for tourism in the regions. The money will continue to be passed via the ETC to the Regional Tourist Boards (RTBs), except in the case of London where the Department will pass it directly to the Mayor of London, while recommending that the London Tourist Board is the most appropriate partner for delivery of the national strategy. [...]

English Regional Tourist Boards

Regional Tourist Boards (RTBs) are companies limited by guarantee and receive their income from a number of different sources. These include government funding via the ETC, local authority funding, income from members and commercial activity. As mentioned in the PQ above, accompanying the transformation of the ETC, was a move to delegate more central government funding to the regions. This is in line with the view that support for tourism - as with many other areas of government services - is better delivered closer to the consumer and industry at a regional level.

The roles and responsibilities of the Regional Tourism Boards, together with arrangements for making funding available to them were set out in a ETC document - Prospectus Under the new arrangements, funding will be based on regional needs, rather than on standard national projects as in the past, and it will allow the RTBs much greater independence and ownership, as well as increased responsibilities and accountability. The ETC invites bids for specific projects that reflect local tourism needs, these proposals are then assessed by two separate assessment panels. In 2000/01 regional tourism in England will receive £5.5 million, a 45% increase over last year. Over £4 million will be used to fund 100 tourism projects, while the remainder will be used for joint programmes such as research. Each region takes a lead in a specific tourism issue.

Scottish Tourist Board

Tourism in Scotland is the responsibility of the Scottish Executive, who fund the Scottish Tourist Board (STB). The STB plays a strategic role as the lead body in developing Scottish tourism, involving undertaking marketing and providing advice on market trends. A new strategy for Scottish Tourism was launched in February 2000 and STB will be working to deliver key elements. The Scottish Minister for Enterprise and Learning, Henry McLeish, outlined the priorities of the Scottish Tourist Board in a press release:

"I am determined that tourism will be at the centre of economic development in Scotland. The Scottish Tourist Board has a major responsibility for

delivering the Government's objectives for the tourism industry in Scotland. "Our New Strategy for Tourism launched in January sets ambitious targets for the industry to achieve and the Scottish Tourist Board has a crucial role to play in helping to deliver these. I look forward to working closely with you on this."

Additional points made in the letter were:

Mr McLeish noted that the new tourism strategy signalled a change in emphasis both for the tourist industry and for the agencies that provided it with support.

The Minister expects STB to pay particular attention to the continued development of the Ossian IT project. He has earmarked a further £3.95 million for the Board and for the Area Tourist Boards (ATBs) for this purpose. STB is required to introduce e-commerce from June of this year so that all accommodation providers who are ATB members can trade in this way if they wish to and are able to do so.

The Board is expected to pursue the longer term development of Ossian through a partnership with the private sector. It is also expected to pay particular attention to the need to develop Call Centre technology to achieve the Government's objective of a single national and international telephone number for tourism information and bookings.

The guidance asks the Board to develop a dedicated industry web-site by June of this year. This will provide information to businesses to enable them to better develop and market their product.

The Government is committed to ensuring that the benefits of tourism are enjoyed across Scotland. The Board is asked to bring forward during the course of this year proposals for developing golf, genealogy and cultural tourism. They are also asked to work with partners at the local level and in particular ATBs to develop local niche products.

The guidance recognises that improved quality of product and of services is essential if the industry is to compete effectively.

STB is asked to establish by September this year, a new team of quality advisors to provide advice to the industry. The Board is also asked to amend its accommodation Quality Assurance scheme so that businesses are required to display clearly information about prices.

Mr McLeish has asked STB to be part of a new Group that will be established to oversee implementation of the Government's strategy.

Wales Tourist Board

As a result of devolution responsibility for tourism was passed the National Assembly for Wales. The First Secretary of the Assembly recently launched a 10-year strategy for Welsh tourism, Achieving Our Potential. This aims to in create an additional 22,000 jobs and increase the industry's contribution to GDP from 7% to 8%, based on forecast tourism receipts of between £3.2 and £3.5 billion by 2010. The strategy is linked into a 49-point action plan, which will cost an estimated £1 billion to implement in full. The key elements of the strategy are:

Create a positive, distinctive and motivating identity.

Improve understanding of the roles and responsibilities of different organisations and develop opportunities for effective partnership working.

Adopt a customer focused approach which will require more useful market intelligence information to be made available to the industry.

Ensure that the tourism industry is able to realise the full benefits arising from advances in ICT.

Develop a well trained and motivated workforce.

Adopt a strategic approach to investment in tourism which identifies development priorities on the basis of market needs.

Support growth in tourism through sustainable means by extending the tourism season; spreading the benefits of tourism throughout Wales; improving business yield and effective visitor management.

In 1999/2000 the Government gave funding of £15.4 million to Wales Tourist Board. This is forecast to remain at the same level for the next few years.

Northern Ireland Tourist Board

The Chairman of the Northern Ireland Tourist Board (NITB) is currently chairing Action for Tourism 2000 Taskforce, which aims to address the deficiencies in the tourism industry in Northern Ireland. The taskforce will "encourage and secure a co-ordinated campaign of action to establish the priorities in the tourism industry, to ensure services are delivered, to co-ordinate various interests, to monitor activities and to provide advice and feedback to the Minister". The Northern Ireland Tourist Board received £9.0 million revenue expenditure grant and £5.0 million selective financial assistance from the Government in 1998/99. Under the Good Friday Agreement it has been proposed that an all-Ireland marketing company will be established. The role of this new organisation will be discussed at a future meeting of the North-South ministerial council.

TOMORROW'S TOURISM

Since entering office in 1997, the Government has undertaken a wide-ranging review of tourism policy. Much of the background work was carried out by the Tourism Forum, a body containing representatives from various sections of the industry, which was established by the Government to assist in developing its strategy. There were nine 'working groups' attached to the Tourism Forum, each of which focused and reported on one particular aspect of tourism. The results of the review were published in February 1999 in the report Tomorrow's Tourism.

It set an overall target for the tourism industry, to match the global rate of tourism growth by 2010, and three overriding objectives:

to provide the right framework for tourism to flourish;

to develop and spread quality; and

to encourage wise growth.

The core elements of the Government's strategy are enshrined in a fifteen-point action plan.

On 1 March 2000 the first Tourism Summit, a meeting between the industry and Ministers, was held to review the progress of implementing the strategy. Each interested party reported back to the Summit on the developments in the past year. The focus of the Summit was the need for Government to operate in a joined-up way in its approach to tourism and to take account of the effects on tourism when making policy decisions. Appendix one sets out each point in the action plan with the progress made on each point. The key points covered at the Summit included:

> *the Foreign and Commonwealth Office is to review regularly overseas visa sections to ensure they are as welcoming and user-friendly as possible;*
>
> *the Department for Culture, Media and Sport is to accept the unanimous recommendations of an industry-led working group on improving price transparency in hotels and will consult widely on updating legislation;*
>
> *the Home Office is to publish a White Paper proposing to modernise the liquor and public entertainment licensing law;*
>
> *the Department of Environment, Transport and the Regions will review implementation of the 1995 guidance to local authorities and the Highways Agency on signing for tourist attractions and facilities in England;*
>
> *a pilot internet site offering visitors public transport information linked to local attractions, will be launched in Cumbria and will provide valuable lessons for a possible extension nationwide;*
>
> *the Ministry of Agriculture Fisheries and Food is working on a project to encourage greater links between local food producers, whose products often have a global reputation, and the tourism industry; and*
>
> *the Government will provide financial and practical support to the industry's second Careers Festival in October 2000.*

8

WORLD TOURIST INDUSTRY

Tourism is the world's largest industry and so is of vital importance to the world economy. It's contribution has risen dramatically over recent decades: in 1950 an estimated 25.3 million international trips were made world-wide, by 1999, the estimated figure was some 26 times higher at over 660 million trips. Even since 1985, the number of trips has more than doubled.

The World Travel and Tourism Council (WTTC) estimate that in 1999 travel and tourism were directly and indirectly responsible for generating across the global economy:

11% of GDP;

200 million jobs;

8% of total employment; and

5.5 million new jobs per year until 2010.

The chart below shows the UK's percentage share of world tourism receipts and arrivals. The share of receipts has been generally declining for the past 20 years, although there has been some upturn over the last five years.

Worldwide, the number of international tourist trips rose by 8.7% per year on average between 1980 and 1997. Fastest growth was in the East Asia/Pacific region (which includes China, Hong Kong, Singapore and Thailand) and in the Americas. The latest 1999 preliminary figures from the World Tourism Organisation suggest the UK has fallen below China to sixth place and that the East Asia and the Pacific region as a whole continued to have strong growth rates and to have recovered from a slight downturn following the financial crisis. Arrivals in the region increased by 10.7% last year. Malaysia was particularly successful, with a growth rate of 43%.

OTHER ISSUES

National Minimum Wage

The profile of employment within the tourism industry (high proportions of female, young and part-time workers) meant that, after the retail sector, the hospitality sector is the sector with most workers affected by the national minimum wage (NMW) which came in to force on 1 April 1999.

The Low Pay Commission undertook some research in to the immediate affects of introducing the minimum wage. A survey of members of the British Hospitality Association found that the impact seemed to be limited to the hotel and catering sectors with nearly three-quarters reporting no effect on their business. The survey found that only 12% of businesses in London and the South East were affected, compared to between 27% and 38% of firms in other regions. The Commission said that introduction of the minimum wage was positively accepted in the sector. It quoted evidence from Tourism South and West Wales who said that a number of employers had expressed the view that "the introduction of the NMW has ensured that we can lay the low wage ghost which has haunted the careers in tourism and hospitality for so long".

The British Hospitality Association's main compliant about the NMW is the lack of regional variation.

VAT on Hotels

There is a general feeling in the tourism industry that one of the reasons that the UK is losing its market share of world tourism (see section VII) is because hotel prices are not competitive. The UK has one of the highest rates of VAT on accommodation in the EU; only Denmark levies a higher rate.

A study conducted on behalf of the BTA by Deloitte & Touche, The Economic Effects of Changing VAT Rates on the British Tourism and Leisure Industry, found the evidence of that international tourism receipts and expenditure are strongly influenced by the price of the UK's tourism services.

The report highlighted the experiences of the Irish Republic whose government halved the VAT on visitor accommodation and restaurant meals in the mid 1980s. Following this reduction visitor numbers increased sharply, generating an increase in foreign exchange earnings of more than 50%. There was also a switch in behaviour of Irish residents who became more likely to holiday in Ireland. The report said that reducing the rate of VAT applying to visitor accommodation from 17.5% to 8%, would cost the Exchequer £400 million a year through the direct loss of VAT receipts. However against this are the gains from additional income and corporation tax receipts and savings in social security payments which would rise from £400 million a year to more than £700 million after ten years. It would also result in the creation of about 50,000 new jobs.

The British Hospitality Association (BHA) has lobbied hard on this matter, Martin Couchman, Deputy Chief Executive, BHA said:

The imposition of VAT at such a high rate has an impact on the industry's prices, and this is holding this country back in the highly competitive international tourism market. We could be even more successful - and attract more visitors - if the level of VAT was reduced. The Government however has made it clear that they are not considering reducing the rate of VAT on accommodation: Mr. Hoyle: To ask the Chancellor of the Exchequer (1) what assessment he has made of the advantages and disadvantages of reducing VAT on hotel room charges; (2) what plans he has to use the taxation system to promote the UK tourism industry.

Dawn Primarolo: The Government currently have no such plans. UK tourism is enjoying record success and the tourism industry is about to benefit from the long term strategy "Tomorrow's Tourism: a growth industry for the new millennium" recently announced by my right hon. Friend the Secretary of State for Culture, Media and Sport.

This issue was debated at length in the Lords on 12 November 1998, when Lord Gordon of Strathblane argued for a cut in VAT on hotel accommodation to 12.5% or 8%. Speaking for the Government Lord McIntosh of Haringey said: [...] The noble Lord, Lord Rowallan, seems to believe that if one cuts the rate of

VAT on hotel accommodation by 10 per cent. one is somehow cutting prices by the same percentage. Nothing could be further from the truth. Only 34 per cent. Of tourism spend in this country is on hotel accommodation. If VAT were cut to 8 per cent, that would be a reduction of 3 per cent. in total tourism spend. If it were reduced to the average of 12.5 per cent., to which my noble friend Lord Gordon of Strathblane referred, that would produce a cut of less than 2 per cent. in total spend.

That is the absolute maximum because 12 per cent. of expenditure on hotels is by UK business visitors who can recoup the tax anyway.

Some £427 million is spent by overseas conference visitors to this country, many of whom can recover VAT. Also, 18 per cent. of hotel expenditure involves establishments that are below the VAT threshold. The effect on prices of cuts in VAT of the kind proposed would be only 1 per cent. or 2 per cent., to be generous. Noble Lords are right to say that tourism expenditure is price sensitive but the claim that matters can be improved by the sort of cut in VAT proposed is not proven. In fact, it is highly improbable. [...]

Licensing Laws

The Government has recently published a white paper containing their proposed changes to the licensing laws, Time for Reform: Proposals for the Modernisation of out Licensing Laws.

The proposals include:

A single integrated scheme for licensing premises which sell alcohol, provide public entertainment or provide refreshment at night.

A new system of personal licences which allow holders to sell or to serve alcohol for consumption on or off any premises possessing a premises licence. (Places providing public entertainment or refreshment at night which does not involve alcohol, would require a premises licence only.)

To minimise public disorder resulting form fixed closing time, flexible opening hours with the potential for up to 24 hour opening 7 days a week, subject to consideration of the impact on local residents.

The Government hopes that the changes will end the confusion of overseas visitors. The Tourism Minister, Janet Anderson said "Many visitors come form countries were liquor licensing laws are quite different. They find our regulations archaic and confusing. They are taken aback when time is called at 11pm in a public house, or told in a restaurant that they cannot order a bottle of wine because it is midnight"

The British Hospitality Association reacted favourably to the proposals:

> *The British Hospitality Association welcomes the White Paper on licensing reform as a major step towards freeing the hotel and restaurant industry from archaic restrictions and regulations concerning the service of drink.*
>
> *"The White Paper is most welcome," says Phil Phillips, the BHA's technical services manager. "It contains many of the amendments to the licensing legislation that we were seeking. For once, government has listened to the industry's reasoned arguments and introduced sensible proposals which treat members of the public as adults. "It will have the added benefit of helping tourism because it provides flexibility. It will enable businesses to tailor opening hours to meet local trade demands and allows visitors to Britain to have a drink whenever they want it - something which has been denied them in the past and which has always been an irritant to them."*

TOMORROW'S TOURISM ACTION POINTS

Tourism Summit

Progress on the 15 Action Points set out in Tomorrow's Tourism

1. A blueprint for the sustainable development of tourism to safeguard our countryside, heritage and culture for future generations Leading role given to ETC, which has set up Task Force and will publish a strategy paper in Autumn 2000. Rural and Urban White Papers to be published later this year.
2. Initiatives to widen access to tourism for the 40% of people who do not take a long holiday ETC has conducted research into holiday non-participation. Research results and outputs from working group sessions will help shape ETC policy. In March ETC will publish "Accessible Britain 2000", a practical travel guide for people with disabilities.
3. More money for a more focused and aggressive overseas promotion programme to bring in more overseas visitors The Government has granted the BTA an extra £5 million over the period 1999-2000 to 2001- 2002. The BTA now has a target to increase from £27 to £30 its return on investment of each £1 of grant-in- aid.
4. New internet systems to deliver more world-wide tourist bookings for Britain and to provide information on attractions and travel options The BTA is on course to launch 36 new websites - one for each country where it is active or has an information service - by early 2000. 19 are already live. Some RTBs now have IT strategies and most regional websites now link to national product databases. Pilot project launched to integrate transport and accommodation data
5. New computerised booking and information systems to make it easier for people to book

accommodation and travel The ETC is promoting Impact Through IT - guidelines for tourism organisations on the use of destination management systems. ETC is also working to secure compatibility of data between different systems. BTA's VisitBritain website now offers on line booking or e-mail enquiry facilities for some hotels and some local pilot schemes are underway

6. A major careers festival and image campaign to raise the profile and promote the image of careers in the hospitality industry Held successfully in June 1999. Reached over 100,000 potential employees. Second festival planned for October 2000
7. A hospitality industry programme to sign up 500 employers to work towards Investors in People standard to help raise the quality of training in the industry 800 have already signed up and 1000 more are going to be signed up. The Hospitality Training Foundation are leading this campaign
8. New strategic national body for England to provide leadership to the English tourism industry The English Tourism Council (ETC) was launched on 12 July with a new Framework for Action. Under the new Chairman, it has reconstituted the Tourism Forum; set up Task Forces to deal with key issues like: transport, sustainable tourism, resort regeneration and future trends; and made progress on other issues including these Action Points
9. A new grading scheme for all hotels and guest houses to give holiday makers and business travellers consistent quality they can rely on The ETC, together with the AA and the RAC, launched

the new quality standards to consumers on 13 September. Participation in the new scheme has continued to grow (self-catering 10%, serviced 13%, from 98/99).

10. New targets for hotel development in London and a further £4.5 million for marketing to\ exploit its potential as a premier location for business travellers and holiday makers and as a gateway to Britain The Government has announced a further £4.5 million for the overseas promotion of London over the period 1999-2000 to 2001-02. Hotel targets are on schedule
11. More integrated promotion of our wonderful cultural, heritage and countryside attractions to enable visitors to enjoy the full range of what Britain has to offer More integration taking place in regional & local destination marketing, and new BTA promotions will help meet this objective. RTBs supporting work on regional & local cultural strategies. BTA co- ordinates UK Cultural and Tourism Group to share experiences and good practice in cultural tourism
12. The development of innovative niche markets, such as film tourism and sports tourism, to unlock the full potential of Britain's unique cultural and natural heritage ETC has completed research on potential niche markets, and will be working on market development strategies for the best markets identified. BTA Movie map was launched in July 1999. "Green Britain" map launched in September 1999. BTA launched the sports tourism strategy in January 2000.
13. Encouraging the regeneration of traditional resorts to allow leisure and business visitors to enjoy high-quality amenities and services The

Government has reflected the needs of resort areas in the new maps proposed for the Objective 2 Structural Fund and Assisted Areas. The ETC is undertaking research, including on best practice. Its Resorts Task Force will consider ways in which resorts can develop sensible, effective regeneration plans and is due to report by the end of 2000.

14. More central government support for the regions to give each part of the country better resources to develop their own identity and strengths Creation of ETC has freed more money to go to RTBs. ETC decisions on RTB bids were announced on 9 February 2000 with allocations made on the merit of individual regional proposals and how they best fit with the national strategy; and lead RTBs identified in key areas.
15. A high profile annual Tourism Summit bringing together industry and government to monitor progress, plan future action and keep all sides working in partnership towards the same objectives Held on 1 March 2000.

NEWZEALAND'S TOURISM INDUSTRY

A key characteristic of New Zealand's tourism industry is its importance to our economy. Tourism has a substantial role in job-creation and export earnings. It is a demand-driven, service-oriented industry experiencing rapid growth and innovation. The industry now faces the challenge of balancing economic, social and environmental dimensions to achieve sustainable growth.

Economic Driver

Tourism plays a key role in the growth of our economy through employment, foreign exchange earnings, investment and regional development. Tourism directly and indirectly contributes almost 10% of New Zealand's GDP.

Tourism is one of New Zealand's largest export industries, with international visitor expenditure in 2002 of $6.1 billion. The most recently available data for Domestic tourism is for the 2001 calendar year, which reports Domestic tourism generated $6.9 billion. See more information on visitor expenditure in the International Visitor Survey and Domestic Travel Study.

Tourism is a vehicle for regional and community development. Many tourists look for unique, unspoilt or 'off the beaten track' locations, so are drawn to small towns and provincial regions that often most need economic development. Tourist interest in the Maori culture also fosters development of Maori communities and businesses.

Substantial Role in Job Creation

The New Zealand tourism industry is made up of 10 major public-listed companies and between 13,500 and 18,000 small to medium enterprises.

Tourism supports nearly one job in ten in New Zealand, with around 90,000 full-time equivalent jobs provided directly through tourism and an estimated 60,000 indirectly. See the Tourism Satellite Account for more information about tourism's contribution to the economy.

Defined by Customer Demand

Tourism is defined by customer demand. When a tourist takes a taxi, for example, that taxi service becomes part of the tourism industry. In this respect, tourism cuts across a broad range of industries, including:

- transport,
- accommodation,
- retail,
- catering and
- financial services.

Many other sectors benefit through provision of goods and services that support tourism businesses, for example:

- construction,
- printing and publishing,
- manufacturing and
- insurance.

As a result, tourism policy issues involve a broad spectrum of areas and interests. Read more about the different policy issues in the Policy section.

Long-Haul Niche Destination

Whilst international tourist arrivals have been growing rapidly over the last two decades, New Zealand remains a niche destination. Our geographic location makes us a long-haul destination - it takes over 8 hours to get here from most countries.

We have a different appeal than high volume tourist destinations like France, Spain, USA and the UK. Research indicates that New Zealand appeals to people seeking adventure, connection with nature, relaxation and revitalisation. Read more about New Zealand's appeal.

Draws on "Public Goods"

Tourism often draws on public facilities and goods such as oceans & rivers, beaches, parks and reserves. By drawing on these resources, tourism impacts on host communities. Careful planning and resource management is required to preserve the quality of these public goods for both tourists and host communities. Read about resource management and sustainable development in the New Zealand Tourism Strategy 2010.

Sold Overseas and Consumed Onshore

International tourism is a unique type of export - products & services are sold to customers overseas but consumed in New Zealand. This presents the challenge of ensuring that the total tourism experience is consistent with visitor expectations when they purchase their trips to NZ. Read more about consumer needs and motivations and perceptions of New Zealand.

Intangible and Perishable Experiences

Tourism largely involves intangible experiences that customers cannot keep, except in photos, videos and memories. Tourism products and services tend to be perishable in nature - for example - excess hotel rooms, airline seats or bungy jumps on one day cannot be accumulated for use at a later date.

Support Networks

There are many tourism associations to support different aspects of the tourism sector. The lead industry body is the Tourism Industry Association New Zealand- a membership based organisation representing the interests of over 3,500 businesses from throughout the tourism industry. Their purpose is to provide leadership, guidance and appropriate services for the benefit of its members in order to contribute to a viable and sustainable tourism industry.

Sector-specific organisations include the Inbound Tour Operators Council (ITOC), Holiday Accommodation Parks Association of New Zealand (HAPNZ) and the Adventure Tourism Council.

CSR IN THE TOURISM INDUSTRY?

For the past 20 or more years, sustainable development has been at the forefront of many government agendas. This debate has concluded that sustainability should be adopted as the way forward to preserve ecosystems and biodiversity, limit growth and improve the quality of life of host populations. Tourism has been put forth as a way to gain income and provide access to market opportunities for small and medium size enterprises, especially in low income countries.

There has also been no shortage of research supporting the need to keep tourism pressures in check, address existing impacts and extend the planning horizon to create more sustainable development in the longer term. The past few years have seen a steady growth in the adoption and endorsement of the principles of sustainable tourism as a development approach which has led to the creation of many initiatives to address concerns such as environmental conservation and protection.

Social issues were brought to the forefront more recently, particularly since Kofi Annans' 10-point Millennium Challenge, and include fair trade, poverty reduction, local and community economic development. Initiatives include codes of conduct, specific guidelines and certification schemes and accreditation. This study is a follow-up to earlier reports commissioned by the World Bank Group which have assessed Company Codes of Conduct and International Standards, Implementation Mechanisms for Codes of Conducts as well as various Foreign Investment Advisory Service (FIAS) reports. The objective of this study was to assess whether the development of national certification schemes may help countries to (a) address expectations of tourists, investors and supply chain actors such as tour operators and travel agencies, (b) ensure the sustainable development of their tourism industry, (c) ensure a localisation of the corporate social responsibility (CSR) agenda by guaranteeing that certification standards are developed in accordance with national criteria and (d) whether certification schemes have contributed to spreading sustainable tourism practices or would align with international criteria or standards.

This report finds a number of limitations as well as opportunities. For a variety of reasons, sustainable tourism has gained increased recognition among industry and governments. However, according to travel trade interviewees, only a small percentage of consumers pay attention to these standards and for all intents and purposes, none are willing to pay extra for adherence to environmental and/or social standards. In spite of this, industry has increasingly focused on sustainable/responsible tourism measures and practices, particularly in Europe. Industry associations, Non Governmental Organisations (NGO's) and governments have been effective in developing guidelines and policies relating to sustainable tourism, but there is a need to focus on the implementation of these guidelines to move the agenda forward.

Through secondary research as well as interviews with over thirty large and specialty tour operators, certification programs and tourism experts, this report found that certification schemes, although increasing in their number and scope over the past ten years, have not enabled Small and Medium Sized Enterprises (SME's) greater access to market opportunities, nor have they moved the tourism industry significantly forward towards sustainability.

Guidelines within the industry are becoming more common, however, implementation and evaluation is still weak. What has been positive is that the efforts of certification programs have enabled companies to reduce costs, mainly related to the environment (water, waste, and energy savings). This cost saving advantage or training aid has helped improve management practices and processes, however there is little incentive to continue being part of a certification label as there is no proven marketing benefit. Certification programs are costly to run and most are subsidised by governments or international funding agencies. They are also costly to join for the individual operations, and so far have not delivered on promised marketing benefits and consumer awareness. Overall, industry awareness of such schemes is negligible. On the other hand, certification in eastern Europe has helped increase awareness of some niche products, such as non-tourism related companies (organic farms), by bringing them into the tourism fold, through agritourism-type packages. This is only marginal and countries are still very much dependant on larger tour operators and travel companies to promote their product.

To date, CSR is largely driven by publicly traded European companies who see it as a way to reduce any potential risks that might negatively impact on the value of their stocks. Thus, they will work with their supply-chain partners to ensure that these, too, will be more environmentally - and increasingly, socially -, responsible in their operations. For transparency purposes, they expect annual reports from their partners that document improvements made, and will usually provide technical/structural assistance (ensure local participation, community involvement and stakeholder dialogue) and expertise to help them tackle improvements year over year. If certification is to continue and be successful, a number of criteria are needed. First, there is a need for one global body to set and monitor the adoption of industry wide criteria. Second, there should be more business to business marketing rather than business to consumer, as consumer awareness and interest are extremely low. Third, demand needs to be created among consumers through increased industry responsibility reporting and educational campaigns. Fourth, if certification is to be successful, there is a need to achieve critical mass.

Currently there are fewer than 1% of companies worldwide that have achieved certification and therefore even those tour companies interviewed that would be willing to support such initiatives do not have enough product to choose from which will not alter their cost base, as tour operators are still driven primarily by price. In the Americas as well as Europe, there have been efforts to amalgamate certification schemes, however the complexity of programs and politics in different countries has not permitted much success. Fifth, quality must be linked with environmental and social management so that certified products can guarantee that a level of quality has been achieved and the 'experience' of the product is still elevated. As this report called for the evaluation of using CSR in the tourism industry, there are a number of recommendations put forward. CSR calls for consistent sets of policies, practices and programmes that steer business operations. For this agenda to be promoted, each stakeholder group must play a critical part. Certification, although fundamentally a positive approach, is not having a significant effect on spreading sustainable tourism practices overall. Initiatives focusing on the larger players will have more impact as the majority of tour operators and hotel groups have operations in developing countries and are key buyers in the industry.

The focus on CSR initiatives, educational and training campaigns for the industry as well as education of the consumer, could have higher initial impacts than attempting to move certification forward to become more mainstream. Overall there is a need to:

- Agree on international standards that can be addressed step-by-step and seen as appropriate by local and international operators
- Build on the work done to date by organisations such as FTO & VISIT (Tourlink), ISO and the European Union Flower
- Link quality with environmental and social criteria in guidelines, reporting and accreditation efforts
- Pressure associations to integrate and implement guidelines
- Consolidate guidelines and charters to be wide reaching and industry specific (tour operators, hotels, etc.)
- Utilise the existing certification framework; however create a brand around local community action and CSR focused initiatives for businesses to see it as a viable business proposition
- Link development monies with CSR criteria so that developers and managers focus on a longer term framework for product life cycles Industry to:
- Adopt and implement sustainable supply-chain initiatives (this will aid SME's in low income countries through a trickle-down and multiplier effect)

- Report on corporate social responsibility initiatives
- Focus on business to business marketing rather than business to consumer marketing (as consumer awareness is currently low)
- Continue to raise awareness to consumers through philanthropy and marketing efforts
- Adopt certification or use certified products through supply chain partners Governments to:
- Develop holistic and comprehensive tourism development strategies in partnership with community and industry stakeholders (including major foreign tour operators or industry associations, where appropriate), that include realistic expectations for the social, cultural and environmental benefits to be reaped from tourism
- Create positive investment structures to support and encourage sustainable development of tourism destinations
- Pressure industry associations to report on how they are achieving more sustainable tourism (e.g. industry associations are asking their members to sign up to guidelines and charters but few are enforcing this as a criteria for membership)
- Legislate for corporate social reporting
- Facilitate arenas to share best practices between sectors (hotels, tour operators, airlines and cruise lines) so that they can learn from one another
- Ensure sustainable tourism measures are seen as a core value in wider development plans and policies rather than solely focusing on economic benefits
- Legislate or provide incentives to businesses who adopt internationally recognised certification schemes or standards within their country.

Previous reports have pointed out disagreements with how far down the supply chain companies should monitor, that there is little standardisation in the monitoring or reporting of companies, and that there is a need to focus on why standards are not being implemented.

This report acknowledges these issues and also recognises that CSR within the tourism industry is behind other industries in all aspects. However, as tourism affects so many other sectors and is a critical economic driver in low income countries, it is believed that great strides can be made to address concerns of poverty alleviation, local economic development and conservation by pushing for greater adoption of CSR. This study highlights current issues for sustainable tourism, certification and codes of conduct, identifies key challenges that tourism will continue to face, and proposes some recommendations for CSR implementation.

OVERVIEW

The worldwide tourism industry currently accounts for 760 million people and accounts for roughly a tenth of global employment and capital formation. In most countries, especially low income countries, tourism is seen as a viable option for economic growth, but current unsustainable tourism practices can impact the health and well-being of the environment and community as well as tourism itself. In many low-income countries tourism is significant to the economy or is growing, and long-haul travel is growing at the fastest rate doubled from 1997-2001)

In most industries, CSR standards and practices have been developed by the private sector to respond to external pressure. In tourism, however, the use of codes of conduct and certification is not widespread and is not based as yet upon agreed international standards. It is difficult to make generalisations about CSR without first examining the context in which sustainable tourism operates, its demand and also assessing the numerous certification schemes, codes of conduct and best practices within the industry.

The purpose of this report is to inform FIAS advisory work on CSR and certification with regards to the feasibility and desirability for low income countries to use certification and accreditation as tools for sustainable development.

BACKGROUND AND METHODOLOGY

This study is in response to the World Bank's research on CSR codes of conduct and social and environmental guidelines. The World Bank's CSR Practice Investment Climate Department commissioned research to determine whether adopting national certification schemes built on private sector standards and whether these initiatives can be used to enhance both the country and visitor experiences.

It is assumed that enhancement would result in better promotion and marketing, which would lead to increased market opportunities through better linkages into the supply chain.

This report is based on both extensive secondary research and a large number of key informant interviews. First, a review of existing research on codes of conduct and certification schemes was undertaken, followed by a review of research on the demand for sustainable tourism. Supplementary interviews with key stakeholders, experts, scheme directors, tour operators and travel providers were then carried out to assess demand for sustainable tourism, the success of certification schemes and consumers' willingness to pay. Companies approached to be interviewed included the largest tour operators, specialty operators in both Europe and North America, certification programs and industry experts (see Appendix A for the full list of organisations interviewed).

It should be recognised that this report is not exhaustive in its nature as not all codes of conduct or certification schemes were analysed. In addition, some potential interviewees could not be contacted, and therefore some opinions may have been omitted. Once codes and certification schemes were identified, they were assessed with regard to broad CSR categories, such as their human rights, labour rights, environmental standards and social and community impact.

The tourism sector's codes of conduct and certification schemes were analysed to gauge their effectiveness and market potential. Interviews with certification players as well as large and eco/adventure tourism operators and travel providers were also undertaken to evaluate the benefits of certification schemes and to determine demand for sustainable tourism.

In the interest of obtaining as much information as possible from interviewees, assurances were given that no direct quotes would be used to identify them or their company. Therefore, all statements are those of the authors' and should not be attributed to any particular interviewee.

COMPONENTS OF SUSTAINABLE TOURISM

Sustainable development has been defined as development that meets the needs of present and host regions while protecting and enhancing opportunities for the future.

Sustainable tourism, in addition to the criteria of sustainable development requires a holistic, integrated perspective that takes into account all the industries and resources upon which tourism relies. The set of criteria or principles that define the conditions for its achievement comprises:

Protect and conserve sustainable resources

Be a multi-stakeholder approach

Be environmentally responsible

Maintain the well-being and involvement of the local population or host

Provide meaningful and fairly remunerated employment for the host population

Have economic benefit

Have a long-term view

Have a triple-bottom line approach (environmental, social and economic)

Be equitable

Government must play a leadership role (e.g., impose a 'greater good' approach)

Obtain optimum guest satisfaction and educate tourists about environmental and social concerns

The definition of corporate social responsibility (CSR) has many similar elements to sustainable tourism in that both focus on how stakeholders should be identified and engaged and that initiatives should be measured to determine their impact on others. Whereas CSR relates to a company's obligation to be accountable to all of its stakeholders in all its operations and activities with the aim of achieving sustainable development not only in the economical dimension but also in the social and environmental dimensions, sustainable tourism was first seen mainly from an environmental perspective and has only recently incorporated social and community aspects. Today, it is commonly recognised that sustainable tourism is more than just environmental conservation of a natural area, but that is must also address the quality of life of those visiting it and those being visited.

Sustainable tourism development is about making all tourism more compatible with the needs and resources of a destination area. Tourism needs to take into account a holistic and comprehensive approach that balances tourism development with other activities yet tourism is made up of many sectors and is very fragmented, therefore effects and monitoring processes through one company or mechanism has been difficult. The supply chain of product to end user is not often controlled by solely one party or individual and different elements are often operated by multiple stakeholders. This therefore has led to difficulties in controlling elements of corporate social responsibility.

At Kotu Beach in The Gambia, staff at the Bungalow Beach and Kombo Beach hotels have helped to make a big difference to the earnings of local people and create a more relaxed environment for their guests. Until recently guests at the hotels were constantly approached on the beach by various local vendors offering them goods such as fruit and fruit juices. The hotel guests so disliked being harassed they were discouraged from using the beach and both the hotels and tour operators viewed it as a major issue. In an innovative project completed in 2002, the juice pressers, fruit sellers and the craft sellers in the local market worked with the local hoteliers to understand and find ways to overcome the problem. It used a multi-stakeholder approach to bring together the informal guides, fruit sellers, juice pressers and craft sellers with the tour operators and hoteliers to discuss how things could be improved. The juice pressers and fruit sellers were keen to reduce the level of hassle on the beach. Each adopted codes of conduct which they now enforce as a group. The hotels also assist the women's' marketing efforts by putting up 'What's On' boards in the hotels to advertise the stall. The women have higher earnings and the hotel guests can use the beach again without being disturbed. Incomes at the craft market increased three-fold between the two seasons - the tourists spend more when they are not pestered in the market and some new products and better merchandising have also helped.

A number of rural communities in Asia have been engaged to make cushions and tapestries for the guestrooms of Banyan Tree resorts. These initiatives complement ongoing efforts by Banyan Tree Gallery to showcase cottage crafts and the work of indigenous artisans at its lifestyle galleries, as well as the Museum Shops, a collection of outlets in Singapore museums from which visitors can purchase a piece of ancient Asian art recreated as contemporary ornaments, accessories and stationery. This arrangement has the two-fold benefit of keeping traditional arts and crafts alive while providing Asian communities with a means of earning a living.

Labour Standards as Part of Sustainable Tourism

Environmental aspects have been the priority of official certification programmes and voluntary initiatives since the early 1980's and only recently have social or community issues been added. Human rights and labour issues have been more focused upon in developing countries rather than in Europe and North

America, partially because social legislation has been more comprehensive in Western countries. Additionally, more advanced concepts such as "the triple bottom line" (environmental, social and economic) are just now being incorporated into definitions and initiatives.

There are a number of labour issues which affect the tourism industry. These include women's rights, fair wages, long working hours, qualification and skills requirements for employees, inability to join trade unions, importing of labour and displacement of traditional employment to benefit from tourism dollars. Tourism workers often do not earn a living wage and are dependent on tips and service charges. Many workers have temporary contracts or none at all, work long hours and are employed in low skilled areas such as waitressing and/or house cleaning.

According to the ILO, tourism workers and managers are often "imported" by the large international hotel and leisure chains (six of the seven leading multinationals of the sector are North American), which pick up the major part of the profits. By contrast, local populations benefit only from low or semi-skilled, poorly paid jobs (cooks, maintenance workers, chambermaids, barmen, gardeners, bus drivers, etc.).

According to a report recently submitted to a tripartite meeting of the ILO, this sector is known for low pay (for example, in the European Union, it is less than 20 per cent of the average salary), difficult working conditions (irregular schedules, Sunday/ holiday work, unpaid overtime), and many clandestine jobs. Women make up 70 percent of the labour force in tourism and there are numerous cases of youth or child workers (half the workers in the sector are up to 25 years old).

Although few tourism codes of conduct, industry policies or schemes (see appendix B, C, D & E) so far have specifically addressed labour or human rights concerns, child labour and prostitution have been widely addressed in the Caribbean, Thailand and parts of Africa through initiatives such as ECPAT (End Child Prostitution, Child Pornography and Trafficking of Children for Sexual Purposes). Awareness of exploitative labour has also increased due to campaigns such as the recent initiative by Tourism Concern: Sand, sea and sweatshops.

Since 2002, major hotel groups, airlines and tour operators have signed up to the code which involves

- establishing an ethical policy regarding commercial exploitation of children
- training staff
- providing information to officials about abuse at various destinations
- and providing information to travellers (in-flight videos and flyers)

Some programs which have developed out of ECPAT include The Youth Career Development Program which has expanded to be the Youth Career Initiative (YCI). YCI contributes towards the eradication of the commercial sexual exploitation of children by giving girls aged 17 to 20 employment training for the hotel and travel industry. The program targets youths from poor communities and the program uses hotel expertise in human resources development to provide disadvantaged youths with the skills to work in the hotel and travel industry. The program started in Thailand in 1995 and has grown from 9 graduates and one hotel in 1995 to 550 graduates and 23 hotels in 2003. The program is now being extended to the Philippines, Romania and South Africa. Governments, NGO's and the industry are only now starting to address these issues, and although environmental elements and biodiversity issues are a crucial underpinning to achieving wider sustainable tourism development goals, it is now being recognised that labour and community equality/ participation issues do affect the success of the tourism product and experience.

DEMAND FOR SUSTAINABLE TOURISM

Within the tourism industry it is generally agreed that there are increasing overall societal and environmental concerns, and that this will increase the demand for more sustainable destinations and travel preferences. These, in turn, will increase the pressure for destination management policies and tour operator responsibility. The destination developments of the 1960/70s, which were the result of overbuilding, are expected to face severe decline as consumers look for more attractive destinations that feature a clean environment and well preserved natural and cultural attractions. Another trend affecting sustainable tourism is health and wellness.

Active or adventure holidays, wellness and spa products and sun destinations are likely to increase in popularity. Authenticity or 'experiential tourism' is another trend. Artificial type destinations (e.g., theme parks), which do not meet higher consumer quality standards, will decrease as the consumer searches for the greater authenticity. Furthermore, there has also been an increase in tourists seeking meaning from their vacation experiences with a resultant noticeable increase in the number of organisations that offer volunteer based travel or educational travel, notably from non-traditional NGO's such as Volunteer Services Overseas (VSO), etc.

The market share of sustainable tourism is difficult to assess as many consumers do not just purchase one type of holiday. During the same year, they may choose a typical package sun and sand holiday as well as one that specifically caters to nature and adventure. Sustainable tourists are approximately 50% free and independent travellers (FIT) and 50% package tour travellers (those travelling with a tour operator)

The majority of tourists seeking nature or adventure type holidays typically travel with niche or small scale operators as mass operators tend to accommodate sun, sea and sand packages. The number of operators offering more nature or adventure tours has increased in Europe over the past few years, whereas in North America, specialty travel operators have existed for over a decade.

Overall, the percentage of consumers who consciously look for sustainable travel packages or ecotourism has been estimated to be as high as 5% of the overall market for travel, although up to 30% feel that it would be 'nice to have' but without an accompanying willingness to pay (World Tourism Organisation-WTO). With increased awareness of general societal issues regarding sustainability, this number is expected to increase somewhat.

Sustainable tourism demand is difficult to assess as most figures are anecdotal evidence of market share. A number of surveys have been completed over recent years which have assessed demand for more sustainable forms of travel. A report by the WTO in 1997 presented information to indicate that ecotourism (not sustainable tourism) accounts for 20% of the world tourism market. The International Ecotourism Society Report, whose statistics were cited worldwide in other reports, indicated that ecotourism contributed US$154 billion in receipts for 2000 and was growing at a rate of 20% per year compared with 7% for tourism overall. This number has not been substantiated in any recent reports.

According to National Geographic, there are 55 million 'geo-travellers' in the United States who are environmentally and socially responsible and have ceaseless expectations for unique and culturally authentic travel experiences that protect and preserve the ecological and cultural environment. 38% of these travellers would be willing to pay a premium to patronise travel companies that use sustainable environmental practices (although it should be noted that only 1% of US travellers take holidays overseas). In Europe, 95 % of Swiss tourists consider respect for local culture to be highly important when choosing a holiday and approximately 87% of respondents in a responsibletravel.com survey suggested they were also interested in locally produced food, local culture and using local guides when on holiday.

The Association of British Travel Agents (ABTA) survey said that it was very important that their holiday did not damage the environment (45%) and that it benefited the people of the destination they were travelling to (for example, through jobs and business opportunities (30%). None of the tour operators interviewed have found that their clientele was willing to pay a premium for these criteria to any substantial degree.

Although consumers may indicate that they expect environmental and social issues to be taken into consideration on their holidays, they do not take it upon themselves to ensure these criteria are being met. Responsibility for ensuring more sustainable tourism falls in the hands of the operator. In the UK, over 80% say tour operators should have responsibility for preserving the local environment and culture and ensuring that local people benefit from tourism.

The same percentage of people are more likely to book a holiday with a company with a 'responsible' travel policy-a 28% increase since 2001. A report in 2000 declared that 55% of consumers believed that travel agents have a responsibility to provide the information, while 48% think tour operators should provide it. Social or environmental considerations, although they may be expected to be addressed in the brochure or on the website of an operator or travel provider, are not demanded when booking travel packages. From interviews with large and specialty operators it was found that no specific consumer requests for specific environmental or social criteria were requested or enquired about when booking their holidays. The only customer issues or questions were regarding stray animals or if there was an animal protection group to look after stray dogs or donkeys clients had encountered. Additionally, environmental and social criteria do not affect most tour operators' choice when selecting their package components as their primary focus is on price and second on quality. In a study done in 2003, almost 70% of tour operator clients expressed no concern or interest in eco-social issues when selecting their products and only 8% expressed a specific interest when selecting their tour Overall, less than 10% of the market booking ecotours in the US is requesting information from their operators on eco-social standards.

Examining eco-tourism, a WTO report in 2002 prepared for the International Year of Ecotourism (IYE) found that ecotourism was closer to 5% of the market compared to 20% as reported in 2000 and although awareness had increased, there was little evidence that ecotourism had been growing, let alone rapidly.

Furthermore, although a 2003 survey of successful ecolodge owners and regional ecotourism experts worldwide found that the U.S. market was cited to be the largest and most significant ecotourism market in the world the GeoTourism study found that less than 10% of the 55 million that were classified as geotourists preferred to travel outside of the United States therefore hardly contributing to tourism revenues in low income countries.

Consumer Motivations

Consumer surveys indicate that there is a willingness to pay for more sustainable types of tourism. In the STI survey (2004) 75.4% of self-declared environmentally oriented consumers declared they were willing to pay $1-20 extra per ticket to mitigate the green house gas effects of their travel. Seventy-seven declared they would switch online travel sites to one that made contributions on their behalf to offset the portion of their emissions. The National Geographic geotourism survey suggested that 61% of those interested in environmentally and socially sensitive travel would pay 5-10% more to use such companies. The Mori (2002) study suggests that package holiday makers would pay more if money went towards preservation of the local environment and reversing some negative environmental effects of tourism (47%), workers in the destination are guaranteed good wages and working conditions (49%), hotels serve food produced locally (36%) or money went to support a local charity (22%).

These consumers said they would be willing to pay up to 10% more for a holiday (1-2% more = 36% of holiday makers, 5% more - 39%, 10% more = 18%). In practice, however, there was no evidence that this research led to actual purchase behaviour. From interviews conducted, there was no indication that consumers were willing to pay more for sustainable tourism products even though they may indicate it in research. As one industry leader noted, "In several surveys done in the last years, a considerable number of people always affirm they would be ready to pay for it. But unfortunately the reality shows that the customer's decisions are often dominated by other criteria, and mostly by price. There is obviously a contradiction between intention and behaviour. It is what we call a cognitive dissonance. However, in many destinations, it is common practice that tourists on an excursion in wildlife reserves pay an extra fee for nature protection activities and this is well accepted". For example, TUI offered a program for ski holiday tourists to purchase a tree to reduce carbon emissions (£10 purchased a tree and a map of where it was planted). Only 1 in 20 bookings subscribed to the program even though it was listed on a full page of the holiday brochure. Specialty operators also did not have much participation, either.

Explore, the UK's largest adventure operator, offered clients to offset their emissions through Climate Care. There has only been a 3% participation rate. By contrast, niche operators see environmental and social issues as part of their core business and often have programs to support such initiatives (see appendix C). These operators are more likely to search for accommodations or areas which are seen as 'green', however, due to a lack of critical mass and awareness by operators, there are few examples of companies using certified accommodations. Sustainability issues are also not perceived to be a key factor in the tourist decision-making process. A report in 2000 notes that surveys have been unable to conclude that environmental, social or sustainability criteria are a key concern in holiday decision-making by tourists - even so-called ecotourists are not often motivated to travel because of interest in being 'responsible' or 'environmentally concerned. It is clear that marketers need to connect consumer motivations with actual purchasing. As one expert noted, "consumers are willing to make a greener choice if the product comes from a company [or destination] they already know and trust, it doesn't require (m)any behavioural changes to use, and it's at least as good as what they're already buying in terms of aesthetics, style, taste, etc.".

The majority of travel globally is still mass tourism which consists mainly of sun, sea and sand tourism package holidays provided by large operators (TUI, First Choice, Mytravel). Price, accommodation quality and personal security rank as the most important considerations of booking holidays. Consumers are susceptible to health and safety issues, however, with cleanliness and quality being major factors in their destination choice. From existing research and interviews with tour operators and other experts, it can be concluded that consumers would change their destination choice as a result of bad press about health (e.g. dirty beaches) or safety issues, but not for lack of environmental or social responsibility on the part of suppliers. If evidence suggests that consumers are looking for more sustainable product in tourism yet are driven mainly by price or health issues, there is a need to rethink a strategy to shift product and packaging so that product offered to the consumer integrates wider issues of sustainability.

OVERVIEW OF CERTIFICATION SCHEMES

Certification can be described as the process of assuring consumers and industry that the company being assessed has met a set of minimum standards. Within the tourism industry, certification started in the early 1990's. Since 1992, a number of schemes have been developed.

The purpose of certification has been to achieve voluntary standards of performance which meet or exceed baseline standards or legislation. The process starts with a body that sets credible certification standards (through standards which are industry relevant, measurable and obtainable). The certification body must be without conflict of interest and the indicators should be recognised by an accreditation body. The applicant or business then is assessed according to the indicators and, if successful, receives recognition, usually through the form of a logo, to inform the consumer that they have met minimum criteria. The aim of certification is to foster responsible environmental, social and cultural behaviour and provide a quality product to consumers. To be considered reliable, certification programs need to have a 3 rd party audit and effective assessment as well as clearly defined accreditation criteria. According to Toth (2002), elements of a credible certification system include:

Adequate, appropriate standards developed/accepted by all affected interests - interpretation of standards;

Trained, qualified assessors - standard defining training and qualifications;

Professional/ethical operations at all levels with no biases or conflicts of interest;

Qualified, financially stable certifying body - if there are multiple certifiers, an accreditation mechanism is needed;

Even-handed certification and accreditation;

Transparency;

Defined procedures;

Appeals mechanism;

Recognition by relevant agencies and/or customers - compliance with accepted criteria (e.g. ISO/IEC Guides) facilitates recognition; and

Acceptance in the marketplace or by regulators - marketing and promotion.

It should be noted that the above definition defines elements of a credible certification system, not necessarily one that incorporates all elements of sustainable tourism. As many schemes do not address social or labour issues in detail, these issues have not been addressed to date.

DEVELOPMENT OF SCHEMES

There are many certification schemes regarding tourism that relate to sustainability. The best known NGO or country initiatives include Voluntary Initiatives for Sustainable Tourism VISIT (Europe-wide), the Costa Rican standard Certification for Sustainable Tourism (CST), Green Deal Guatemala), and Scotland's Green Tourism Business Scheme (GTBS). The best known industry certification programmes are Green Globe and Blue Flag. Green Globe offers product as well as destination certification, while Blue Flag certifies beaches. There are two industry based standards which do not solely address tourism: ISO 14001 which addresses environmental impacts and ISO 9001 which addresses quality assurance (both mainly used by larger hotels rather than small operators or accommodations). The majority of funding and attention towards certification has addressed tourism-only schemes. These are the 'eco' schemes that focus mainly upon SME's. A number of eco certification projects are in the pilot or development phase such as Mexico, The Caribbean, Sub-Saharan Africa and Peru and countries such as Kenya and Botswana are considering them.

The majority of European ecolabels have related to environmental criteria, however, developing countries such as the Americas and South Africa have included social and cultural aspects as major components. Development of certification and eco-labels has been irregular and although there are benefits of putting forth such programs to set baseline standards, programs are not world-wide, nor is there a critical mass of certified products. There are few programs in low income countries as 2/3 of the approximately 7,000 certified tourism products are in Europe. Approximately 40% of programs started before 1996 with an additional 40% between 1996-2000 and a number of new initiatives developed since 2000 (European Centre for Ecological and Agricultural Tourism (ECEAT), eastern European programs and Central and South America).

Programs and practices vary region to region. Most schemes are national in scope, such as the CST, Guatemalan Green Deal and South Africa's Fair Trade Tourism label. The model for certification in Latin America is the CST and this is now being expanded to become the Network of the Americas to include Guatemala, Brazil, Ecuador and other newly proposed schemes. Most countries in this region have implemented (or plan to such as Mexico & Peru) a national program using the CST as a model 'although the costs of starting and operating a certification program have meant there has been little progress'. Although publicised as a model for tourism certification, the CST program has few certified products and the Network of the Americas does not have many in total (e.g., only 21 products have been certified in Guatemala).

In Europe, the VISIT program has created ar inclusive system to raise standards and cooperation among current European programs, and markets approximately 4,000 certified products through ethical trade fairs (green travel market) and to tour operators. The most successful certification program, Blue Flag, has extended its program outside Europe to the Caribbean, North America and Africa although this program only applies to the certification of beaches.

Green Globe is an industry standard which currently operates out of Australia but has certified properties worldwide. Destination certification has been gaining momentum in recent years due to issues of sustainable destination management and Green Globe's program offers a comprehensive approach for multiple players. Measurability and implementation of this scheme, however, has been questioned. Green Globe is one scheme that does offer certification of more than just ecotourism or small scale products as they offer services for tour operators, hotels, destinations, etc. Some larger scale companies have obtained certification (all-inclusive resorts such as Sandals, Casuarina Beach, Almond Beach and some Hilton and Marriott properties). In 2002, a project called the Sustainable Tourism Stewardship Council (STSC) was set up with the aim of harmonising and providing mutual recognition of schemes, and to set up an international accreditation agency - but little progress has been made since its inception. Reasons include the lack of an over-riding body to adopt international certification, confusion of existing criteria and competition between existing schemes (who did not want to merge their labels).

The majority of certification schemes accredit accommodations (approximately 63%), whereas only 7% address tour operators, mainly ground operators specifically dealing with ecotourism. Approximately 40% of the criteria or indicators in standards relate to management issues and the remaining 60% relate to specific actions such as environmental benchmarking (34%), economic indicators (8%) or socio-cultural criteria (12%). The majority of programs to date (with the exception of Green Globe, Blue Flag and ISO) have targeted small operations or ecolodges rather than larger scale tourism accommodations.

Standards can be divided into product standards (reflecting the appropriate characteristics a product is expected to have) or process standards (reflecting the appropriate characteristics from products to final distribution).

Larger tourism operators, mainly hotels, have few connections with smaller certification schemes and opt instead for international standards such as ISO 9001 which provides a quality assurance accreditation or ISO 14001 which provides environmental accreditation. These schemes are not widely adopted, however, due to a lack of awareness and marketing and many larger chains having their own internal monitoring or benchmarking systems.

Benefits and Issues

The benefits of certification are seen to be widespread although the majority of programs uphold marketing and training as their primary benefits. With the designation of a logo, certification is thought to give companies a competitive advantage and increased linkages into the distribution chain and to consumers through marketing (inclusions on web sites, travel fairs, brochure recognition), all of which would be assumed to give businesses competitiveness. Additional benefits perceived from certification include:

The ability to distinguish sustainable tourism from 'greenwashing'

The encouragement of voluntary improvements

Showcasing best practices

The use of the standard as a blueprint for future development

Training of management procedures

Cost savings

Peer recognition

Achievement beyond legislation compliance

Determinants of success of schemes have been linked to marketing which to date, has been largely unsatisfactory with the exception of some ECEAT schemes due to the small number of certified products and therefore reduced appeal to large operators to use them in their product choice. Also, the sheer number of schemes and labels makes it difficult for tour operators to incorporate them as they would have to educate the consumer about the standards behind each one and differences among them. This is beyond what tour operators deem practical for hard copy brochures. Larger certified operators (through organisations such as Green Globe or ISO) have seen cost savings and overall improved management structures. Some benefits to the community are improved environmental conditions of facilities or infrastructure improvements such as new access roads (although often larger hotel chains build water or sewage plants only for the hotel complex rather than the community or village at large). As most certification schemes do not include labour or social/community issues, the local community has not greatly benefited. In addition, companies have not generally seen marketing benefits, and therefore have participated in schemes largely for cost savings or reporting purposes.

Ecolabels in Eastern Europe were developed to promote organic farms and rural accommodation and promote them to the increasing number of tourists visiting these regions. The Czech Republic's scheme has seen 135 accommodations certified which have been promoted through publications of the Countryside Holiday Guidebook and or the Heritage Trails. As many visitors to Eastern European countries have been VFR (visiting friends and relatives) or independent tourists, farm stays and rural accommodation was a unique and relatively new type of tourism which has since led to the growth of agro-tourism in Europe. The newest initiative is the new "national ecolabel for tourist services" which has been accepted by the Czech Government three weeks ago and will be used as a tool for the new governmental "Tourism Policy" since 2007 (because of the EU programming period 2007-2013).

Failures of certification schemes

Issues around certification are widespread and varied. As Font (2003) suggests, the majority of certification schemes for tour operators address ecotourism operations rather than large mass market operators who supply the majority of the world's tourism and have the main access to the market. Therefore it has not helped respond to industry pressure as most operators have not heard of the numerous schemes or choose their product based on price. Additionally, there is a lack of critical mass as less than 1% of tourism businesses are certified. Thus, tour operators do not have enough products to choose from and often schemes do not ensure quality standards in their accreditation. Issues include:

Lack of critical mass (too few certified products, certification is not wide-spread)

Too many certification programs and other industry awards have led to confusion Lack of awareness by industry, consumers and government

Lack of unified brand (too many programs compete against each other, duplicate efforts, yet vary in their criteria)

Low consumer demand and a general tiredness with labels of all kinds

Lack of credibility (local certification schemes with no international recognition)

Lack of proven marketing benefits (and lack of marketing by certification bodies)

Lack of incentives for hotels or businesses to join

Lack of readiness to disclose information (Businesses do not wish to disclose information to obtain certification)

Cost of adherence (e.g., Green Globe, ISO) and perception that recognition/label can be 'bought'

Types of and Participation in Schemes

The most successful certification program to date has been Blue Flag, an internationally recognised program for measuring the health of beaches. Over 2,700 beaches have been certified. Success can be linked to health and safety as tourists do not want to bathe on polluted beaches. As noted earlier, beach health and cleanliness is a motivating factor in choosing a holiday therefore, having an internationally known system that assures beach health is an economic incentive for a hotel owner near a beach. The Blue Flag program greatly reduces the cost of evaluation by using existing infrastructure to take measurements of the environment. Overall, certification within the tourism industry has been difficult to achieve because tourism is multifaceted and includes a mix of services and products. Most certification and supplier development is voluntary (between 10-25% of suppliers have met the voluntary sustainability related standards), but there is little consensus that certification is actually viable. There are also few accommodations or organisations that have been certified. In Europe, where the most ecolabel or certification programs exist, less than 0.5% of accommodations have been certified. The four best known certification programs for ecotourism and SMEs (ECOTEL, CST, NEAP and Green Globe) have less than 2000 members in total. In Costa Rica only 5% of hotels have been certified, with only 46% of them advertising their certification.

It has been suggested by the new InterAmerican Bank MIF project for a Sustainable Tourism Certification System that certification for sustainability of tourism will increase competitiveness and market access of small and medium sized enterprises in Latin America. The EU has funded the VISIT scheme and the Green Travel Market to promote certified products and the Cooperative Research Centre for Sustainable Tourism (CRC) in Australia has partnered with Green Globe. However, a thorough review of existing reports on this topic shows that there are no market demand studies available to support this assumption.

Many programs also focus specifically on eco-lodges or other small scale accommodation, such as agro-tourism accommodations. Although this form of tourism can bring positive benefits to the areas in which it operates, its very nature does not make it suitable for mass tourism operators who control the vast majority of travel. There is also a lack of awareness among businesses, although the GTBS in Scotland affirmed that they had good take-up over the first three years, and that their membership is now increasing by about 30% per annum. In Costa Rica, initial participation in the program was also high, however, to date there are few hotels that have achieved a full five star rating. The CST stated that the department was receiving approximately 300 requests for certification per year before the 'oath of legality' (must be notorized by a Public Notary) was put into place. Now they are only receiving 10 requests per year.

There is also a lack of awareness among consumers. In Christchurch, New Zealand, interviews with 295 visitors found that only one-fifth recalled any place with ecolabels, and only 13% had ever heard of any tourism ecolabel. In a survey of 100 tourists in Australia, not one of them chose his or her hotel based on Eco-Australia certification. It is estimated that less than 1% of consumers were aware of the existence or criteria of any tourism certification program (for consistency). Some certification programs assessed did not claim to attract increased business but focused instead on improving management procedures and reduce cost savings. The GTBS said applicants have higher occupancy rates than average for Scotland. This, however, must be accepted with caution as these applicants tend to be well managed companies who would likely achieve these results even without certification. In Guatemala, companies gain more through management techniques to reduce costs and improve efficiency than they do through marketing.

There are also problems with transparency as some businesses in Guatemala do not want to disclose their practices in order to obtain an ecolabel. Certification cannot be seen to counter the problem of 'greenwashing' as schemes are mainly small scale and there is not enough industry pressure to make a difference. There is no world-wide method of monitoring certification and therefore overall compliance and improvement is hard to gauge.

Roles and Costs

Approximately 60% of certification programs are led by private tourism organisations or NGO's; the remainder are government led. The investment for the development of eco-labels differs from the maintenance of the programs. Development of programs is almost evenly split between NGO's, public and private sector (1/3 each, respectively), whereas almost 2/3 of programs are engaged in a multi-stakeholder collaborative approach regarding decision-making and advice giving. The costs of developing certification programs are often put upon governments, however, large governance structures are pricey and programs may need a further layer of organisations to help industry implement the standards. There is a high cost for SME's to apply for certification unless it is subsidised by government (application procedure and operation of program), and it is often not the priority of the government to run these schemes. Past studies showed that examples from Fiji, Dominican Republic and Venezuela failed in their early attempts to set up programs. NGO's are not able to afford the start-up costs of wide-scale certification projects and are therefore either government subsidised or address specific areas (e.g. Ecuador's Smart Voyager program in the Galapagos, PAN Parks in Europe, Kenya lodge accreditation). Unless subsidised, not all firms will have the same potential access to become certified.

Most programs have addressed these issues through scaled fee structures which are linked to overall company turnover or number of staff. In Costa Rica, the government has successfully subsidised first time applications to the CST. In Australia, costs are kept low but this then impacts the amount of marketing possible. Green Globe, as an industry run program, has higher costs and is linked to the stage of certification. While some certification programs can provide sufficient benefits, cost is an issue for both the company (who may find it costly to implement criteria to become certified) and the program itself as it needs to run its operations and audit the companies applying.

Some companies find ways to repay the fees as they find that meeting some of the criteria make them more eco-efficient and therefore they can justify further certification costs based on the savings realised. For smaller companies, certification programs might need to consider encouraging applications from co-operatives of small firms or under a destination umbrella. Costs are seen by many businesses as high due to the time needed for site visits and filling out forms and questionnaires. Certification can help reduce operating and management costs, although it should be noted that not all adherences to social criteria reduce cost.

Research has shown that substantial energy, waste and water savings can be realised by implementing sustainability criteria into operating processes and procedures. Credible environmental tourism certification programs, with respected standards and rigorous criteria, should be careful in considering broadening their approach to include social issues. 'A tokenist introduction of social issues might instead lead to criticisms for being environmental programs under a sustainability label' and could also raise costs and expertise needed to administer them. It is generally quite difficult to measure social/community impacts through certification.

If certification is to continue to move forward, sustainability criteria need to be assessed alongside health and safety standards as quality assurance is critical to selling a better product. Although eco-certification claims to address environmental and sometimes social criteria, basic health and safety factors are not always considered and some certified ecolodges in Central America have been found to lack basic hygiene and safety. Although ISO 9000 addresses quality assurance, it is not linked to other schemes and has only been adopted by some hotels rather than entire chains or others in the tourism sector.

The main selection criteria for customers to choose their travel packages remain price, safety and quality. Environmental and social criteria will only be considered when these primary criteria are satisfied.

STAKEHOLDER ROLES AND GOVERNMENT INVOLVEMENT

Government roles have mainly involved providing an institutional framework as well as grants or loans. An advantage of government led schemes is that they are usually longer term in focus. Promotion of best practices has also taken place and there is an expectation that governments will take a more active role. Through the assessment of schemes, however, there is no evidence to support that governments are effective at marketing such schemes and often there is a lack of willingness to share information or cooperate with other schemes. There are few motivations for governments to be involved in certification.

There is no market potential as the number of consumers actively supportive is minimal, and most often governments have adopted schemes as part of their wider development strategy (e.g., Costa Rica's Chamber of Commerce (CANATUR) was instrumental in setting up the scheme but has had no part in marketing it). From previous research on the subject and discussions with existing certification programs, it has been suggested that international governmental bodies need to play a more active role. One is a cooperative arrangement with the WTO, and the other a more integrated relationship. An International Sustainable Tourism Commission (ISTC) - an autonomous body functioning as an executing agency of the WTO - has been proposed. There is no evidence, however, to suggest that there would be an increase in certification if this were to be the case as many countries who already offer programs do not want to give up their brand and there is currently a lack of global criteria used in certification.

NGOs

NGO's have also been responsible for running some certification programs, however the high costs of operations questions the feasibility and long term sustainability of this option. The role of NGO's has been to raise awareness and apply legislative pressure. As certification schemes need large upfront and ongoing investments, subsidies are required, and often NGOs partner with industry associations to implement programs. Politically active NGOs are also exerting pressure, particularly on public companies, to take more of a leadership role with respect to CSR.

Industry

There are some industry schemes such as Green Globe, ECOTEL, ISO and CERES. Industry also plays a role in operating schemes such as Guatemala's Alianza Verde (Green Deal). Positive aspects of independent certification are that programs are self-sufficient and would not be relying upon government support. Industry- led schemes are also more willing to share information and partner with other certification schemes to move towards a wider brand and reduce costs for themselves and operators.

Future Involvement

Certification incentives could help build industry buy-in. Interviews with tour operators and existing research suggests that tax write-offs, preferential access to areas (e.g., beach property or remote parks) and preferential marketing for supporting schemes would be beneficial, however, the majority of businesses use certification as a means of cost savings, improving management practices and to comply with the requirements for corporate reporting. The main weakness of certification is the overall lack of reporting and monitoring. Certification has been seen to positively affect resource management but does not necessarily deal with labour or social issues and therefore most companies who promote their certification also provide additional forms of reporting.

Certification also has mainly addressed small companies rather than larger operators, accommodation providers and other service providers who make up the majority of the market.

The Spier estate comprises a 155- room hotel, conference facilities, golf course and winery. Their triple bottom line approach to sustainability has the vision to create a sustainable "micro-ecology" which enhances heritage and culture, generates wealth for all stakeholders, helps meet social and economic needs, and provides the infrastructure to encourage new community lifestyles compatible with the vision for the Winelands. Over 150 indicators measure aspects from compliance with employee regulations, energy and water usage, to the impact of the HIV/AIDS prevention and treatment initiatives. Some of the ways that Spier has contributed to CSR initiatives include:

- Procurement of natural gas from local, black owned business
- The establishment of a crafts market on the estate where individuals sell their craftwork
- obtaining the S.A. Fair Trademark (FTSSA)
- reduced wastewater by 20%
- created 19% new employment abiding by laws of equal opportunity
- given 65 hectares of land and water to 16 small farmers from historically disadvantaged backgrounds (as part of a wider land-reform program)

To advance certification schemes a number of options have been put forward by NGO's, industry and government. The WTO guidelines call for higher government intervention to move sustainable tourism forward. National and regional certification schemes declare there is a need for higher government intervention through the establishment of a global set of criteria, promotion and monitoring. They have also noted that a joined-up government approaches to policy development in destinations (participation from both government and industry associations) is needed to help promote certification and that the overall supply chain needs to be focused upon. Interviewees have been suggesting that overall awareness and one overarching standard is needed if certification is to continue but that financial incentives, verification procedures and mandatory reporting are the most effective means to ensure participation and compliance. Since larger brands and companies dominate the sector, they can have more influence than small scale, bottom-up, locally based initiatives in the adoption of sustainability criteria and reporting. Currently it is the NGOs, politicians and the financial market which are pushing for sustainability measures to be incorporated. Publicly traded companies, in particular, are being forced into compliance since financial analysts want to avoid risks at all costs; these companies are benchmarked against other global players such as Cendant, Marriott, Hilton, Carnival Cruises, etc., and CSR is therefore seen as key for their investor relations. However, the majority of the certification initiatives within the tourism sector to date have focused on the small scale voluntary initiatives that are not facing pressure to conform.

Operators within the supply chain that report their compliance are in many ways better monitored than if they were certified. TUI, in particular is very strong about tracking and demonstrating continual improvement, and assisting their suppliers through expertise in achieving these improvements. Accor, an international hotel chain also monitors through its purchasing organisations in each country.

In 2002, Accor's Purchasing Department Developed a Sustainable Development

Purchasing Charter which aimed to promote and monitor good labour and environmental practices in the 15 countries where it has a purchasing organisation.

In 2003 the charter was sent to Accor's 2,000 preferred suppliers (the group's total spend is more than 1 billion Euros) who were asked to complete a questionnaire in order for the company to monitor supplier compliance. In 2003, Accor also set out a new Subcontracting Charter that clearly defines working conditions for outside cleaning personnel in hotels managed directly by Accor, covering areas from work schedules to training programs and the calculation of hours paid.

CODES OF CONDUCT AND ROLES OF REPORTING

Codes of conduct were first developed in the 1970/80's and were predominantly focused on visitor management and environmental management. Their aim was to raise awareness in industry. There are a number of these codes within the tourism industry, put out by international bodies (WTO, UN, TOI, TIES, etc.), however, there is not industry wide awareness nor is there any monitoring of compliance. The tourism industry is fragmented and difficult to monitor due to the complexity of stakeholders in the value-chain. Codes of conduct tend to be voluntary or informal and vary considerably from sector to sector (hotel, cruise, airline, and operator) and in what they cover (labour, environment, social, economic). There are two types of codes of conduct. One is put out by organisations such as the WTO or industry associations and the latter are self-imposed guideline of what the corporation deems ethical business behaviour and it's done to reassure investors and consumers.

This research supports a recent World Bank Group report that there is virtually no effective monitoring or implementation mechanism yet in place for CSR practices, and that even defining sustainable tourism can be difficult as criteria are interpreted differently by different stakeholders. There are, however, a growing number of guidelines and charters on sustainable tourism which have been put forth by both government and industry.

CODES OF CONDUCT-ROLES AND PARTICIPATION GOVERNMENT

Governments have endorsed the concept of sustainable tourism and signed on to multiple charters, such as the Lanzarote Charter for Sustainable Tourism in 1995 or the EU's 'Working Together for the Future of European Tourism'. However, few charters or country codes actually outline specific measurable targets, as most tourism policies have been driven by economics and divorced from environmental and social costs. There has been raised awareness by destinations in mature stages of development that conservation and social issues could be a challenge as many communities were economically dependant on tourism. There has also been an increase in the adoption of Local Agenda 21 principles for destination management in the past few years. Currently no government body has regulated the need for reporting in the tourism sector.

NGO's

NGO roles have been mainly to put pressure on development agencies and governments to address issues of sustainability, to put pressure on supply chain and distribution channels to change methods of procurement and to develop codes of conduct such as Conservation International's Marine Recreation Guidelines for water sport supplier procurement or the International Tourism Partnership's Siting and Design Guidelines for new hotel construction. Tourism Concern has been a leader in the pressure applied for the inclusion of human rights and labour issues to improve working conditions in tourism destinations. Over recent years, NGO's have called for businesses and governments to report on their environmental and social practices to ensure transparency of operations but currently these are only in the form of advocacy.

Industry

Many individual operators are working toward incorporating sustainability into their products and almost ¾ of tour operators or travel industry associations interviewed (and niche adventure/nature specialty tour operators) had a responsible or sustainable tourism code or policy, although not all evaluated or monitored compliance. Currently, a number of large scale tour operators are developing sustainable supply-chain policies. European tour operators tend to be most active in this regard, possibly due to the initiatives by the Federation of Tour Operators (FTO) and the Association of Independent Tour Operators (AITO) and the fact that most of the larger ones are publicly traded companies. Although becoming popular, there is a lack of uniformity of codes in spite of the growing number of associations that are making charters or codes mandatory. Elsewhere in the world awareness is much lower.

The Netherlands Association of ANVR tour operators implemented a Product Oriented Environmental Management System as part of their Responsible Tourism Program. The program is obligatory for all of its 200 members. It includes an action package with steps tour operators need to take: internal management and involvement of staff, purchasing, and contract management for the provision of transport, accommodation excursions and entertainment in the destination. The association believes that success factors for travel organisers depend on intact nature, clean beaches and authenticity of destinations. The ANVR, a federation of 3 membership associations: Association Air and Business Travel Agents (VLZ), Association Travel Agents (VRA), Association Travel Organisers (VRO), is focused on outbound tourism. Committed tour operations showed interest in working with certified products even though this cannot always be communicated effectively to clients. Most companies have set their own standards rather than use certification labels as these do not exist in all destinations where tour operators work and there is not enough product that is certified to choose from. Tour operators also feel that the number and variety of different schemes makes it very difficult to educate their customers or their staff. The most successful initiatives which have helped spread more sustainable practices are those for supply chain management. Through the development of association charters or standards such as TUI or the Accor Group, many SMEs worldwide could improve their access to market if they abide by these criteria and offer their services to these buyers (who will need to replace suppliers who are non-compliant if they are to uphold their commitment to their initiatives).

Hilton has adopted a new Standard for Business Partners and Suppliers which includes standards on child or forced labour, employee representation, health, safety and environmental management, discrimination, disciplinary practices and employee compensation and working hours.

Hotel chains have been addressing their environmental concerns for some years. A number of them set up the International Hotel Environmental Initiative in 1992 which focused on environmental improvements and is now starting to address social and community issues. Most of the larger hotel chains comply with environmental standards and have environmental policies and standards ranging from in-house benchmarking systems (Accor, Hilton Group, etc.) to environmental standards manuals (Rezidor, Starwood, Fairmont, etc.). Although not widespread in adoption, some hotels are now promoting when they achieve international certification such as ISO 9001 and 14001 (some Taj, TUI, ITC Hotels, Sol Melia, Baja Inn Hotels). Some hotels have subscribed to local certification systems (such as Rezidor hotels in Scotland attaining the Green Tourism Business Scheme or Rezidor and Scandic hotels in Scandinavia receiving the Nordic Swan ecolabel), however they are few in numbers. There are growing examples of hotel companies who have helped sustainability through backward linkages in lower income countries (see box 9), but to date hotels and large tour companies are not pressured into having to receive a social and/or environmental license to operate as most communities and developing destinations do not have awareness of tourism, let alone the negative issues which may surround it.

Orient-Express inherited a large plot of land as part of the staff accommodation complex in Aguas Calientes, Peru. Orient Express employees who live within the hotel complex and local church workers have started growing their own vegetables which they sell back to the hotel, the Machu Picchu Sanctuary Lodge. In this area of Peru, the hotel had problems finding quality food items, especially vegetables, and now purchases these from their employees.

Reporting

Industry has historically suggested that it will respond to consumer demand for sustainable tourism and that this is where the demand must come from, however, there is evidence that increased CSR is the result of the increased pressure by NGOs, politicians and the financial market to monitor or evaluate codes of conduct or tourism policies which address sustainable or responsible tourism. Reporting comes from constant need for ongoing-communication with suppliers. A notable organisation that is driving progress in this area is the Global Reporting Initiative (GRI), which aims to 'raise the level of sustainability reporting to that of financial reporting'. The Tour Operators' Initiative, in cooperation with the GRI, developed a Sector Supplement to the GRI 2002 Sustainability Reporting Guidelines providing Tour Operators' performance indicators. Forty-seven indicators were developed to measure tour operators' performance in addressing the environmental, economic and social impacts of their business operations. The tour operators' supplement adds to, but does not replace, the 2002 GRI Sustainability Reporting Guidelines' section on performance indicators. The supplement was not designed to capture sector-specific aspects of the various service industries associated with a package, such as transport, accommodation, and other tourism services.

Many companies produce reports that are aimed at their own employees, in order to help explain and support the roll-out of a company's new sustainability policy. Some companies also report for reasons of reputation; such companies are keen to capture their leadership work and/or combat negative perceptions that may have arisen about their sector or brand. A social report can also be a useful communication tool to highlight responsible business practice across a company's worldwide operations. Publicly traded companies need to report on CSR initiatives as part of their investor relations and to demonstrate that they are proactive in reducing potential risks. Thus, larger hotel chains, for instance, have moved significantly towards CSR reporting and have been included in the Dow Jones Sustainability Indicator and FTSE4GOOD index (Accor, Hilton and Intercontinental).

Industry association-led initiatives include the Tour Operators Initiative (TOI) and the IHEI. Both these organisations do not have a specific code of conduct but rather coordinate efforts of tour operators or hotels, respectively, to harmonise performance indicators, monitoring, reporting and tools to assist supply chain partners. The three-year programme aims to standardise sustainability checklists with those of certification programs. The project's goal is to merge/assimilate criteria of the FTO with VISIT (VISIT covers mostly environmental criteria, whereas the FTO includes social and labour issues). The aim is to achieve transparency, a cost-effective distribution system, and to link different supply chain initiatives to provide a common toolkit for travel providers.

CSR AND LOW INCOME COUNTRIES-RECOMMENDATIONS

It must be recognised that without political stability, security and basic infrastructure, tourism will not be fostered by any of the larger international companies, as risks to customers would be deemed too large, and therefore CSR cannot be considered in largely non-democratic countries.

Certification Conclusions

Certification has resulted from confusion over terms in tourism such as 'sensitive, green, and eco', and the desire to legitimise them has led to multiple schemes being developed worldwide. While certification schemes may be described as ways for SMEs in lower income countries to obtain access to market, interviews with both major and specialist tour operators, travel providers and certification programs do not support this view. Most of the certification schemes have only certified small numbers of attractions or businesses and have not linked into the wider distribution channels due to low awareness and lack of critical mass. In addition, the majority of certification schemes address ecotourism operations rather than large mass market operators who supply the majority of the world's tourism and have the main access to the market.

There also remains considerable variety in standards, criteria and indicators in certification usage. From this study it can be ascertained that although Costa Rica and other countries have widely known and recognised schemes, they are not able to keep up due to lack of staff and finances for operation. Voluntary standards have not been found to increase access to trade unless governments have assisted with mandatory legislation or trade access structures. Industry is cynical about government taking responsibility for the implementation of sustainable tourism practices and also that investment into better social and environmental performance will increase access to market.

There are a lack of internationally accepted principles for certification criteria (although programs such as VISIT and the Network of the Americas are a partial attempt to overcome this) and there is currently a lack of critical mass of products. Certification was also found to be unsuccessful in allowing greater access to new market segments with the exception of some Eastern European countries who noted that organic farms and rural based accommodations gained an increasing number of tourists (providing they were in accessible locations with other amenities/attractions nearby). The lack of awareness about certification programs and the low incentive for international operators or larger players to take part are largely to blame. Certification schemes at their very best will only allow access to niche market segments, unless they become more widespread and focus on more than just ecotourism and small scale ventures. Operators and certification programmes and research studies have suggested that a global brand is needed if certification is to be pursued more seriously. One brand would help certification to be internationally recognised and also comply with generally accepted international criteria, and thus have a stronger chance of brand recognition in industry. However, no single approach has so far been put forward successfully due to the varying degrees of infrastructure in countries and the lack of sufficient markets to attract certifiable product. If certification is to be moved forward, there is a need to link certification with quality.

"Case after case has demonstrated that consumer demand develops long after a certification program is well established," according to Amos Bien of The International Ecotourism Society (TIES). The recent report on ecotourism certification suggests that consumer demand takes between 8-15 years (sometimes as long as 20) to develop and that quality, safety and price must be satisfied before the consumer will consider other factors. There is also a need to create demand for sustainable tourism among the travelling public through the linkage with existing quality standards. One example where quality has been linked to certification programs is Green Globe, which has partnered with Australia's

AAA to award green stars to products, thereby using an existing quality standard to promote eco friendliness. Their advertising notes research that suggest 62% of travellers say that endorsement will encourage them to consider one accommodation over the other.

Although ISO 9001 is a quality standard it is not linked with other certification standards. In addition, the education of governments about the benefits of long-term planning to ensure sustainability of the destination will also provide them with the skills to understand that long-term planning can ensure a more quality rather than quantity focused approach. Most industry players noted they would be willing to abide by a national level certification scheme as long as it was transparent, did not raise costs of product and achieved a critical mass of certified products. In order to achieve effective certification schemes or guidelines in low income countries, a multi-stakeholder participatory approach was suggested that included international organisations, such as tour operators or industry associations, to represent individual companies and contribute to the development/adoption of schemes. Recommendations also included that there needs to be an assurance that Government engages with effective systems and builds proper partnerships and that there is a long-term commitment to the process. Industry is not willing to increase its costs unless it can be translated intc increased profits or the cost can be transferred to the consumer. Incentives for gaining participation into schemes by larger operators who could push certification through their supply-chain were suggested, particular tax incentives, preferential access into natural areas and marketing incentives.

It should be noted, however, that there are a number of issues within certification schemes themselves which need to be addressed before governments propose this on a wide scale to industry. For certification to advance it needs to be credible, demand driven, open and transparent, self supporting, accessible and link into a consensus of international standards.

Recommendations

This report advocates that countries with more developed infrastructure are better placed to reduce negative effects of tourism than the development of certification schemes, and that adopting CSR and measures of reporting will have a greater positive effect on industry overall. In many low income countries there are problems of lack of tourism planning, established tourism ministries as well as clear roles and objectives. Therefore focusing on public-private partnership to forward the CSR agenda should have a greater overall positive impact and advance sustainable tourism in the industry. However, if certification is to continue, recommendations include:

Rather than develop new certification schemes in each country, have governments endorse existing and internationally known standards, such as ISO 14001 and 9001 and ILO standards

Continue with efforts to merge certification systems and provide for recognition or convergence of schemes to ensure wider participation and the inclusion of labour and community elements within certification and evaluation initiatives Create a more homogenous market and avoid overregulation in service sectors For elements which are not covered by international agencies (ISO etc.) develop or adopt one internationally recognised brand with baseline criteria to cut down on confusion and multiple criteria Focus on larger tourism companies and international brands operating in developing countries in addition to ecolodges and SMEs to promote wider scale adoption Promote existing industry codes of conduct or guidelines to ensure they are widely disseminated, implemented and monitored/ evaluated

Move towards mandatory certification and reporting (for national recognition of sustainable tourism, a critical mass must be achieved) Integrate quality assurance and health & safety standards into schemes or link with other programs (e.g. GTBS links to a quality assurance accreditation scheme)

Focus on capacity building and awareness campaigns primarily to engage business-to-business marketing and government-to-business marketing and awareness.

Ensure that local certification is implemented through a credible local or regional association to ensure participation and ease of access (but still linked to the overall global brand)

Award achievement rather than commitment (to ensure confidence)

Encourage individual business reporting which would improve awareness and obtain confidence in the credibility of certification initiatives

Recommendations for Achieving Sustainable Tourism and Access to Market for Low Income Countries Supply Chain Initiatives

In order to enhance sustainable tourism development in low income countries, there is a need to focus on elements of the tourism industry which can affect a greater number of products and businesses and contribute environmentally, socially and economically to lower income countries. SMEs as well as larger businesses in developing countries need to align themselves with European and North American buyers through abiding by CSR and sustainable tourism initiatives that are widely adopted (for example, TUI has made clear that they will not rely upon external auditors for checking accommodations in their programs; therefore businesses reporting on achievements will help link them to buyers who are looking for conformance). Restrictions or initiatives for more sustainable tourism may not come from low income countries as they are more than ever dependant on the free market economy. Restrictions must come from buyers in Northern Asia, Europe and North America and there need to be incentives for industry to apply supply chain CSR/sustainable tourism standards. Supply chain initiatives can aid in creating more sustainable forms of tourism through:

- Employment: commitments from tourism companies to employ local people at fair wages and provide job training
- Local economic linkages: local procurement of food, supplies and services
- Minimising negative cultural and environmental impacts: through sustainable charters and codes adopted by large industries (such as abiding by international environmental and social regulations which may be ignored or not monitored in local destinations). Also through corporate reporting, education to consumers and businesses on traditional cultures and behaviour will be promoted
- Participation in planning and decision-making processes: through the procurement of local operators and services, community and local views will be fed back through the supply chain

- Linking quality assurance and certification: if buyers adopt criteria for their suppliers, suppliers may use certification programs to obtain the necessary training and knowledge to attain baseline or minimum standards

Recommendations: Encourage SMEs to focus their criteria to match those of international buyers so that they can align themselves with buyers who demand CSR criteria.

Governments should increase pressure on industry associations to ensure supply-chain practices are publicly accessible Provide standards for reporting, including common terminology, disclosure of information, methods of evaluating performance, quality management systems and assessment of evaluation bodies

Provide incentives for both small and larger tourism businesses to adopt supply chain sustainable tourism/ CSR criteria. Incentives suggested include:

* Rewarding good practice or suppliers that meet minimum standards set
* Facilitating more business to business marketing - through distribution channels; instead of business to consumer marketing as this is not yet strong enough to influence the consumer
* Promoting best practices that showcase that success needs to include Profit and Returns on Investment in order to build the business case for the industry

Ensure low income countries incorporate tourism into their development policies and provide incentives for larger international companies to adopt certification measures and supply chain guidelines which will benefit SMEs and the local community.

Reporting

Business reporting on social and environmental issues has potentially helped increase loyalty and a sense of distinctiveness. Some businesses ascertain that promoting their responsible/sustainable business practices can give them a better market position by distinguishing and differentiating their approach.

Initiatives must be industry led as labour standards and other elements of sustainability are not visible to the consumer but crucial nonetheless to the long-term wellbeing of the destination. CSR reporting means a company is more transparent and accountable to external stakeholders, enabling investors to avoid risk and consumers to support more sustainable businesses, therefore having a multiplier effect. Reporting was deemed essential by the corporate interviewees to ensure that efforts are maintained, and initiatives continued. It also makes it possible for others in the supply chain and at destinations to duplicate successful practices. Currently there is low brand loyalty as consumers make decisions primarily based on price; CSR initiatives could potentially lead to increased brand loyalty and product differentiation. As there is currently little consumer support or awareness, information databases need to be linked so that environmental and social criteria can be provided to the client when they are booking their holiday.

Recommendations: Governments should focus their capacity-building efforts on suppliers, using such methods as legislated compliance (e.g., environmental, reputation and business probity), ensuring that resources are available for training and learning by suppliers and, where needed, fill resource gaps Increase public-private partnerships of training for environmental and social awareness and mitigation strategies Offer incentives and reporting guidelines to the tourism sector distributed through industry associations. Support training and sharing of best practices Encourage industry associations to make adherence to sustainable or responsible tourism policies a condition of membership and to report on progress Encourage CSR reporting from tour operators, airlines, cruises, hotels and destinations themselves so that they can understand the impact they themselves are having. Reporting will also provide measurable criteria by which companies and destinations can be compared.

Providing for a Sustainable Industry

To ensure that a more sustainable form of tourism is pursued, there is a need for stricter legislation coupled with joined-up government. Both industry and certification bodies interviewed noted that a such an approach adopts a concerted effort using all the arms of government - central, regional and local government and public agencies, as well as the private and voluntary sectors to form private/public partnerships. Integration into wider sustainable development plans as well as destination management plans is imperative, and a bottom-up as well as a top-down policy approach is needed. Pressure on governments to incorporate tourism into their wider development policies may help raise awareness about the need for sustainable tourism and the benefits of long-term planning approaches, however there is a strong need for training of employees and industry players at the local level. Stricter legislation in low income and developing countries is often fraught with issues of corruption, lack of monitoring and lack of governance, as there are often neither tourism master plans that incorporate sustainable tourism practices or measures nor incentives for industry to adopt them on their own initiative. To date, few developing countries have imposed social or environmental criteria to foreign investors, seeing only short term economic gains instead of long-term, holistic, sustainable tourism development.

Recommendations: Ensure transparency through a multi-stakeholder process Include sustainable tourism in all levels of policy formulation from national tourism policy to local destination management plans Recognise the difference between local vs. international stakeholders and the incentives or encouragement they need to adopt more sustainable forms of tourism practices Ensure that tourism is seen as a core or pillar in countries' wider development plans and policies

Ensure that development of tourism in low income countries includes education and training of local communities Provide for sustainability experts to be included in new tourism developments to ensure social and environmental criteria are considered in proposals and funding Ensure stakeholders are identified and consulted throughout the tourism development process and play an active role in decision-making Promote positive investment structures for integrated tourism master planning -focusing on risk mitigation through sustainable development and planning of tourism.

CONCLUSION

Sustainable tourism can help overcome many of the negative impacts associated with tourism development. Based on the interviews conducted, it is clear that guidelines alone are not strong enough to overcome the short-term profit motive of many operators, governments and destinations. At the same time, national certification programs are too numerous, with too many varying criteria, and not enough accredited product to be effective at this point in time. The analysis indicated that there are emerging trends and recommendations to be gained from this examination, however, it is not suggested that these codes or schemes are standardised within the tourism sector, nor is there a convergence of themes within them with the exception of the International Labour Organisation (ILO) and environmental criteria which often addresses similar issues of waste, water and energy management.

In summary, the conclusions of this report are fourfold. First, there is little overt demand for sustainable tourism therefore more research is needed to determine how product can be shifted to include sustainability. If the consumer and the industry are driven by price then there is a need to re-think the strategy of how to include sustainability within current cost structures. Second, there is low awareness and success of certification programs to date. There is a need to further develop the concept of an international certification label for the travel and tourism industry that is inclusive (environmental, social, cultural etc.), affordable, monitored, and reported. As there are already a number of recognised and internationally accepted schemes, these should be promoted to extend their reach rather than developing new schemes which add to the confusion of both the industry and the consumer. Third, in order to achieve more sustainable forms of tourism, it needs to move away from voluntary measures towards reporting where progress can be measured and buyers and suppliers held accountable for their actions. Fourth, CSR could help with a number of issues facing tourism with regard to promoting sustainable tourism practices, however, industry must see government involvement and support if they are to increase their own involvements in CSR. There is a need for governments to step up to the challenge of ensuring more sustainable forms of tourism will be supported and to reassure investors and players in the tourism sector that government will support and encourage sustainable tourism management and development.

Sustainable Tourism Diagnostic Checklist

The purpose of this checklist is to attempt to align CSR practices within the tourism industry and public sector development of tourism. It contains a series of criteria that strive for optimal roles for good business practices and development. It should be noted that different criteria will be different for each sector of the industry (for example airlines would not be operating tours or tour operators would not be gaining acquiring land). In addition, due to the nature of the tourism industry, many businesses within this sector may be too small to fulfil all criteria and this tool should be used as a guideline only. A number of elements of this checklist are critical to ensure the development of a sustainable tourism industry. This does not mean that other elements are not important, however, the elements marked with an * are the minimum standards for which broad enforcement/compliance is desirable and realistic. It should be noted that different countries will have different laws and regulations, and that basic international standards as set out by ILO and other such organizations should be followed in due process.

Economic

General Policies and Planning

- Policies to accommodate cultural customs, traditions and practices of staff throughout the organisation*

- Disclosure of loans, monies and taxes from third parties*
- Policy to support voluntary eco-labels and certification where possible
- Public disclosure of health and safety policy for operations, staff, end-user and management in accordance with national and international laws*
- Annual environmental, social and economic report available in public domain*
- Policy and compliance of anti-corruption measures*

Management Systems

- Governance structure*
- Management systems*
- Corporate accountability and risk assurance committee
- Compliance with local laws and regulations*

Employee/HR Principles

- Clear policy and guidelines on labour standards in accordance with local labour law *
- Established working hours and terms of overtime, sick leave*
- Abolishment of child labour, sexual discrimination, forced, bonded or compulsory labour*
- No tolerance of physical, psychological violence or verbal abuse*
- Recognition of right of employee to be represented by trade unions or other associations and recognition for negotiations on behalf of associations*
- Recognition and access for employee feedback and established mechanisms for grievances, redress, appeal

- Respect for human rights (including indigenous and tribal people)*
- Compliance with ILO conventions on child and forced labour*
- Recognise freedom of association; non-discrimination; programmes to combat sexual exploitation of children and to combat and mitigate the social impacts of HIV/AIDS; citizen participation in planning process*
- Provide evidence of recruiting local residents (including destination nationals) for destination posts including management positions (in accordance with local and international law)
- Preference to local employment (within legal constraints)
- Established wages consistent with national standard*
- Honoured reasonable employee benefits - Access to health care, dental, vacation pay, maternity rights, meals or food allowance, transportation allowance, travel, performance bonuses*
- On-the job training for skills and upgrading of skills
- Training for environmental and cultural sensitivity - both within community, corporate culture and to tourists*
- Fair redundancy, compensation and termination terms*

Note: Many labour standards should reflect compliance with ILO standards Supply chain / procurement procedures

- Provision of purchasing of local food and equipment from local community

- Creation of networks of environmentally/socially responsible businesses within the destination area
- Use of locally sourced and produced materials, foods, etc. (within legal constraints)
- Describe processes through which suppliers, by type, are consulted during development and implementation of the supply chain management policy,
- Description and disclosure of supply chain policy and targets for social, environmental and economic measures
- Description of suppliers who have sustainability policies and implemented a sustainability management system and/or have a staff person with management responsibility for corporate sustainability.
- Adoption of fair competitive practices for procurement and service contracts*
- Provision of information on quality of products and quality standards
- Fair payment of contracts and service agreements within national legal standards*
- Applied health and safety practices in accordance with national and international laws for suppliers and purchasers*
- Promotion and public encouragement of environmentally and social practices within supply chain
- Published supply chain practices code
- Promotion of labour standards through supply chain

Environmental

Environmental Reporting/Management Systems

- Established policy and compliance with local and international environmental management, transport and hazardous waste principles*
- Established formal Environmental Management System (EMS) (performance based)
- Disclosure of improved EMS management, operations and organizational structures (attempt to integrate EIA into standard EMS)
- Annual environmental report
- Policy and timely disclosure of environmental reporting to shareholders and public stakeholders including:
- Assessment of significant risk of products, services and/or operations*
- Incorporation of risk assessment and mitigation*
- Conducted and application of environmental impact assessment (EIA) in all new building or construction in accordance to international and local laws*
- Conducted independent EIA to assess and avoid conflict for both environmental implications as well as social/community implications - obtain clear permission/license to progress from both environmental and social community*

Environmental Management

- Incorporation of published standards for new siting and design for new construction, refurbishment and renovation of property
- Consultation with affected stakeholders regarding risk mitigation

- Disclosure of environmental risks to affected stakeholders within reasonable timeframe*
- Established effective procedures to address environmental damage to resources and risk mitigation plan to overcome hazards or deterioration*
- Environmental impact assessment checklist or guideline to assess adverse social impacts
- Support of conservation efforts
- Standard training of risk management, environmental awareness of products and services*
- Established tour size (tours or excursions group sizes for tours are kept to minimum size (under 16 passengers)
- Established tourist/resident ratio on peak days or season*
- Established standards for impacts for specialized tourism products/services (golf, diving, beaches, hiking, heritage sites, etc.) *
- Use of sustainable forms of tourism for touring or use of low emission gasoline
- Established measures to increase public access, visual and landscape impacts
- Assessment and measures for protection of local Flora y Fauna, wildlife, open spaces and forest, biodiversity, marine/eco/terrestrial habitats, water, air and noise*
- Establishment of Green areas and gardens
- Mitigation of visual and landscape impacts
- Established appropriate scale for design and building of tourist facilities/accommodation

- Use of appropriate building materials (aesthetically sensitive to area and renewable where possible)
- Environmental education to staff, management and consumers of risks and possible reduction of energy, water and waste

Water

- Efficient use of water*
- Reporting on usage of potable water
- Re-use of grey water

Energy

- Use of renewal energy sources*
- Reduced use where possible of energy intensive practices*
- Reporting on fuel usage cost, CO_2 emissions Usage of alternate and other energy sources, including solar, wind, geothermal, biomass, small-scale hydro energy, and methane based composting systems
- Waste
- Compliance with national and international regulations of hazardous waste*
- Provision of consumption of annual waste
- Optimal use of Non-corrosive biodegradable chemicals / cleaning products*
- Recycled / eco-friendly products, Post-consumer recycled paper and products
- Established recycling program
- Reduction of non renewable resources where possible *

Pollution

- Assessment and mitigation of noise and air pollution
- Assessment and mitigation of air quality

Social

Guests

- Encouraging responsible use of alcohol
- Evidence of environmentally friendly materials for guest/client promotional materials
- Education to consumers about local traditions/ cultures*
- Education of ecological and biodiversity to guests*
- Assurance that guests do not purchase products made from endangered species*
- Responsible advertising customer satisfaction and feedback
- Encourage customer engagement through
- feedback systems
- awareness and education means surrounding environmental and social issues and protection Community engagement and benefit
- Training programs extended to local community
- Planning gains- infrastructure or public building (e.g. hospitals) that are donated through development
- Appropriate land acquisition *
- Accessibility for public and local community to beaches and attractions and special consideration given regarding local rates and membership*
- Established and accessible community feedback system for feedback and participation in new development*

- Disclosure to employees and community of health and safety risk as well as occupational hazards/ diseases/health risks
- Established policy or guidelines for community engagement and non-commercial stakeholders (community groups, NGOs, non-shareholding government authorities, universities etc.)*
- Recognition and protection of the integrity of the community social structure*
- Recognition and respect for local tribal and indigenous groups*

Health and Safety

- Accident and insurance prevention*
- Senior management accountability
- Regular training*
- Systems to respond to and prevent threats
- Clean bathroom, potable water and food storage
- Established house keeping standards
- Clear policies and guidelines established for health and safety measures including accidents and disease*
- Clear policies and guidelines developed for fair and equitable hiring/termination
- Clear policies and guidelines developed to address social issues (e.g. aids/HIV, etc in accordance with national standards) *
- Established effective management system for promoting health and safety*

Accessibility

- Accessibility measures for the handicapped
- Consideration of environmentally sound mean and modes of transport

Contribution to Local Development

- Evidence of changes in tour package or hotel operations to minimise negative environmental and social effects on local community
- Charitable donations to socio-cultural projects
- Charitable donations to environmental or conservation projects
- Contributions of annual hours of in kind / volunteer to local communities
- Describe measures taken to identify and offer commercial opportunities and assistance to non-contracted suppliers that support community development*
- Indicate total funds (in cash and estimated value of in-kind contributions) for conservation and social development projects.
- Describe programmes for philanthropic and charitable donations in relation to conservation and community development projects.
- Deployment of market research, distribution networks and retail channels to support community-based enterprises
- Provision of emergency assistance (e.g. for natural disasters)
- Rescue and protection of Historic-Cultural Patrimony

9

MANAGEMENT STATUS: TOURISM AND RECREATION

OVERVIEW

Tourism is the largest commercial activity in the Great Barrier Reef Marine Park (GBRMP), generating up to A$4.2 billion per annum (see Chapter 4 of the Industries, Land Use and Water Quality in the Great Barrier Reef Catchment Research Report released by the Productivity Commission in February 2003). The marine tourism industry is a major contributor to the local communities along the coast of the GBRMP and the Australian economy. It is estimated that private recreational use on the GBRMP contributes at least an additional $240 million (Productivity Commission 2003). Since initial establishment of the GBRMP in 1975, tourism on the Reef has transformed from some small operators in regional centres to a multi-billion dollar industry focussed offshore from Cairns, Port Douglas and in the Whitsundays.

The marine tourism industry is very diverse, offering a wide range of products, from day trips, to cruise ships, sail-your-own yachts or kayaking in coastal areas. There are approximately 730 tourism operators with 1500 vessels and aircraft permitted to operate in the

GBRMP. The overall number of visitors on commercial tourism operations has been relatively stable since the mid-1990s, with approximately 1.8 million visitor days in 2001. Private recreational use of the GBRMP is focussed on recreational fishing.

There is limited information on the number of recreational visitors or their patterns of use. Management of tourism and recreation in the GBRMP is focussed on ensuring ecologically sustainable use of this outstanding natural area. Management by the Great Barrier Reef Marine Park Authority (GBRMPA) is conducted in partnership with the marine tourism industry and relevant governments agencies, especially the Queensland Parks and Wildlife Service (QPWS). In general, tourism operators demonstrate a strong commitment to protecting the GBRMP, as it is fundamental to their business future.

CURRENT STATUS TOURISM ON THE REEF

There is a diverse range of tourism operations in the GBRMP. These include:

day tours, often to a permanently moored pontoon adjacent to a coral reef

overnight and extended tours

diving and fishing charters

long range roving tours

aircraft or helicopter tours

bareboats (self-sail)

cruise ships

beach hire

watersports

passenger ferries

The tour vessels used by operators range in size from small sailing vessels, which typically take fewer than 20 people, to the large wave-piercing catamarans, which carry up to 400 people.

There are also an increasing number of cruise ships visiting the GBRMP, with bookings to cruise ship anchorages increasing from about 200 in 2000, to nearly 600 in 2002.

Around 40 per cent of Great Barrier Reef tourists are serviced by the 10 largest tourism operations. Destinations include coral reefs, continental islands and coral cays. Over 85 per cent of visitors go to the offshore Cairns, Port Douglas and Whitsunday areas that make up less than ten per cent of the GBRMP.

In Cairns and Port Douglas, the tourism industry focuses on day visits to pontoons and moorings and extended diving and fishing charters to offshore reef destinations. There are also aircraft and helicopter overflights. The Whitsunday operations focus largely on visiting resorts and island bays. Australia's largest bareboat yacht fleet operates in the waters around the Whitsunday Islands.

An audit of the use made of tourism permits during the year 2000 demonstrated that a large number of permits were rarely used. Of the approximately 1500 permitted vessels and aircraft in the GBRMP, only 40 per cent were used more than 50 days in that year and 45 per cent were not used at all.

This potential, or non-use, of tourism permits is known as 'latency'. The amount of latency was higher in the less popular regions of the GBRMP, although still significant in the Cairns Area and in the Whitsundays.

Visitors to the Reef

International, national and regional visitors are drawn to the Great Barrier Reef and for many of them the tourism fleet is their primary means of experiencing the Great Barrier Reef and learning first hand about its World Heritage values. For those visitors accessing the Great

Barrier Reef on a commercial tourism operation (tourists), their reasons for visiting include wanting to learn more about nature and experience its beauty, looking for relaxation and pursuing exciting activities.

The Cooperative Research Centre for the Great Barrier Reef World Heritage Area (CRC Reef) has undertaken comprehensive surveys of reef tourists since 1995 to establish baseline knowledge of the visitors to the Great Barrier Reef and examine changing patterns of reef tourism. Reef tourists can be grouped in three main categories:

> *"First time - potential enthusiasts" who have an active interest in nature. They seek variety in the locations visited and activities undertaken and are concerned about impacts on the environment.*
>
> *"Reef enthusiasts" who are seeking different nature-based experiences in their repeat visits and are concerned with the perceived quality of the natural environment.*
>
> *"Once in a lifetime" visitors who are Australian families and older couples, less interested in active nature-based pursuits but possibly attracted by the iconic image of the Great Barrier Reef. About half of the tourists visiting the GBRMP are international visitors. There is little information*

available about the characteristics of private recreational visitors to the GBRMP. Research on recreational fishers shows that they are mostly male and rarely younger than 30 years old.

Changes in Overall Numbers: The number of visitors carried on commercial tourism operations in the GBRMP along with a breakdown of visitors to the Cairns Area and the Whitsundays. Tourism numbers have been relatively stable since 1994.

The minor decline in 1997/98 is attributed to the Asian economic crisis. In 2001, the Cairns area recorded a notable increase, which is attributed to post-Olympic interest in Australia. There has been a 43 per cent increase for the Whitsundays since 1996.

Preliminary figures for 2002 indicate that international events such as terrorism have affected international visitor numbers, but may have also contributed to increased domestic tourism. In 2003, outbreaks of Severe Acute Respiratory Syndrome (SARS) and the conflict in Iraq appear to have caused a decline in international tourist numbers but the extent of this decline and its effects have not yet been assessed.

Since 1995, there has been a fall in visits to the GBRMP by vessels greater than 100 passengers, steady growth in the 51-100 passenger category for Cairns and major growth in the 16-50 passenger category in the Whitsundays.

The extent of private recreational use of the GBRMP cannot be so accurately quantified. However, based on recreational vessel registrations in adjacent coastal communities, it can be assumed that private recreational use of the GBRMP is increasing gradually.

Trip Satisfaction: Tourists who visited the Reef in 2001 and 2002 reported high levels of overall satisfaction with their reef experience. Eighty-five percent of visitors gave their trip a rating of 8 or higher out of 10, with an average visitor satisfaction of about 8.7. Features of the reef trip that were rated highly for satisfaction included staff knowledge and friendliness, tour facilities, water quality, fish, coral, other marine life and information about the tour and about the reef generally.

MANAGEMENT

The GBRMPA, in conjunction with the QPWS, employs a number of management tools to provide for a range of tourism and recreation opportunities throughout the GBRMP, and to minimise the impacts of tourism and recreation activities on the marine environment.

The legislative basis is provided by the Great Barrier Reef Marine Park Act 1975 and its

Regulations, and Zoning Plans for each of the major Sections of the GBRMP. More specific management strategies in the key areas of offshore Cairns, Port Douglas and the Whitsundays are contained in Plans of Management. These plans are designed to:

provide environmental protection, particularly at high-use and sensitive sites;

separate different uses;

resolve conflicting use; and

limit use where necessary.

Tourism and recreation use is also managed on a finer scale through specific management initiatives for popular reefs and bays, with a focus on co-operative strategies developed in close consultation with local users. Management is supported by a set of policies, addressing key issues such as moorings, cruise shipping and bareboats.

Every tourism operator is required to hold a permit for the operations being conducted in the GBRMP. This permit is jointly issued by the GBRMPA and QPWS and covers activities in the GBRMP and adjacent State Marine Parks.

Through these permits, the activities that may be undertaken by each operator are defined and any necessary conditions are described. Each permit application is assessed by the managing agencies. If considered necessary, applicants may be required to prepare an Environmental Impact Statement or to provide public notice of their intentions.

This is more likely where the proposal includes the installation and operation of structure within the GBRMP. The GBRMPA also works with the marine tourism industry to encourage and facilitate higher standards, through the adoption of best practices.

A number of industry associations and recreational groups have adopted their own voluntary codes of conduct. Some training courses are available for tourism industry staff. An Environmental Management Charge is levied on commercial tourism operators in the GBRMP.

This includes operators conducting tourist programs and those operating facilities. The majority of tourism operators pay the standard tourist program charge equivalent to $4.50 per visitor per day, subject to concessions and exemptions.

In 2001-02, Environmental Management Charge payments provided over $6 million that was directed towards GBRMP management and research, including visitor use research conducted by the CRC Reef.

A Tourism and Recreation Reef Advisory Committee (TRRAC) was established in 2000 to provide the GBRMPA with expert advice on the management of tourism and recreation.

The TRRAC consists of 18 expertise-based members and an independent Chair. The TRRAC has played a key role in providing advice on contemporary approaches to management of tourism and recreation in the GBRMP.

Management Issues

The GBRMPA is committed to fostering a sustainable, diverse and world-class tourism industry in the GBRMP and to ensuring a range of tourism and recreation opportunities. Tourism and recreation have been identified as critical issues for the Great Barrier Reef and there is a dedicated Tourism and Recreation Group within the GBRMPA addressing priority policy matters in close cooperation with the tourism industry and other stakeholders.

The GBRMPA recognises that the tourism industry plays an important role in the GBRMP. Marine tourism operators are the principal means by which the Great Barrier Reef and its World Heritage values are presented to national and international visitors. They provide natural history education and are regular and wide ranging users of the GBRMP who can be 'eyes and ears' for Park management. Furthermore, most tourism operators have a strong sense of stewardship for the GBRMP, particularly around their preferred sites of operation.

In managing tourism and recreation use in the GBRMP, particular attention is given to:

Protecting coral reefs and other habitats, such as seagrass, from anchor damage, poor diving practices, waste disposal, reef walking and collecting (for more information see Environmental status - corals)

Protecting turtles and sea birds from disturbance, especially during nesting seasons.

Minimising the environmental impact of facilities and structures.

Respecting the cultural importance of the GBRMP to Aboriginal and Torres Strait Islanders.

Minimising conflicts in access within this multiple use marine park.

Informing the community about the Great Barrier Reef and its World Heritage values.

Encouraging the adoption of best practices by tourism operations and private recreational users.

Assisting the marine tourism industry to contribute to management initiatives and monitoring programs.

The Tourism and Recreation Group is undertaking a number of projects to address high priority tourism and recreation issues.

Management of tourism permits, including allocation, latency and tenure. The GBRMPA is seeking to improve the management of tourism permits and is developing policies that will provide a more business-focussed approach that encourages best practice. Important components of this program include:

an equitable system to allocate permits, particularly where there is a capacity limit;

measures to reduce the number of latent permits, especially where there is hoarding and speculation affecting entry into the sector and expansion of existing operations; and rewards to recognise high standard operators and incentives to encourage other operators to achieve higher standards.

Cruise Shipping

The increasing number and diversity of cruise ships visiting the GBRMP has prompted the GBRMPA to work closely with the cruise ship industry to improve management of this tourism sector and facilitate their access to the GBRMP. A series of cruise ship anchorages have been designated along the length of the GBRMP to assist in accessing safe and interesting reef and island locations.

Management of Moorings

Many tourism operators install and operate moorings when they visit the GBRMP. In addition, a series of public moorings at high use sites throughout the GBRMP help Reef users, both commercial and recreational, to minimise their impact on fragile coral communities. The GBRMPA has developed a policy on moorings in the GBRMP and is implementing improvements to moorings management.

Health and Presentation Value of the Reef

The overall health of the Great Barrier Reef is crucial to the future of marine tourism as it affects the presentation qualities of the Reef for visitors. Issues of major concern include global warming and the consequent bleaching of coral, the quality of water flowing from coastal regions into the GBRMP, and the pressures placed on the reef ecology by fishing. The GBRMPA has a number of major programs underway to address these issues.

There are also localised issues that can affect the value of the GBRMP for tourism:

Events such as cyclones and crown-of-thorns starfish infestations can devastate a reef or a region, placing pressure on local operators. The Commonwealth and Queensland Governments have provided substantial support to the tourism industry to help control crown-of-thorns starfish numbers at key tourism sites.

Future Directions

The GBRMPA, with advice from the TRRAC, the tourism industry and other stakeholders, has been exploring new ways to deliver ecologically sustainable, cost- effective, responsive and equitable management of tourism and recreation use within the GBRMP.

The TRRAC has focussed its attention on developing a 'Cooperative Framework for Sustainable Use and Management of Tourism and Recreation', which it has provided as advice to the GBRMPA. The GBRMPA is using this advice as a basis for improving tourism and recreation management.

The primary components of the TRRAC Framework advice are:

Reef-wide legislation and policy that underpin the other components;

an entry system where all users are informed and educated about appropriate use and requirements;

a set of standards for tourism and recreation use;

a broad spectrum of opportunities for tourism and recreation activities, including capacity limits on some opportunities where necessary;

an open and transparent mechanism to allocate limited tourism opportunities;

a cost recovery and resourcing system for Park management;

a range of initiatives to foster best practice, based primarily on industry co-operative management;

performance monitoring and censure arrangements; and

environmental and social monitoring and research.

Fundamental to improved management is a strong partnership with the marine tourism industry. In fostering a sustainable and world-class tourism industry, the GBRMPA will be working with the industry to ensure there are opportunities for improvement and innovation. We will also be exploring ways to further engage tourism operators and recreational users in programs to keep the GBRMP a healthy and well-protected resource.

BIBLIOGRAPHY

Abram, Simone: *Tourists and Tourism: Identifying with People and Places*, New York, Berg, 1997.

Andrew Holden: *Tourism: A New Perspective*, London, Prentice Hall, 1995.

Andronicou, Antonios: *Tourism in Cyprus*, New York, Oxford University Press, 1979.

Apostolopulos, Y., S. Lewadi: *The Sociology of Tourism*, New York, Routledge, 1996.

Ashworth, Gregory J.: *Marketing Tourism Places*, London, Routledge, 1990.

Baldacchino, G.: *'Global Tourism and Informal Labour Relations: The Small-scale Syndrome at Work'*, Mansell, UK, 1997.

Baum, T.: *'Human Resource Issues in International Tourism'*, Butterworth Heinemann, UK, 1993.

Bennett, O.: *Financing for Tourism Projects in Developing Countries*, England, Wiley, 1994.

Bevan, D. L., and D. W. Soskice: *Appraising Tourist Development in a Small Economy*, London, Heinemann, 1976.

Boissevain, Jeremy: *Coping with Tourists: European Reactions to Mass Tourism*, England, Berghahn, 1996.

Boniface, B.G. and Cooper, C.: *Geography of Travel and Tourism*, Butterworth Heinemann, UK, 1994.

Brogan, E.: *Human Resource Development in Tourism: The Scottish Perspective*, England, Wiley, 1994.

Bruce, David : *Tourism Strategies for Rural Development*, Sackville, New Brunswick, 1993.

Brunt, P.: *Market Research in Travel & Tourism*, Butterworth Heinemann, UK, 1997.

Butler, R., Hall, R. and Jenkins, M.: *Tourism and Recreation in Rural Areas*, Wiley, UK, 1998.

Byran, H.: *In Tourism Alternatives: Potentials and Problems in the Development of Tourism*, Philadelphia, University of Pennsylvania Press, 1992.

Chambers, Erve: *Tourism and Culture: An Applied Perspective*, Albany, State University of New York Press, 1997.

Conlin, M. and Baum, T.: *Island Tourism: Management Principles and Practice*, Wiley, UK, 1995.

Cooper, C.: *Tourism: Principles and Practice*, London, Pitman, 1993.

Cooper, C.P.: *Progress in Tourism, Recreation and Hospitality Management*, Belhaven Press, UK, 1990.

Creque, Darwin: *A Study of the Tourist Industry in the U.S. Virgin Islands*, North Carolina, Amalie, 1964.

Dane, Suzanne: *Share Your Heritage: Cultural Heritage Tourism Success Stories*, Washington, DC, National Trust for Historic Preservation, 2001.

Daniel, R.: *Recent Advances in Tourism Marketing Research*, New York, Hawthorne Press, 1996.

David W.: *Tourism Planning*, Chicago, Council of Planning Librarians, 1995.

David, L.: *International Tourism Policy*, New York, Van Nostrand Reinhold, 1990.

David, W.: *Tourism Planning*, Chicago, Council of Planning Librarians, 1995.

Davidson, R.: *European Business Travel and Tourism*, England, Wiley, 1994.

Deegan, J. and Dineen, D.A.: *Tourism Policy and Performance: The Irish Experience*, ITBP, UK, 1997.

Douglas, C.: *Heritage Tourism is in the Future of Many Alabama Communities*, Auburn Univ., Auburn, 1991.

Douglas, Pearce: *Change in Tourism: People, Places, Processes*, New York, Routledge, 1995.

Edward, M.: *In International Tourism: Identity and Change*, London, Sage, 1995.

Foley, M.: *In Tourism: The State of the Art*, England, Wiley, 1994.

Forbes, A. H.: *Tourism and Transport Policy in the European Union*, England, Wiley, 1994.

Frew, E.: *International Charter Travel—a New Opportunity for Australian Tourism*, England, Wiley, 1994.

Garfield, Donald: *Partners in Tourism: Culture and Commerce*, Washington, DC, American Association of Museums, 1997.

Gimblett, Barbara: *Destination Culture: Tourism, Museums, and Heritage*, California, University of California, 1998.

Gorman, Michael: *Design for Tourism: An ICSID Interdesign Report*, New York, Oxford University Press, 1972.

Harrison, David: *Tourism and the Less Developed Countries*, London, Belhaven, 1992.

Heise, Dorothy: *Promoting Tourism in Rural American*, Maryland, National Agriculture Library, 1991.

Holden, Andrew: *Tourism: A Commodity of Opportunity for Change?* Chichester, England, 1994.

Howard Green: *Tourism and the Environment: A Sustainable Relationship*, New York, Routledge, 1995.

Huit, Groupe: *The Sociocultural Effects of Tourism in Tunisia: A Case Study of Sousse.* New York, Oxford University Press, 1979.

Inskeep, E.: *Training for Tourism in Developing Countries*, Chichester, England, 1994.

James Makens: *Marketing for Hospitality and Tourism*: New Jersey, Prentice-Hall, 1998.

Jenkins, C. L.: *Tourism in Developing Countries: The Privatisation Issue*, Chichester, England, 1994.

Jeremy, B.: *Coping with Tourists: European Reactions to Mass Tourism*, England, Berghahn, 1996.

John Sem: *A Training Guide for Rural Tourism Development*, Minnesota: Rural Tourism Center, 1995.

Knox, J.: *Tourism Research Priorities in Hawaii and the Pacific*, Honolulu, University of Hawaii, 1979.

Komilis, P.: *Tourism and Sustainable Regional Development*, Chichester, England, 1994.

Koth, Barbara: *A Training Guide for Rural Tourism Development*, Minnesota: Rural Tourism Center, 1995.

Kotler, Philip: *Marketing for Hospitality and Tourism*: New Jersey, Prentice-Hall, 1998.

Lawrence, R.: *Rural Tourist and Non-Tourist Communities in Massachusetts: Quality of Life Patterns*, 1980-1990, Pennsylvania, Northeastern Forest Experiment Station, 1993.

Lloyd, E.: *Tourism: A Shrinking World*, Columbus, Grid, 1980.

Martinus J.: *Tourism by Train: Its Role in Alternative Tourism*, Philadelphia, University of Pennsylvania Press, 1992.

Mary, E.: *A Heritage Tourism Tool: National Register of Historic Places*, Radnor, Pennsylvania, 1993.

McConnell II, D. W.: *Nature-Based Tourism and Rural Coastal Development: Observations, Options, and Trends,* South Carolina, Clemson University, 1990.

Mieczkowski, Zbigniew: *Environmental Issues of Tourism and Recreation*, Lanham, University Press of America, 1995.

Muzaffer Uysal: *Recent Advances in Tourism Marketing Research*, New York, Hawthorne Press, 1996.

Richard, W.: *Tourism and Recreation in Rural Areas*, Chichester, U.K., 1998.

Ryan, Chris: *Recreational Tourism: A Social Science Perspective*, London, Routledge, 1991.

Soskice, D.W.: *Appraising Tourist Development in a Small Economy,* London, Heinemann, 1976.

Stephen F.: *Linking Tourism, the Environment, and Sustainability*, Ogden, Utah, 1995.

Stephen, C.: *Tourism in the Navajo Country: Resources and Planning*, Winslow Rock, Navajo Tribe, 1967.

Valentine, Udoh: *Tourism Development: A Research Note on Africa,* Connecticut, Praeger, 1996.

Victor T. C.: *Sustainable Tourism: A Marketing Perspective,* Woburn, Massachusetts: Butterworth-Heinemann, 1998.

William W. Swart: *Planning for Tourism Development: Quantitative Approaches*, New York, Praeger, 1976.

INDEX

D

E

F

G

M

N

O

P

□□□